WORK

AND

OTHER SINS

WORK

AND

OTHER SINS

———■———

Life in New York City and Thereabouts

CHARLIE LEDUFF

THE PENGUIN PRESS

NEW YORK

2004

THE PENGUIN PRESS
a member of
Penguin Group (USA) Inc.
375 Hudson Street
New York, New York 10014

Photograph Credits
Page xx: Vincent Laforet/New York Times; pages 86, 108,
154, 270, 302, 334, 346: Edward Keating/New York Times; page 182:
Charlie LeDuff/New York Times; page 226: Fred R. Conrad/New York Times.

Library of Congress Cataloging-in-Publication Data
LeDuff, Charlie.
Work and other sins : life in New York City
and thereabouts / Charlie LeDuff.
p. cm.
Compilation of articles originally published in *The New York Times*.
ISBN 1-59420-002-5 (alk. paper)
1. New York Region—Social life and customs—Anecdotes. 2. New York
Region—Social conditions—Anecdotes. 3. Working class—New York
Region—Anecdotes. 4. New York Region—Biography—Anecdotes. I. Title.
F128.36.L43 2004
974.7'1043—dc21   2003054945

This book is printed on acid-free paper. ∞

Printed in the United States of America
1   3   5   7   9   10   8   6   4   2

Designed by Claire Vaccaro

ALL MY RELATIONS

The word *newspaper-writer* means, at the very least, a scoundrel. I am one of them. I work with them. I shake hands with them. I'm even told I've begun to look like one. But I shan't die as one.

—ANTON CHEKHOV

Contents

Introduction   *xv*

Work   *1*

Good-bye to Mr. Hello and Good-bye   2

The Michelangelo of the Hard Sell   5

Mother's Day? Florists Love and Love It Not.   9

He's No Bob Dole, but He's Still a Celebrity   12

A Mohawk Trail to the Skyline   14

"Rasputins"   20

Gravediggers' Gallows (What Else?) Humor   22

How Time Goes By on West Forty-third Street   24

Where Sinatra Fills Your Ears, If Not Your Eyes   26

A Bleaker Santa's-Eye View   28

A Barber's Soothing Aria   32

Harlem Nocturne for a Still-Beautiful Chorus Girl   34

On Top of the World   36

Where Is King Kong When a Bulb Goes Out?   36

Stray Thoughts at 1,454 Feet   40

In the Pit   42

Hauling the Debris, and Darker Burdens   42

A Night Shift to Numb the Body and Soul   46

Hard Hats and Soft Hands at a Ground Zero Bar   51

On the Corner   53

Hard Work in Hostile Suburbs   53

Brooklyn Poles and Jews Refashion Old World Ties   61

On Land and Sea   64

Last Days of the Baymen   64

Springtime for the Harbor Police   74

The Man to See for Raccoon Pie   77

So It's a Lighthouse. Now Leave Me Alone.   82

THE SLAUGHTERHOUSE   87

At a Slaughterhouse, Some Things Never Die   89

JOINTS   109

At This Bar, Everything Is on the Table   110

Schlitz on Draft   112

A Bar on Rails   114

Smile for the Camera   116

A Beer Hall with Homegrown Czech Nostalgia   118

The Harbor Light Stays On   120

The Lights Are Bright, the Hours Always Happy   122

Stars, Stripes and Insults   124

No Ferns, Please   126

A Real Fireman's Bar   128

How Diplomats Drown the Sorrows of the World   130

A Steak Pub Missing a Central Ingredient: Steak   132

Join the Navy and See the Light   134

The Scene   136

Looking for Mr. Dreamy   136

A Life off the Books   139

Manners, Morals and Money at a Room Salon   141

Never Trust a Man Who Kisses His Own Fingers   143

The Life of the Party   145

Shimmering Beauty in a Sweltering City   150

A Valentine's Story: Take out Your Handkerchiefs   152

REGULARS   155

If Glasses Are Half Full, Wallets Are Half Empty   156

A Merry, If Pensive, Old Soul at Just the Right Bar   158

Big Shoes to Fill with Wine and Whiskey   160

Wheels of Fire, Beards of Gray   162

"The Saloon Priest"   164

Geeks and Freaks   166

Absolute Dunleavy   168

The Roar of the Beer Suds, the Smell of the Fish   170

An Actor Awash in Ambition and Merlot   172

Frankie and Johnnie, Together Again   174

A Tasteful Mix of Blood, Beer and Dirty Pictures   176

The Piers, a Blind Man and an Old Seaman's Eyes   *178*

Fifteen Minutes of Fame Where Black Is the Color   *180*

Mr. and Mrs. Nobody   *183*

The Pair of Bickering Brothers Who Made
    Coney Island Hot   *184*

"Hero" Label Lifts a Life   *186*

Society's Throwaways, with Booze and Attitude   *188*

Saluting the Fourth   *190*

Her Queens Days Will Become Moscow Nights   *194*

A Jazz Rhapsody Turned Sour   *196*

Saturday Night Fever: The Life   *201*

Dot-com Fever Followed by Bout of Dot-com Chill   *213*

Runaway Girl   *218*

Sinners and Victims of Domestic Hell   *222*

The Hustle   *227*

You Can't Buy a Thrill   *228*

The Exchange Rate Behind Bars   *230*

The Hustling Life   *236*

What's a Few Bloodstains? It's an Apartment!   *246*

The Shantytown of the He-Shes   *249*

Raffle to Benefit a Charity Close to His Heart   *254*

The Way to Live? With Your Feet on the Table.   *257*

Fame Stinks   *259*

The Gambler   *261*

Squad 1   *271*

Dave Fontana's Legacy   *272*

The Empty Coffin   *276*

The First Holiday   *280*

A Jacket, an I.D.   *284*

Star Without a Script   *287*

Hero Fatigue   *292*

A Lonely Son   *297*

The Sporting Life   *303*

The Champ   *304*

A Lifetime of Lifeguarding   *308*

The Ring   *312*

Landing Jabs to Pay Bills   *312*

Borrowing Mailer's Car, and Other Ring Tales   *317*

The Diamond   *319*

Free Swinger on the Hudson   *319*

In Stadium's Shadow, Waiting for the Opener   *323*

A Telescopic Lens on a Baseball Legend   *325*

Diamonds Aren't Forever   *329*

There Goes the Neighborhood   *335*

Nickel and Dime and Quartered to Death   *336*

Elks (Clubs) Becoming Extinct   *339*

Before There Was Dumbo, There Was Pedro's   342

Bridge of Sighs   344

Words to the Wise   347

When Those Dancing Days Are Over   348

Latin Lovers with Free Advice   350

Homeless but Not Helpless by the Harlem River   352

A Mentor Shares a Secret That Really Wasn't   354

The Quantum Leaps of a Pretty Nice Mind   356

INTRODUCTION

Among the more fantastic nobodies hanging from my family tree are a pair of heavy-drinking lighthouse keepers, a sleepy morphine addict, a grave robber, a rumrunner, a streetwalker, a numbers maker, a dean of a sham college and a police informant. A few of these relatives are still living, a few lived long lives, a few died young by misadventure or of self-neglect. Those are sad biographies ending with "done me wrong."

My grandpa Roy was the bookmaker for the Detroit Race Course, which no longer stands. Like everything else, it has been replaced by a shopping mall, I think. They say Grandpa was a math genius. Maybe, but he never struck me as one. He was a sharp dresser with a thin pencil-trim mustache, a sophisticated and sociable man, but a math genius? I can't say. He did make a lot of money in his time, but when the president of the Teamsters and the underboss of the Bufalino family were your dinner pals, you didn't really have to be that good with the numbers.

Grandma insists that Grandpa was not a gangster but the most decent and honorable man she had ever met. I believe her, but I wonder why she kept the photos of Grandpa and Jimmy Hoffa at the bottom of the trunk, above the one of Grandpa and a strange woman laughing it up in a fishing cottage somewhere far away. I am working from memory here, since relations of mine stole that trunk and most of the rest of my grandma's things and sold them away to strangers.

But this is not a memoir. There are too many of those. I give you some family background as a way of credentialing myself, to show you that everybody's got a history, that most everybody comes from nowhere and that in every family there is a cousin no one wants to admit to. This book is about such people: New Yorkers almost exclusively, working people most definitely.

The dandies I know say I write about dives and losers, but they are wrong. I write about the people who live in neighborhoods, crowded apartments and dreary ranch houses. These are the people who shovel their own snow and have fat aunties who wear stretch pants with stains on the ass. This is not a book about the people who have doormen but a book about doormen. It is about the laborer, the dreamer, the hustler, the immigrant—whether he is a writer from Michigan or a waiter from Michoacán. I suppose in all of this I'm trying to find myself and justify him, to you.

When the cocktail set tells me they enjoy the cast of losers, I never mind them. I smile and drink their liquor. They don't know work.

The elders in my family told me our stories. The better stuff has come more recently, pried out with the crowbar of old age. Nobody likes to admit he cheated his way to the middle. As far as I know, our stories of half-breeds, half-asses, half-truths, crawdaddies from the Louisiana swamps and kicking birds from the Great Lakes have never been written down or chronicled except for that newspaper photograph of Grandpa and Jimmy Hoffa standing on the picket line in front of the track two generations ago.

That picture, that one piece of acknowledgment and notoriety, is lost to my family. The stranger who bought the trunk has no idea that the thin man standing next Hoffa was known along Woodward Avenue as the Duke.

That American nobody is somebody to me. He's the guy who taught me about horses. You will not find recollections of him in these pages, but he is here. Pete the Gambler and I spent hours at the Aqueduct Race Track in Ozone Park, Queens, talking about my grandpa, about his handicapping system and his philosophy on horses. That philosophy: Stay away from the track. But it doesn't work that way and so there you have it.

The nice thing about being a reporter is that you can show a gravedigger your press card and ask him: "You mind if I watch?" He lets you watch for a while. He will let you try his shovel until your hands start to blister and your back starts to ache. You hand him back his shovel and you watch some more and it dawns upon you to ask, "Doesn't that hurt your hands and back?" Usually, people try to make their lives sound better than they are. But that falls away after a while, and the longer you hang around, the less they realize you're around and eventually you get at it.

Reporters like to tell themselves that they are doing something socially and culturally important and that in the best of circumstances they are doing some good—righting wrongs, exposing crooks and such. That's what they tell each other over free drinks at the awards ceremonies, anyway.

The truth is, we reporters are window peepers, suck-ups, people too ugly for the movies. That's what normal people say. That's the bad part. The good part is the job beats manual labor.

The stories in this book appeared in *The New York Times* at around the turn of the century. Chronologically, they end with September 11 and its aftermath. I wrote some stories about Squad 1, a firehouse in Brooklyn that lost half its men. Rereading them now, these stories seem salty and cold to me, like watering eyes in the wintertime. There was so much more to be said, but I could not say it, because life in those moments was hard enough. I hope the stories at least seem limber, that something good can be gotten from them by somebody.

New York is a glamorous city, constituted mostly of nobodies. They crave the lights, and if they tell you differently, they're lying. Only dreamers come to New York. As a matter of course, few people have control of their lives. You live at the whim of your boss, your landlord, your grocer, the stranger, the judge, the bus driver, the mayor who won't let you smoke. On the other hand, you live at the whim of your whims, and that is the most exciting thing there is.

New York is a lot like a shit sandwich. The more bread you have, the less shit you taste, and this town would tumble to the ground without money. For those who don't have it, there is always the hope of getting it. This book is meant for them.

Work
and
Other Sins

WORK

WHEN I WAS a cub reporter at the *Times,* I was talking with an editor about a strike at an auto-parts plant in Flint, Michigan. There was some story in the paper that day about workers who were spending their idle time antique shopping and speeding around the lakes in their powerboats.

"Since when is it bad to have a boat and make good money?" I asked.

The editor, a smart guy with a weak chin, put his palm to his nose and said: "Those people had about this much foresight. They should have seen the writing on the wall and gone to college."

That's what he said.

But if we were all poets, we'd starve on words.

Good-bye to Mr. Hello
and Good-bye

Robert E. Mitchell will retire on March 29. He will take his belongings and his doorman's pension and go back home to New Orleans, where he plans to grow old on the front porch with his relations.

No one need apply, as Mr. Mitchell's job was filled just days after he announced his retirement. "That's the way it goes," he said at four one afternoon as he dragged his broom and dustpan around the perimeter of 801 West End Avenue, a prewar building with seventy apartments on the west side of the avenue between Ninety-ninth and One Hundredth streets. "Time moves along and things are forgotten. Including the memories of you," he said. There are, after all, eight thousand doormen in the city.

And maybe the new guy will make the residents of 801 forget that for thirty-three years, Mr. Mitchell was the man who mopped their hallways and shoveled their snow. Or that he was the man who took their children by the scruff of the neck when he saw them doing wrong. Or that he was the man who ran down the wig-wearing mugger who attacked their mother. Or that he was the man who discovered their dead locked away behind the doors.

But it seems unlikely, if the card the six-year-old girl gave him the other day is any indication. *I love you. Please don't go, Robert,* it read.

Nearly every block in New York has its mayor. Some acquire the title through milk-crate endurance, passing away the hours in the same spot on the same corner, becoming such a fixture and spectacle that people just start calling out, "Hey, Mayor." But others earn it by giving of themselves.

"He was my second father after my father moved away," said Beck Lee, forty, who grew into a man in apartment 1B. The neighborhood was tough in the sixties and seventies, Mr. Lee said. Schoolchildren were robbed so often that their fathers gave them broken watches and expired bus passes to give the muggers. But the children developed their own method of self-defense. They learned to stall, pat their pockets and wait for Mr. Mitchell to catch sight of the larceny from his perch near the building's column.

In the seventies, there was a parade of fathers who packed their bags and walked out through the marble foyer for the last time. Mr. Mitchell was there to help them with their bags. And he was there to help the women put a fresh coat of paint on their apartments and move their furniture around. He was there to teach their kids the curveball. He was, Mr. Lee said, a surrogate man of the house.

Mr. Mitchell cut a handsome figure in his gray uniform with white piping. He wore a colorful sweater, a threadbare tie and smooth hair the color of the uniform. At sixty-five, he is thin and stands erect. When the neighborhood started changing in the eighties and the silk-stocking crowd moved in, they asked him to wear a hat. He refused. He has never worn a hat on the job and is proud of it. They do that on the East Side. He's a West Side doorman.

"I opened this door so much they'd run out of numbers if they attempted to calculate it," he said, standing in the cold foyer in thin shoes and no coat. "I'm going to miss this building. It's been my whole life for half my life."

September 28, 1967, was the beginning of that life. That's when the unemployment office sent him to the building's superintendent. "The super told me, 'If you like it, you've got the job for life,'" he said. "I been here ever since."

The true gentleman never insinuates himself into other people's business, Mr. Mitchell said. He keeps to his own, never talks about things unless asked and never talks about people in the building, period.

"Which doesn't mean I don't know what's going on," he said. "I know just about everything that goes on around here. If I didn't, I wouldn't be a good doorman."

Maybe the people of 801 West End Avenue will forget him, he said. But he'll be thinking of them on his porch down in Louisiana.

The Michelangelo
of the Hard Sell

Tony Razzano is a used-car salesman on the Gold Coast of Long Island. He is moving high-end, hey-notice-me cars, even in these spooked economic times, because, he says, he understands a basic concept of Long Island life: "You are what you drive."

He is one of eight salesmen at Champion Motor Group, a dealership that specializes in the "slightly used" Jaguar, Porsche and Rolls-Royce. The car market caved after the September 2001 attacks on the World Trade Center and the Pentagon. Car sales rebounded to record levels in October, due in large part to interest-free financing deals.

"The big companies are giving their cars away below cost," Mr. Razzano said. "You won't see me giving away the store. I need to make money to make dreams happen."

He sold sixteen luxury cars, including a $300,000 Bentley, between September 11 and the beginning of November. He accounts for 25 percent of sales off the lot. To prove this, he pulled a stack of sales receipts from a drawer and tossed them on his mahogany desk while continuing to speak to a customer on the other end of the line.

"Look. Two and two are four. If you want it to be five, God bless you," he told a man named Richie, who worried that he could not manage the finances on a '98 Bentley, at 6.8 percent interest, which translated into a monthly payment of $3,657 and a lump sum of $160,000 due at the end of five years. "Whatever you want. Just come see me. You know I love you, Richie."

Tony Razzano bleeds ego. He hung up the telephone, smiled and recited the well-worn psalm of the showroom: "I could sell ice to an Eskimo."

The products sell themselves, Mr. Razzano said, but these days he helps the Mr. Joneses and Mr. Smiths of the world make their decisions with a devilish pitch.

Terrorists and anthrax, he reminds them. "Why would you wait for tomorrow to get what you want today, when tomorrow may never come?" he asks. "Do what the president asks of you. Go out there and spend and be a patriot."

Tony Razzano is forty-nine and engaged to a twenty-eight-year-old blonde. His hair is swept back and gray around the temples, his dress is impeccable and his jewelry, silver. He tans twice a week, is short of stature, and his presence is announced by the metal taps inlaid into the soles of his shoes. *Tickety-tap, tickety-tap, tickety-tap.*

He is the type of man who cannot tell you the make of his shoes but will tell you that they cost seven hundred dollars. He drives what he calls a young man's car, a black Mercedes coupe with black tinted windows, and has a cell phone glued to his ear. The conversation is usually not about automobiles but about how to pay for one.

And there lies the foundation of Mr. Razzano's livelihood, which he says is around a quarter million dollars per annum—creative financing. There are three ways to get a car, he says: the conventional loan, balloon financing and the lease.

The conventional loan, according to Mr. Razzano, is preferred by Solid Joe America, a hardworking man who wants to make payments on his car and who after five years wants to own it. "He's got a wife and kids and wants to own something by the end of the deal," he said.

Then there is balloon financing. This is for men—rarely women—who want to look like big shots but in reality don't have the money to be big shots. (He compares them to "a fancy home without furniture.") For them, balloon financing is a way to buy a car with little money down and to stack the big payment three years down the line. The car is usually sold before the big payment comes due, a new car is purchased, and the process begins anew. It is akin to rolling over credit card debt.

"A guy like that I own cradle to grave," Mr. Razzano said. When he makes that kind of sale, he calls it "taking him down."

The other road to car keys, the lease, is recommended for the man who has bad credit or a short attention span. Banks are getting out of the leasing business in this tattered economy, since a bank cannot recoup its losses on a repossessed car sold at auction. But Champion Motor Group has an arrangement with the banks that allows for lease swapping. Luxury cars hold their value better than run-of-the-mill Chevrolets. So, instead of the auction yard, the cars go back to the Champion showroom, where they are resold. The dealership keeps its customers interested, and paying, by letting them swap one car for another.

So while other salesmen starve, Mr. Razzano eats. "Men with good credit, they're an easy sell," he said. What he specializes in is the man with poor credit and rich tastes. A car costs the same for everyone; it's the payments that differ.

"For instance, the reverend wants a Rolls," he explains with a true-life story. "I say, 'Reverend, you can't have the new Rolls, but you can have a slightly older one. Who's going to know the difference? Pass the basket around and pray to the Lord, because your credit smells worse than roadkill and you're going to need to come up with an extra five grand.'"

And when the reverend does, Mr. Razzano sends him away in his Rolls-Royce with a bottle of good wine and not one but two Cuban cigars. The reverend is happy, and, as Mr. Razzano says, he owns him for life.

"I understand how badly somebody wants to be Somebody," he said while sitting in his office decorated with roses, good liquor, a humidor and a photo of himself and his blonde on the beach. "I'll help this kind of person. And if he doesn't make the payments, I'll take his car, his ego, and still make a profit."

Mr. Razzano does not promise things he cannot do. He tries to avoid a lease where a man cannot make the payments. "Every one of my applications is a Michelangelo," he said. "I work the bank over as hard as I work the customer. That's what makes me so good."

A man is shaped by his circumstances, and Mr. Razzano is no different. His grandfather was an Italian immigrant who sold groceries to the robber barons of the Gold Coast. His father did some time at the grocery store and died young. When Tony Razzano speaks of him, he gets misty-eyed. "He was an artist, a man who loved life." Mr. Razzano calls his eighty-two-year-old mother at least twice a day.

He was born lame, clubfooted, and eventually had his ears surgically removed and reattached because they stuck out so unnaturally. He grew up in nearby Westbury, attended morticians' college and began working at his uncle's Pontiac dealership on the side. He found he was good at the vocation, and his life became sales.

"I understand that a guy wants to be something else," Mr. Razzano said. "I'm a good person deep down inside. I try to love people, treat them good, you know? Like I'd want to be treated. Black, Italian, Catholic, Jew—it doesn't matter."

Except for the know-it-all. Mr. Razzano hangs up on this type. But before he does, he works him over a little.

"He calls and says, 'Beat $659,'" Mr. Razzano explained. "I can't beat $659. I say, go buy it. I call him the get-a-life guy. He spends his whole day calling twelve dealerships. Three guys have told him the same quote within ten dollars. I don't have time for that. 'Why you coming out to Long Island?' I ask him. 'Either you're bored or you're lying or you're a loser.'"

Mother's Day?
Florists Love and Love It Not.

There is a type of man who will walk into a flower shop and say he's in trouble. He's done something wrong or forgotten someone, and he needs a special flower to make it right.

At this time of year, this type of man will ask for a mixed bouquet. He does not care what goes into the arrangement as long as it's cheap. After the man's mother receives the bouquet, she calls the florist to complain in a shrill voice that she absolutely hates lilies. Lilies remind her of death. "My son spent a lot of money on me," she says. But she feels cheapened by the lilies.

The truth is that the son has spent the bare minimum. And after hanging up with the woman, the florist knows why the son sent her the cheap bouquet.

Few people ever consider that the florist is a mother, too, a widow who is not likely to get flowers on the second Sunday of May.

Mary Tryforos, sixty, has spent the last thirty-three Mother's Days standing on her feet in her little shop, Tryforos & Pernice Florist in Bronxville, New York, making the day happen for other women.

"You work so hard over the holidays that sometimes you want to cry," she said. "That gets forgotten. It's a tough holiday. You're physically broke."

It is a crucial time of year for Mrs. Tryforos and the twenty-five thousand other flower-shop owners across the country. She put in fifteen-hour days last week, since the business for this holiday accounts for 15 percent of her yearly receipts. A good Mother's Day gets you through the dog days of summer. A bad holiday can get you on this year's bankruptcy list with the other sixty-three hundred flower shops. "You have to remember that nobody buys flowers on Father's Day," she said.

"Working on Mother's Day, it sort of takes the fun out of it," Mrs. Tryforos said as the front doorbell sounded, the telephone rang and the deliveryman shouted for directions. There are thorns in the roses, the smell and dust of pollen and floral foam, the swollen joints from being on your feet all day. People suffer so that others may enjoy flowers.

Then there is the psychology of the flower business, the human nature of it. Not only will some men—and most times they are men—ask for the cheap bouquet; they will ask the florist to write out the card for them. They will recite something like: "Dear Mother, From your son, John Smith."

There will be no love to it. *John* will not even be signed in John's hand—it will be a computer printout. As the florist, you sometimes puzzle over it. What sort of relationship is behind that card? It seems as though the mother and son are almost strangers.

"There is the beauty to it, too," Mrs. Tryforos said the other day in the workroom of her shop. "On Monday, the calls come in. You've made women happy. That's gratifying."

Mary Tryforos raised and fed two children from this flower shop. She sent them through college. The children, Gary, thirty-eight, and Anna, thirty-seven, did not appreciate the business then. When asked to work, they did so grudgingly. It was boring, they said. It was unfair. It seemed to them then that they never had a good Christmas or Easter, because the shop always came first.

They can admit that now, since they got fed up with the corporate world, quit, came home and went to work in the family business.

"I took it for granted," said Anna Kenney, the daughter, as she put together one of those conspicuous bouquets. She used to market diet pills and Kool-Aid. "I never realized that dinner came from here. I tried to avoid working here. Now I even enjoy it sometimes."

Gary Tryforos returned in 1987, when his father, James, fell sick with lung cancer. He quit his big insurance company job and came home to help his mom for a while. He never left.

"My dad didn't want me working here," he said. "Why work seventy hours a week for such a small return? No pension. No benefits. If he were living, there's no way I'd be in this business. But he's not. I guess I've inherited my father's life."

James Tryforos died in 1988. There were many flowers from his family and his friends in the business. His widow still remembers how the coffin was covered in white phalaenopsis orchids.

The Tryforos family has been in the flower business for more than a hundred years. The original shop was in Harlem, on East 125th Street. The current shop is thirty-eight years old and sits in a nice brick building on Pondfield Road in Bronxville, a pleasant village in southern Westchester County where drivers stop and wave to pedestrians.

Mrs. Tryforos plans to work until two P.M. today and then have a barbecue with her grandchildren. "To tell you the truth, I would prefer to dispense with the flowers," she said.

He's No Bob Dole,
but He's Still a Celebrity

The manager of Golden Lady, the landmark gentlemen's club in the South Bronx with the fifteen-foot neon marquee of a woman swimming in a martini glass, did not immediately realize there was a celebrity in his midst.

But soon, word percolated down the abandoned recesses of Bruckner Boulevard. "Yo, man, that's Vinnie Viagra." Pito, the manager, asked, "You really Vinnie Viagra?"

"It's true," L. J. Gancer said. "Page sixty-five of the George Clooney, Julia Roberts issue of *Esquire*."

Mr. Gancer is paid to be the white, average face in magazines and on billboards whose life has been uplifted by the impotence-curing pill. There is also a Latino Vinnie, a black Vinnie and so forth. L.J. is short for Little Jim. "But don't call me that," the poster boy said.

Pito welcomed him warmly. The cover charge was waived for Vinnie Viagra, and his first drink was on the house. It began to dawn on Mr. Gancer that there may be some advantages to this new celebrity, that perhaps there were other rubber carpets waiting to be rolled out upon his arrival.

The interior of Golden Lady had two pool tables, wall-to-wall mirrors, a coin-operated snack machine, a long stage with two brass poles and a number of men sitting around the horseshoe bar. Mr. Gancer is an actor with a face of indeterminable age; he guards his age as a trade secret. His hair is slightly gray and thinning on the crown. He has average-size hands, a long waist and rounded shoulders. He is married with two children.

He ordered Scotch.

For the man who enjoys a drink but wants to remain vital, Mr. Gancer suggested alternating between glasses of liquor and tap water. "New York water, I find, is very refreshing," he said. "It's from the mountain rivers, and it's full of vitamins and minerals."

Mr. Gancer had a few drinks, but never the water, and periodically the dancers came by to introduce themselves. Soon comfortable, Mr. Gancer confided the odd twist of being Vinnie Viagra.

It seems that as a teenager, his first dozen encounters with women ended badly. His superego mocked him in the voice of his father, B.J., Big Jim, castigating him for ruining his life. "I put a lot of mental pressure on myself," he said.

It was the early seventies, and while flipping through his father's *Esquire,* he saw an article: "The Impotence Boom."

He clipped that story and kept it for a number of years, until he conquered the voice in his head. "Now look at me, how many years later?" he said, swirling his ice cubes. "I'm in the same magazine, but I'm the face for the cure. Life's weird."

A Mohawk Trail
to the Skyline

The paychecks come on Thursday. When the walking boss calls quitting time, the ironworkers stuff their tool belts into empty bolt buckets and stash them near the columns.

They cram themselves into the freight elevator, and someone is wearing cologne. They descend to the dressing shacks and change into their street clothes. Some go to the bank and cash their check and put the money in their pocket. Others go directly to the saloon and see the bartender, who takes 5 percent. They line up at the bar, and slowly the backaches and joint pains are dulled by cigarette smoke and beer bubbles. The white men joke about their ex-wives, their alimony checks and their bad habits. The Indian men also drink on Thursday, but never on Friday.

At quitting time Friday, the Mohawks will pile into their Buicks and Fords and drive four hundred miles to Canada to visit their wives and children on the Kahnawake [pronounced ga-nuh-WAH-gay] Reservation, eight miles from Montreal, on the south shore of the Saint Lawrence River.

It is the spring of 2001, and there is a construction boom in New York City. All over town you can hear the sounds of pneumatic guns, hammers tolling against steel girders and ice cubes clinking in whiskey glasses. Three skyscrapers have gone up in Times Square in the past two years, and there is enough work scheduled to last three more. Local 40, representing twelve hundred city ironworkers, is at full employment. Nonlocal men like the Mohawks have "boomed out"—chased the work—and landed in town, earning $33.45 an hour plus benefits.

They are the grandsons and great-grandsons of Mohawk iron-workers who helped build the Empire State Building, the George Washington Bridge, the Triborough Bridge, the Waldorf-Astoria, the Henry Hudson Parkway, the RCA Building, the Verrazano-Narrows Bridge, the World Trade Center and all the other major projects in New York that involved heavy steel construction.

The Indians of past generations had a bustling neighborhood of their own in Brooklyn, supported by the construction dollars. But then came the building bust of 1985 to 1995. While the locals were kept employed with bridge-repair work, there were no jobs for iron-workers like the Mohawks, whose union ties were on the Canadian side of the border. So they boomed out to places like Kentucky and Detroit, where power plants were going up and bridges were needed to span water.

They went wherever there was money to be had and hell to be raised. Some went home and retired. When there was absolutely no work anywhere, some trafficked in cigarettes from the United States.

They are back. There are about 250 Mohawks from Kahnawake working in the city. They are working on the Brooklyn courthouse, the Ernst & Young building in Times Square, the 155th Street over-pass in the Bronx, Kennedy Airport—wherever new steel is being laid. And in April, work should begin in earnest on the massive AOL Time Warner building in Columbus Circle that will be 2.1 million square feet and have double towers. It will be a monument to this generation of ironworkers, just as Rockefeller Center is to their grandfathers.

At three-thirty Friday afternoon, the Phillips cousins—J.R., thirty-one, and Jeffrey, forty—and Joe Horn walked briskly from the Ernst & Young job site to a nearby parking lot. They climbed into an old Bonneville and rolled out for Kahnawake. The trip would take seven hours, slowed by the snow and a burning Jeep that stopped traffic for two miles. A Mohawk would be smashed by a tractor-trailer that evening, and by sunrise the news of it would pass around the eight-thousand-person village like the measles.

They rolled past the Canadian Pacific Railway Bridge silhouetted in the moonlight. It is a double-humped cantilever bridge built in 1886 that spans the St. Lawrence Seaway and runs through part of the reservation.

It is the bridge that gave the Mohawks their start in ironwork. In exchange for running a railroad through Indian territory, the company hired the Mohawks as laborers, allowing them to tote pails but not to work on the bridge. But when the foremen were not looking, the Indians began climbing all over the span as if they had been born to it. Soon they were working the iron. It took them away from their lives as timber rafters and traveling-circus performers. (The Phillips name, in fact, was purchased in 1885 from a rodeo timekeeper for $2.75 in Philadelphia. Their great-grandfather, Kanadagero, was a Wild West performer. Their grandfather, James Taheratie Phillips, was an ironworker who fell two floors and crippled his knees while working in Detroit.)

They drove past the iron cross on the western edge of the reservation, erected in honor of the thirty-five Mohawk men who died in the 1907 Quebec Bridge collapse. Five Kahnawake family names went down with the bridge: Leaf, Lee, Blue, Bruce and Mitchell.

"It nearly wiped out the village," said Stuart Phillips, a white-haired elder, former ironworker and tribal historian. "But instead of scaring the men away from the work, it attracted them to it."

Ironwork became the stuff that Mohawk men were made of, offering a little excitement and big money. "When the bridge collapsed, the women of the village decreed that all men may not work on the same job, eliminating the possibility that the reservation would be made up solely of widows and orphans," said Mr. Phillips, who is J.R.'s father. More than a thousand men from Kahnawake are iron-workers or are drawing pensions from that work. It has become as much a part of the Mohawk tradition as the longhouse in Brooklyn.

More than seven hundred Indians once lived near the Local 361 Union Hall in Boerum Hill, a Brooklyn neighborhood. They brought their wives, their children went to public school, and they attended Roman Catholic Mass. During the summers, after a season of saving money, they piled into their cars and made the twelve-hour trip back home to the reservation.

Then they were gone. Extinct, it seemed. Local mail-drops like the Wigwam Bar closed, and the last Mohawk at 375 State Street, an apartment building where for decades there was a Mohawk name on every buzzer, moved out five years ago. The Indians just packed up and left.

There was the building bust. But before that, the neighborhood went bad with drugs and crime. And in 1967, the last 172 miles of the extension of Interstate 87, also known as the Northway, were completed. The men no longer needed to tear their families away from home. They began to leave them and make what was now a six-hour commute on the weekends.

Instead of brownstones, the Indians nowadays take rooms in boardinghouses or cram themselves into apartments or shabby motels. They are scattered across the metropolitan region, living in places like New Rochelle, New York; Hoboken, New Jersey; and the West Village. About seventy men live in Bay Ridge, Brooklyn.

And on Friday night, as the Phillips cousins pulled into the reservation, the lamps burned bright in the living rooms of the square white homes. The man of the house had arrived, and he had a fistful of American money for the wife and toys in his bag for the kids.

These men will tell their children later, maybe over breakfast, the stories from the city, and then tell them that they must work hard in school. But the older boys do not pay attention. It doesn't make sense. They know where they are going: up on the steel.

Some men went to bed when they got home; others went down to the Legionnaires' Hall to drink beer with other ironworkers. A group of women danced in the back of the hall without men. The bar gave twenty-six Canadian dollars for twenty U.S. and everyone in the place knew it was a swindle, but the men wanted to drink and catch up. They complained, like older men do, about the younger generation.

"It took a lot of years and a lot of lives for the Mohawk to develop a reputation as good as it is," said an ironworker known as Bunny Eyes McComber. "The truth is, the white guys—the Irish and the Norwegians—work as good and hard as the Indians. The problem with our younger guys is that they don't understand that. They walk on the job demanding respect because they're Kahnawake, which they do not deserve. This destroys the whole thing, see?"

The hall was filled with portraits of the warriors who served in the Canadian and American armed forces, as the Indians are allowed to cross the border freely. The names are Phillips, McComber, Jacobs, Diabo, and at least half of them are—or were—ironworkers, said Jeff Phillips, himself a former paratrooper with the 82nd Airborne.

On Sunday, he watched movies with his children and then ate a traditional meal of steak and boiled bread, called ka-na-ta-rok. As the evening grew long, his children cried as they do every Sunday. "Daddy, please don't go," they said. And he kissed them and sent them to bed.

He looked through his father's things. His father, Michael, was a movie actor and an ironworker, and he died last year. Mr. Phillips caressed his father's old Bible, wrapped it in plastic and put it away. "He was a very good man," the son said of the father.

At midnight on Sunday, the village lit up with headlamps and the rides arrived and the dogs in the village howled. Mr. Phillips kissed his wife, Wendy, good-bye, and the steelwork took her man away as it will probably take her son.

They drove all night and arrived at the job site just in time to begin the workday. They were bleary-eyed, worn-out and homesick.

"Rasputins"

With liquor on his breath, Alexei Dmitrich whispered at the bal-
lerina, clutched for her wrist and missed.

She was beautiful in the stage lights, her lithe body veiled in green
chiffon, her eyes sparkling coquettishly. She came close and then she
danced away, only to come close again. She smiled sweetly and stole
the heart of Alexei Dmitrich. This tease maddened him, and he
pounded his fist on the table.

"So much beauty," he said in thick, soupy English. "Such a piece
of happiness."

He was rather stout, and sat in a sturdy middle-aged manner. He
had light blue eyes and razor nicks on his square but not unhand-
some face. He sat erectly, holding his knife like a pitchfork, possessing the self-satisfaction of a man who knows he has done well for
himself.

"Like so many other Russian men," he explained, "I have made my
money in America as a businessman in the import-export trade."

A former Muscovite, he was doing so well, he said, that he had
taken an entourage to Rasputin's, the opulent nightclub on Coney
Island Avenue near Brighton Beach, Brooklyn, as a matter of magna-
nimity. They ate a six-course dinner of beefsteak and salmon, caviar

and pickled cabbage. The glasses were crystal. The men wore dark suits and the women glittering dresses and furs. But it was the marvelous dancing women and the sweet violin and perhaps the vodka that made Alexei Dmitrich's chest swell, nearly sending him to tears.

"Something sad about we Russians," he said. "The beauty, the artists have left for the benefit of America. And these women, these beauties, with their terrible eyes."

He promised he would wait near the backstage door. "They must not dance for money," he said. "They dance for the soul."

Backstage, behind the illusion, costumes hung on hooks and the violin lay on a bench. The dressing tables were missing lightbulbs.

On the mirrors of these tables, the scrapbooks had already begun. There were pictures of babies and husbands. There were others with the women standing cheek to cheek. They dance for the art, the women said. But they also dance for the money, and in the belief that a man with a nice suit and a good deal may be waiting at the door.

"So many are looking for something bigger," said Anna Litvinova as she sat at the mirror wiping away the makeup from the eyes that had bewitched Alexei Dmitrich. "I do this for the money. But I want to go to the moon or further."

She dressed, put on her coat and slipped through the kitchen exit, beyond the reach of Alexei Dmitrich, who was standing at the backstage door.

Gravediggers' Gallows
(What Else?) Humor

A. Berg was buried last week. His remains were laid to rest in a hole dug two feet wide, eight feet long and four feet deep, in accordance with Jewish law.

His was the seventh funeral of the day at Mount Hebron Cemetery in Flushing, Queens. His grave was dug precisely, by hand, and a mourner admired its craftsmanship and square corners. "Say, that's a very nice grave," the mourner said to the burial gang.

"Thank you very much, sir," said Armando Malave, a twenty-eight-year-old gravedigger, standing at a respectful distance, his shovel against his shoulder like a military cadet, his voice low and rueful. "I'm sorry for your loss."

"Well, back to the grind," the mourner said as he brushed some imaginary dust from his palms. Then he put his hand around a woman's waist and they turned and walked away.

The gravediggers scrambled toward the hole as though it were last call at an all-you-can-eat buffet. The day was hot and humid and it made no sense to be working in the sun longer than necessary.

"Come on, Willy, hurry it up," Mr. Malave said to William Taylor, a man in his fifties, with more than thirty years on the job.

"It don't matter," Mr. Taylor said, going as leisurely as you please. "He's already dead. He ain't going nowhere."

Mr. Taylor lost his shovel speed after he was stabbed by a replacement worker who crossed a picket line in 1998 during a strike over wages and benefits. The strike was settled after seven months, but Mr. Taylor has never been the same. He doesn't go out for drinks anymore, for one.

Some of the other men do. The gravedigger's credo: After a long day of putting cold ones in the ground, you look forward to putting a few cold ones down.

"It's gallows humor, I know," says Johnnie, the foreman. "But you've got to have it if you're in a business like this."

When their work is done, Mr. Malave and Sammy Acevedo head to Hollywood, at Main Street and 58th Avenue in Flushing. It is one of those cheerless cracker-box-type bars that blanket the city. It has too many television sets and looks as though it was decorated by a beer distributor.

When death is your occupation, death is your conversation, and the gravediggers make for grim fellowship over burgers and chicken wings and beer.

"The babies, those are the hardest," said Mr. Acevedo, thirty-five, a big man who has three children. "You have to get in the hole with the casket, it's so small. It's like you're staring down at your own kids. That's when I go home and give my kids a kiss."

Equally disheartening are the cheap particleboard coffins. "They come straight from the nursing home. No rabbi comes, no family, and you're wondering how this person must have lived," Mr. Malave said.

He rubbed at the calluses on his hands, souvenirs from more than a thousand burials.

"New York can be the saddest place on earth," he said.

How Time Goes By
on West Forty-third Street

Jaawani Abdu was once a handsome man. His face was wholesome and his gait vigorous, until he began working at the parking garage.

They call him Jimmy, and Jimmy has been the flagman at the garage, on the south side of Forty-third Street next to the Hotel Carter, for eleven years. He once was so good that admirers who watched him waving his red flag would call out, "Baryshnikov!" Jimmy would treat them to a pirouette.

Eventually, Jimmy's feet went flat and exhaust fumes settled into his pores. He took to drinking from blue paper cups. He is forty-five, his shoes are old and he wears no socks. He spends his days in an upholstered office chair in front of the garage. He is semiretired.

"I don't like to do the flag," he said the other night, which happened to be Halloween.

Jimmy was melancholy, and he drank a little more than usual. He said his father, Abdessalam Abdu, had recently died of an asthma attack in the old country, Morocco. Jimmy needed the drink tonight to filter out the unjustness of life.

"I bought him the best doctors and nothing," he said. "I'm so sad."

"When did your father die?" asked Ali, a cabdriver who drank coffee from a similar blue cup.

"Four years ago," Jimmy said.

"I remember eight years ago, and you said your father died then," Ali said, suspicious.

"Yes, five years ago," Jimmy answered.

The men come from Casablanca. They are Muslims who drink alcohol. They sin, Ali admitted, the same way that some Jews eat pork and some Catholics cheat on their wives. "The difference is, we do a little bit and people say we are terrorists," he said.

The night was warm and Jimmy sat in his chair and thought back to Casablanca, where he said he used to drink at Rick's Café, the same bar where Humphrey Bogart drank in the movie. He even remembered the address: 45 Jaafa Ben-Aatia.

"What's this?" Ali asked. "Forget about it. That's a Hollywood set. The movies have nothing to do with Morocco, and there is no Rick's Café."

"No?" Jimmy asked.

"No," Ali said.

"Well, I still don't like to do the flag."

They have friends in Morocco who, unlike them, studied rather than caroused at university. Those friends are now people in high places.

"Me? I'm okay with my life," Ali said. "Now, Jimmy here. I told him he could make twenty bucks more doing the flag in Jersey. But he won't go. He kind of likes it here."

"Yes, I like it," Jimmy said. "But why am I having to do the flag? I'm Jimmy."

Where Sinatra Fills Your Ears,
If Not Your Eyes

Here's what the critics say about Cary Hoffman, the Sinatra interpreter who can be heard every weekend at the Carnegie Club on West Fifty-sixth Street in midtown: "Dead On!" raves *The New York Times*.

"He'll Blow You Away," claims the local television station New York 1.

"I like salsa and meringue but he's all right," says Antonio Varela, a busboy at the Carnegie.

Here's what at least one critic thinks of Steve Lippia, a construction worker turned Sinatra stylist, who recently finished a week at Birdland: "He was silly, like an Elvis imitator," says Chip Defaa, a music reviewer for the *New York Post*. "He didn't even look like the publicity photo. He was fat and short and he wore elevator shoes. Hoffman is better. He's just more sincere."

Cary Hoffman arrives to his show with sweat on his brow. It's been eighteen solid weeks of standing room only, but now these two-bit Sinatra impersonators are starting to crawl out of the walls.

It's these kind of hacks, Mr. Hoffman says, that make you sweat. They make you work harder. They turn your homage into fromage.

It's like playing the Catskills.

"He didn't sound anything like him," Mr. Hoffman, fifty-five, says of Mr. Lippia. "And he dressed like a bum. He was strictly an imitator."

You can call Mr. Hoffman Old Four Eyes. Call him anything you want. Just don't call him an impersonator.

"There is a fine line between the Rubenstein bar mitzvah and art," explains the pepper-haired Mr. Hoffman as he sits down for a preshow Coke. "I am, I must say with all humility, an artist."

There is an earnest quality in his voice and there is true virtuosity in his fifteen-piece orchestra, which plays the original arrangements of those old Capitol Records songs of the Chairman.

It has been a long road to the top for Mr. Hoffman, who started with Sinatra records in his Long Island bedroom. He worked his way to crooning gigs in Catskill lounges. He wrote television jingles. He hit the country charts in the late sixties with "Congratulations" and "The Last Person to See Him Alive." In 1986, he crossed over into the business side of entertainment by opening the comedy club Stand-Up NY in Manhattan.

But now it's all about the music, Frank's music. To prepare for his show, Mr. Hoffman takes a steam shower, dresses in a starched shirt with studs and a tuxedo and hums to himself for half an hour.

The first show begins at nine-thirty P.M. It costs twenty dollars, and there is a two-drink minimum. He plays to the locked-out-of-Broadway crowd: Japanese, Germans, suburbanites. The orchestra wheezes to life, and curious faces from outside stare into the plate glass and then flicker away like ghosts in an old movie.

Mr. Hoffman begins by saying something like, "If you're mad at your girl, if you're unhappy when the boat busts loose, you're on Whiskey Rocks Mountain."

And he slips neatly into "I Could Have Danced All Night."

Sadly, Cary Hoffman is stuck being Cary Hoffman. But he does sound like Sinatra, and the couples get so close you can smell them. And over in the corner, Antonio Varela, the busboy and music critic, is tapping his hands on the bar.

A Bleaker Santa's-Eye View

There is a street-corner Santa who works Fifth Avenue at Rockefeller Center with a bell in his hand and a red chimney with a money slot at his side. He is the Santa who works on one knee.

His name is Maurice De Witt. He is a calm, patient man who says he loves the Christmas season and the noble profession of nickel-and-diming because, in some small measure, the profession imparts a sense of importance and self-worth upon him. Mr. De Witt, formerly of no fixed address, has rung the charity bell for the last eight years and, predictably in this holiday season, he has noticed a subtle yet perceptible change.

"The normality is not there," Mr. De Witt said as he perched on one knee and posed with Mommy's little baby, a Doberman pinscher. He attributed the change to the post-traumatic stress of September 11.

"The parents will not let the hands of their children go," he said. "The kids sense that. It's like water seeping down, and the kids feel it. Their reactions to Santa are not natural. There is an anxiety, but the kids can't make the connection."

There are other changes in the holiday crowd. The manner of dress has been toned down. No fur or pearls this year. Moreover, there is no blockbuster toy that children are asking for. Mostly they want traditional things, like Barbie for the girls and robots and puppies and video games for the boys. The colors of preference are red, white and blue.

"Many times the children don't know what they want at all, and that is strange," Mr. De Witt said. "Usually they have a list."

Occasionally he gets an emotional request, like the one from the firefighter's son who wants Daddy to be happy.

Another doesn't want his parents to get divorced. A man in a wheelchair wants new legs. A bundle of rags asks for some new shoes.

The donations are down, and people are asking more questions about their purpose in the wake of the Red Cross decision (since retracted) to apply part of the September 11 donations to other causes, Mr. De Witt said.

There have been some changes in Santa, too. For one, Mr. De Witt does not accept letters anymore. "I'm afraid of anthrax and spreading it to the children." He is afraid of the hot dog vendors, who are banned from Rockefeller Center until six P.M. Many are Arabs. "They could have a bomb in those things," Mr. De Witt said. The Secret Service has come and asked him to pull down his beard. There are no trash cans in the vicinity, for security reasons. There are scant tour groups and fewer children overall.

"At first, I didn't want to do it this year," he said. "But then I figured, if one candle is lit in the dark, you have light." Santa has a hole in his mitten. He wears gold glasses, steel-toed boots and a white belt that distinguishes him from freelance Clauses. He is sixty-two years old and five-foot-ten, weighs 220 pounds and is blind in his left eye from a shrapnel wound suffered in Vietnam. Because of the ravages of age and diabetes, he gets a haggard look as the day wears on. Occasionally he can be found leaning on his red chimney for support. They are weary days of flat feet and swollen knees.

Santa does not live at the North Pole. He lives uptown, in a single-room-occupancy hotel. Maurice De Witt is a black man, though many people do not recognize this fact immediately. They will first pose for a picture and then turn to him and stare into his eyes and exclaim with a little start: "Oh! You're black." To which Santa will reply, "Last time I checked, yes." This does not worry Maurice De Witt whatsoever. He has given thousands of hugs, stood for thousands of photographs, collected thousands of dollars for the army of homeless in whose ranks he once marched.

"Most times of the year, I'm a big black man," he said. "People are scared of me. All colors of people. They cross the street away from me. They draw their women closer. They put their hands over their wallets. This suit breaks the barriers where people can share a common love.

"I've been homeless, I've eaten out of cans," he said. "And, oh man, those hugs and kisses and kindness—that keeps me alive for the next eleven months."

Santa said he would like something for Christmas: a computer for his diabetes club at his hotel.

Children fill up his heart, he said. Sometimes they brush him with a hand for good luck, as if he were a talisman or perhaps a mirage. Santa does not live with the reindeer. He does not sleep with the elves. The truth is that Santa is lonely—he lives by himself.

Life has gone by. He rarely speaks to his blood son.

"We've talked twice this year," Mr. De Witt said. "Once when my mother died and once when the World Trade Center collapsed. He's doing good, though. I wish it could be different. So does he."

Standing, Mr. De Witt sees drabness and gloom, the good cheer muffled by job worries, a feeling that peace on earth is unattainable. The view of the world from a knee, however, is one of children and dogs and the down-and-out, he said, a private place whose denizens make eye contact and smile.

"It's peaceful down here," he said. "You don't have to get with the complexity of the adult world. There is no class down here. No judgments."

Unlike the department-store Santa, Mr. De Witt has no product to sell, no company to represent. There is no time limit per child. He is paid fifty dollars for an eight-and-a-half-hour day.

There are some rules to being Santa, however. No drinking. No smoking in public, and if you do have to smoke, do it at a loading dock and do not smoke through your whiskers or they will get yellow and smell.

Mr. De Witt also has some personal rules of conduct in the uniform. When using the bathroom, opt for the stall. "Children are curious," he explained.

Never go into a store or a bank with your whiskers on; you'll set off the bells.

Respecting the uniform pays off. By the end of the day, he is warm from the love, and the chimney is packed full of dollars. He takes the subway home and the women get on their toes to kiss him. Sometimes, he said, he gets dates.

Santa arrives home to a single room with a sink, well past dusk. He puts on the Drifters and takes off his boots. He empties the ashtray and lights himself a cigarette. He eats his pills: one for his blood pressure, one for his blood sugar and a vitamin to be safe. He pulls down his suspenders and rubs ointment into his aching joints. He sits in his easy chair, massaging his feet, thinking about his son and his poor dead mother.

A Barber's Soothing Aria

Pepe Sanseli is an East Side barber, the coiffeur to titans of industry, lawyers, poets, playwrights and some minor journalists. He has good hands constructed of long, fine bones, and when they are at work, his scissors make the *tick-a-tack* sound of a teletype machine.

"I am an artiste of both-a the hair an-a the mind," says the fifty-five-year-old Sicilian, who studied under the great Giuseppe Martino in the village of Santo Stefano di Camastra and began his apprenticeship lathering faces at the age of thirteen.

There is a certain unspoken kinship between a man and his barber, and an appointment with Mr. Sanseli is akin to having your back sponged and powdered by a psychologist. Among the East Side elite, Mr. Sanseli is considered nothing less than the Signore of the Sideburn, the Maestro of the Mustache. He is Herr Hair.

His simple three-chair shop, Salon 61, is located in the rear of the foyer of 170 East Sixty-first Street at Third Avenue and he is so keen at his craft that a dozen times a year he is flown to Florida by retired New Yorkers with bald patches and drooping hairy ears.

"The hair never a-changes, really. You do," Mr. Sanseli philosophizes in an accent dripping with excess vowels. "It grows a-long a-maybe, but that's it. It never looks different. It's-a just that there's something a-bothering you. That's when-a you go to the barber. You sit down and have a drink an-a a talk about it.

"Of course there is the cruelty of a-baldness. That's something else."

Mr. Sanseli has noticed a saturnine affectation creep into his clientele since September 11, and to calm them he will take a bottle from the refrigerator and pour a cup of good Scotch.

"They're not-a so happy anymore," he says. "They're very tortured about what-a happened. New York is to look good and to dress good. Maybe a haircut helps them a little bit."

Mr. Blechner, a salesman, arrives early for a trim and a manicure. "Pepe, I'm still depressed about the whole thing," he confides. "So much death. It's depressing. The closer you live to it, the more depressed you are. My nine-year-old grandson talks about wiping them out and paving over Afghanistan into a parking lot."

"Everything is-a going to be okay, don't a-worry about a-nothing," Mr. Sanseli soothes.

The salesman is offered the Scotch but refuses it.

Sinatra plays. The salesman laments. "If life could stand still . . . if Sinatra realized that."

"Hey!" the barber lets out. "Don'a feel bad. He did it his a-way."

"That's true." The salesman shrugs. He considers the cruel, unfair events of history and gets out of the chair with his left hand protruding, waiting for the nail polish to dry.

Harlem Nocturne for a
Still-Beautiful Chorus Girl

They weren't average men who used to stop by the Flash Inn.
They were Harlem's most sophisticated. They were men of ways
and means. Doctors and lawyers, masters of the political machine
and warriors of the ring. They were well dressed.

Sometimes they came for the cocktails and the chops. Other times
they came to see her, not knowing they may have seen her before,
dancing the boogie-woogie at the Apollo behind Cab Calloway and
Count Basie and Duke Ellington. They lingered outside a moment
before stepping in. Some smoked cigarettes under the red awning at
the corner of Adam Clayton Powell Jr. Boulevard and Macombs Place,
on the bluff alongside the 155th Street viaduct. They were casual.
They tried for a glimpse of her through the plate-glass window.

"She was a stunner," said Joe Merenda, who owns the Flash with
his brother Danny and whose father hired her way back in 1956.
"Everyone around was trying to put the make on her, but she was
always nothing but class, always conducting herself in the proper way."

Those men are gone. Now it's the old ladies who walk by the window, stop, stare and cackle, "The Flash Inn. Lord have mercy!"

Cleo Hayes, the chorus girl, is still here. She is still a stunner,
pouring drinks every Thursday and Friday, noon to six. She still gets

her crowd. The first of the month is Social Security day. First, the rent gets paid, and then the cocktail gets drunk, and silver-haired women sit at the circular bar and talk about grandchildren and no-good men.

"I've been places and seen things," said Ms. Hayes, who at eighty-six may be New York's oldest continuously employed bartender. She is striking in the dim light cast from the bar, dressed in purple velour, silk and stones.

"Nonconformity gets you in trouble and I'm a nonconformist," she said.

"Venturesome." That is the way she describes her life. She was born on August 18, 1914, in Greenville, Mississippi, the grand-daughter of a freed slave. Her mother died young and her father took his leave.

She grew up in her grandmother's white house in the country-side with a piano in the parlor. She left for Chicago when she was seventeen.

"Everybody left, more or less. It was the Depression," Ms. Hayes said with no note of sentimentality. "I wanted to dance."

She went to Chicago in 1934 and within months made the jump to New York, because "that's where everyone was going who wanted to dance."

She was onstage in 1934 when the Apollo Theater Rockettes made their debut. Prohibition was just a bad memory by then. The Champagne was flowing, and the pay was $22.50 a week for six shows a day. She drank stingers: cognac with crème de menthe and ice.

"We danced with all the great bands," she said, staring out through the plate glass, smiling at the memory of it. "We would get five or six encores. We were the backbone of those shows."

The Apollo got rid of the chorus girls in the early 1940s. Time and changing tastes did away with most of the rest of them by the end of the decade, and Ms. Hayes took to bartending to support her daughter.

"That was the end of the dancing," she said.

———————◼———————

Where Is King Kong
When a Bulb Goes Out?

It was a cold and windy evening, which doesn't mean much unless you are one of the men hired to change the lightbulb at the pinnacle of the Empire State Building.

The ten-inch, 620-watt aviation beacon went dark in October, around the same time that a man waving a wooden musket and wearing a puffy pirate's outfit plunged from the observation deck and met the maker on the outcropping of the twenty-first floor. This interesting bit of synchronicity was related by some engineers who were congregated on the eighty-fifth floor, where they make their offices. "Next time, he should try the door," said a rotund radioman, who was halfway through his second jelly doughnut.

Deke Johnson, thirty-eight, a Kentucky-born gamecock whose job it was to scale the 1,454 feet and 6$\frac{9}{16}$ inches from the street level to inspect the filament in the bulb, shook his head in mock horror at their conversation. "They sure know how to take the thrill out of the thing," he mumbled to himself.

The official job title held by Mr. Johnson is antenna tuner. He is the son of a good Christian man, he said, an insurance salesman who donated his life to the occupation. The son tried the business as well, discovered he was no good at it, and found this job paying him

$17.50 an hour with medical benefits and a 401(k). He did not know, and did not seem to care, that New York union men make twice as much.

"Hell, I'm just an old high school boy, and I made it to the top of the Empire State," he said in a thick Dixie drawl as he zipped his freezer coat up to his chest early on a Saturday morning. The winds would reach perhaps thirty miles per hour at the summit and the temperature would hover around zero. "The only wind and temperature gauges up there's your hind end," he said. "But it's pretty accurate."

He was to be joined on the steel needle by Keith Unfried, forty, an antenna installer, and Tom Silliman, the boss.

Mr. Silliman has a reputation as one of the best antenna men in the world. A stout and robust man of fifty-five, he is a designer and manufacturer of commercial antennas, a competent welder and electrician and, above all, an able climber. He has made more than a hundred trips to the top of the Empire State, beginning in the early 1970s.

To maintain his reputation and business relationship with the building, Mr. Silliman had to get the work done in the appointed time: two days. During normal operation, 17 million watts are pumping from the antennas at the top of the building; for the men to accomplish the repair work, four television stations had to be shut down and sixteen radio stations rerouted through other antennas. The weather had to be ignored and fear left on the ground.

"You climb up there when it's a live wire and it'll cook you like popcorn," Mr. Silliman said around one A.M. as he separated his tools and wires while the television stations were taken off the air. "But you have to remember that a television station isn't making money when all you're seeing is a black screen. Time is of the essence here."

They came by plane and then by a bus and then by the subway train. They came from Chandler, Indiana, a small rural town in the southwestern corner of the state, which is the headquarters of Mr. Silliman's concern, Electronics Research, Inc.

They are simple men and they dressed in leather and canvas and thermals and whiskers. Their faces were red and lined and wind-whipped.

Excepting the forlorn, the seventy-year-old building has good luck for the working person. While the building was erected over one year and forty-five days—ahead of schedule—only two ironworkers fell to their deaths, and no window washer ever has.

The tower begins above the 105th story, the original mooring mast for dirigibles and 1,250 feet from the ground. A hatch opens out into the evening air, and from here the lightbulb—which can burn for two years—is 204 feet away. Just 117 feet of this climb is enclosed ladders and platforms built of U.S. steel; the spire grows narrower and narrower until a crow's nest is reached about 87 feet from the bulb. The crow's nest is less than four feet wide and has no railings, and it is a straight plummet to a certain death.

There are few sounds besides the howling of the wind, and when a man urinates, he will watch it disappear into the night, calculating that it will take minutes before it rains in Brooklyn. The men strapped on their gear, including manila safety ropes. But they could not use those ropes until after they had free-climbed the remaining eighty-seven feet on four-inch bolts welded into the antenna, much the same way a high-wire diver must.

The humor was pickled, but the work, like their footing, was precise. They claimed that they were not concerned with heights, but when it was time to go up, Mr. Unfried took a deep breath and said to himself, "I hate this part."

Once on top of the vibrating antenna, which is about the width of a softball, they locked their ropes into place and the blue sparks from the welding began to fly, giving the appearance that the men were being struck by lightning.

Only the welding of new tuning brackets and heating strips that keep the antenna free of ice and in proper frequency would be done that night. It was not until the next afternoon, during sunlight hours, that they tightened the radio antennas into position and solved the light problem. It turned out to be a broken electrical line, not a broken lightbulb, and the beacon was restored at 4:31 P.M. Saturday. As it happened, the beacon would not blink as it usually does, because the fuse that makes it do so had burned out. Another job for another day.

When the light came back on, the men lingered for a few minutes, and Deke Johnson lit a cigarette and leaned back on his heels. They admired the Statue of Liberty and they admired a city that they would never want to live in. Then they scaled back down, took off their tools and headed for the bar.

Stray Thoughts
at 1,454 Feet

Tom Silliman climbed to the pinnacle of the Empire State Building early one morning in December 2001, to change the lightbulb.

The bulb had burned out eleven months ago, and Mr. Silliman had fixed it then, too. Why it went dark again, exactly, remains a mystery. But without a flashing red beacon, the building is in violation of federal aviation law. Then there are the thousands of children who are sure to be disappointed on Christmas Eve when they don't see Rudolph's blinking red nose. The new bulb did not help, as the problem was deeper than a filament under glass, and Mr. Silliman, fifty-six, hoped the city's children would not blame him for ruining Christmas. He climbed down the antenna, now the highest point in the city, and sat on the metal decking, 1,367 feet above the world. He hung his legs over the side.

"I love this old place," he said, his body illuminated by the red and green holiday lights that shine on the building from below. Mr. Silliman, the highest man in New York, stared south toward Ground Zero.

"If I could make it like before," he said, "I would."

The site still smoked, and with the floodlights, it looked as though the rubble was covered in a muslin cloth. New York did not seem itself that night. No sirens, little traffic, even the rivers did not move. But Lady Liberty still burned orange and the city still shimmered.

Mr. Silliman sat quietly for some time. From here, words seemed to be flat and slippery things, like flounder. He had been to this roost countless times, and still he marveled at the spectacle, so far away from his hometown, Chandler, population five thousand, in the rural southwest corner of Indiana.

"Wow, what a view," he finally said. "I feel really privileged to come up here and see this. I feel so sorry for all those people who died. It's like my whole town got wiped out. Everything."

Mr. Silliman has worked on jobs around the world, including the huge antenna that once capped the World Trade Center. He had a relationship with the twin towers, and on September 11, he watched them disappear on a television set from his office in Indiana.

"When I come up here, I feel it all over again, thinking about those people like ghosts," he said. "But then when I'm elsewhere, I hardly think about it at all, like my life is moving back to normal.

"I don't know. Do other people feel like that?"

Hauling the Debris, and Darker Burdens

SEPTEMBER 17, 2001

The crews come silently to work now. The rescue operation at Ground Zero has become a job. The ironworkers and truck drivers are under contract. At shift change, there is order where before there was mayhem.

For the truckers, it has become a funeral procession of sorts. It wends from the mound of the World Trade Center, still smoking like the wick of an oil lamp, and goes through the Brooklyn Battery Tunnel. It continues over the Verrazano-Narrows Bridge and ends on the peak of Muldoon Hill at the Fresh Kills landfill on Staten Island, where the bones of the skyscrapers are dumped. The trip is a slow one: ten miles and at least ten checkpoints. There are other things in that load, too. Grisly things that federal agents in hazard suits are paid to rake through. When they find these things, they separate them and tag them for later identification. At this point the truckers don't linger anymore. They don't want to see it.

Dennis Gartland, thirty-five, has been hauling wreckage since Wednesday. They found a torso in his load on Friday. It knocked him off center, he said. The thought has crossed his mind that he is little more than a hearse driver.

"It just really freaked me out," he said of the body as he idled at Ground Zero waiting for his rig to be loaded. "I got friends who died in here, you know? Firemen. That could have been my friend. This whole thing's got me beat down."

As of September 14, fifteen hundred truckloads, or nine thousand tons, had been moved to the landfill, which was closed permanently earlier in the year but reopened after the September 11 massacre.

The men who make their career of tearing down and building up the city estimate it will take about a year to clear the wreckage and lay new roads. Giant I-beams from the buildings have punctured the subway tunnels, and the tunnels have filled with groundwater.

"There's a lot of work here," one hollow voice said over the CB radio. "But there's a lot we're never getting back."

The mood among the truckers is a surly one. The adrenaline has given way to fatigue. Though there is little chance that anyone in the wreckage is still alive, the drivers are still holding out for the chance of a miracle.

"I've heard stories of people living eleven or twelve days under collapsed buildings," Mr. Gartland said. When asked when and where these miracles occurred, Mr. Gartland said he could not remember. Still, he has heard about miracles and he believes in them. "It's ironic, though," he said. "We're taking the whole mess to a place called Fresh Kills."

It's unsettling to see a grown man cry, but Bob Vagnier, fifty-eight, said those weren't tears welling in his eyes—it was the dust. He, like many of the truck drivers, is a veteran of the armed forces. He is one of those hardened men, the type who does not cry at his own mother's funeral.

"But this—this is different," he said, his hands in his pockets and his foot on the running board as he looked out onto the carnage.

"What about those young Staten Island girls who took the ferry to work? The ones who wore the panty hose with the sneakers? Gone, I guess. It don't make sense."

The cleanup job is under contract now and the drivers are paid about twenty-eight dollars an hour. But they would do it for free. They did do it for free, in fact, until late last week. And now there is a gigantic new job. There is money in war.

The truck drivers—at least the union men—did not have to run out and buy American flags to show their support and unity. They already had the Stars and Stripes sewn onto their jacket sleeves. They wore them those short weeks ago when times were still good. And underneath the patches of those union truck drivers is stitched the motto PROUD TO BE AN AMERICAN.

"They hit the World Trade Center," one driver said on his way to the dump. "They hit the Pentagon. But they missed America."

The scene through the windshield Saturday was one of chaos. There were thousands of volunteers sitting around with nothing to do but eat donated cookies. There were the crash-site crazies who posed as marines and priests and firemen. There were reporters milling around disguised as construction workers. There were men drinking in bars that had had windows blown out. There were tens of thousands of photos taken. Some people stood and smiled and posed. There was too much traffic for the trucks to move in and out effectively.

By sundown, somebody with an efficient mind had taken charge and the streets were clean and the work was brisk, the trucks hauling debris from the south end of Trinity Street.

There was an esprit de corps at Ground Zero, a respect for one another and the work they were doing. There were inquiries about families and concern for one another's safety. "Get some sleep, pal," they told each other. They wore the flag on their helmets.

"It's all about the working people now," said a National Guardsman standing sentry at the rubble to keep the crazies out. "It's about truckers and ironworkers now."

At dusk, while driving over the Verrazano Bridge, one could see that the harbor was nearly empty and that the Coast Guard was searching each cargo ship thoroughly.

Over the CB radios, some truckers, who had no knowledge of the serpentine downtown streets, were in a panic. "Lost on Rector!" a man shouted. "Maybe it's Rector? I can't tell. The signs are blown off."

"Keep making lefts, Jimmy," came the answer.

"Frank. That's called a circle."

Eventually the drivers did get their loads to Muldoon Hill, the graveyard for the twisted carnage that has become the roost for ten thousand birds.

A Night Shift to Numb
the Body and Soul

DECEMBER 10, 2001

There is no exact starting time for the graveyard shift at Ground Zero. The crews work on staggered schedules determined by the jobs they do. The gangs of ironworkers go until midnight. The excavators labor for twelve hours at a stretch and the firemen often come in their spare time, and so on.

The simplest gauge is sunset, about four-thirty P.M., when Eddie Reinle hits the switches on the false lights and the Pit takes on the look of a lunar landscape. "The winter days are long and dark and cold," said Mr. Reinle, who earned the lighting privilege after thirty years of operating heavy equipment. "They're fourteen-and-a-half-hour days now. Maybe in the summertime, I'll get some sleep. If I live that long."

There is no extra money for working the night shift, though there are extra physical and psychological challenges.

There are the strained marriages, the spotty eyes from the flood-lights, the cold and the wind. At night, the tourists don't line up to take your picture or slap your back. The movie stars rarely visit. It's a Friday night and people are partying.

At night, it is all about the work, work that the men and women at Ground Zero consider an honor to do. It is their defining moment, just as it was for their grandfathers when the Empire State Building went up.

About half the rubble has been removed now, the foremen estimate, perhaps six hundred thousand tons of steel and debris. The south side of the site is as clean as a parking lot, and the only thing left of the two towers is a section to the north, about two hundred feet high and twelve columns wide. Most of the work goes on below ground level now, and compared with the initial wreckage, the scene looks almost sanitary.

The workers, though, do not count their success in metal or tonnage but in bodies. Despite pressure from the contractors in charge of the site and decrees from City Hall, it is still a recovery operation to them, and it will be until the end.

At six P.M. Friday, the work stops: two uniformed bodies are found in a stairwell near the elevator shaft, their faces still discernible. They are firefighters, and their remains are bagged and covered with a flag and taken out of the Pit through a double column of mud-stained firefighters. A salute is given, a prayer offered, and finally they are driven away to the temporary morgue on Liberty Street for identification.

James McKee, fifty-nine, watches. Ironwork is in his blood. He worked three and a half years on building the Trade Center; he watched his brother Gerard fall to his death while helping to erect the Verrazano-Narrows Bridge; his father was crippled by ironwork and his great-uncle Jimmy Sullivan was the first in the family to join Local 40.

"All these people died, for what?" Mr. McKee wants to know. "Let us not forget about the civilians who died here and those who lost them. Who salutes them?"

When the bodies are gone, the work resumes and all the undramatic things familiar only to the Ground Zero crew assume their proper places. The excavators claw through the pile. The ironworkers are hoisted up in a bucket to burn away the remaining wall. It rains fire, pressurized water dissipates into mist and the blowtorches produce an eerie green vapor. The Pit fumes a white stinking smoke. Men shout. The falling metal makes the sound of the ocean booming as it breaks over the shore. The smells are of burning wires, dankness from the subway tunnels and the sweet, acrid, cherrylike smell of death.

There are small amulets: crosses welded together from the steel and piping, Christmas wreaths attached to the grills of dump trucks, Mass cards hung in the cabs of the cranes as a favor to the relatives of the missing.

Around eight-forty P.M. on Friday the bodies of two more uniformed men are found in a stairwell of the south tower. Work stops again and the ironworkers, who have been cutting steel beams, emerge from the hole.

Andy Jacobs is among them, looking numb. Mr. Jacobs is a thirty-six-year-old Mohawk from the Kahnawake Reservation near Montreal, and in the tradition of that territory, he followed his father and grandfather into the occupation.

"I'm Indian, so I can adapt," he says, staring down toward the nightmare. "Those are human beings, eh? But you got to detach yourself. I try to think of them as big stuffed dolls."

Lunchtime comes at nine P.M. for the ironworkers. Some eat the free grub in the Salvation Army tent. They have coffee cake and pepper steak and nearly anything you want there except a change in scenery.

Some of the gang takes lunch at the pizza parlor on Greenwich Street, next to the Pink Pussycat, outside of which streetwalkers also work, because capitalism abhors a vacuum. In the back of the pizza parlor, there is a little bar where the women talk friendly and are more friendly if you pay them.

The ironworkers and their foreman, Larry Keating, take their coffee outside and smoke cigarettes. They are covered in pockmarks from where the slag sparks from the burning metal have smoldered into their necks and arms and eyelids. One of them, Al Benecke, goes back to the night he first got to Ground Zero. He grows animated and frightens a man in white shoes and a clean overcoat who is walking out of the Pink Pussycat. The size and volume of the ironworkers upsets the man, who has the look of never having suffered prolonged physical discomfort, hunger or cold. He tosses a sheepish grin and gives a wide berth to the group of substantial men.

Another man, similar to the first, walks out of the club alone, similarly dressed, and soaks his foot in a puddle, which causes Dennis Telford to howl with laughter.

"Haw-haw, did you see that?" It is the freest, most boisterous laughter all evening. Laughing, screaming, even drinking coffee are not done in the Pit.

The work goes steadily to midnight. More debris is removed and two more bodies are recovered. A group of ironworkers stand on a gnarled beam, one end of which juts out over the Pit like a gangplank. They stand with their arms folded and they can smell the bodies. A chaplain attends to every corpse. No one goes to the morgue unaccompanied, without a friend. Mr. McKee, the signalman, looks at his watch and confuses ten-forty with seven-fifty.

"You lose track working at night," he said. "When I wake up, I don't know if I should eat eggs or dinner."

Midnight comes, the half-moon is low in the sky and the ironworkers don't linger. Most run to their cars and drive home to Long Island or New Jersey. A few go to the Blarney Stone: Bars seem to be the only nighttime businesses in the general vicinity to have recuperated.

There they find a Friday-night crowd. They study their fellow patrons, listen to their worries and small concerns. A couple hug and kiss, soul music plays, the ice cubes tinkle. The sign above the bar reads SMOKING AND BREATHING SECONDHAND SMOKE IS DANGEROUS TO YOUR HEALTH.

At the Pit, the work never stops. Early in the morning, between three and four o'clock, workers found two more bodies, and when they pull them out, Martin Riley, a gigantic man with ears set low on his head, lingers in the cab of his excavator, shattered, whipped, numb.

The halt in work gives him a moment to gather himself, and when the uniformed men pray, Mr. Riley thinks not of the dead but of those yet to be, his unborn child, those who remain.

Mr. Riley had taken the last three days off to be with his wife, having been at the site since the beginning of this calamity. The regular life, the poinsettias and the groceries and the housework, had softened him. Now back on the job and looking at those bodies, he understands how difficult it is to be the master of one's emotions when under distress. And as he shivers, someone asks, "You okay, Mo?"

At some point, all of them need a crevice in which to catnap. The ambulance drivers do it in their rigs, the foremen in the construction trailers, the morticians in the morgue. Many go over to St. Paul's Church, on Broadway, to sleep in the pews. Nearby, on the corner at Fulton Street, laborers stand around waiting to be chosen for office-cleaning jobs.

Inside the church, the morning coffee is brewing. When you put your head down to rest, you see the backs of the pews covered with letters and drawings from children across the country, and you fall asleep reading good things about yourself.

"The sausage and pancakes are really good," one police officer says. His breakfast is interrupted by a call. More bodies.

And at six-thirty, in the waning darkness, the seventh victim of the evening is exhumed, and a Port Authority police officer, who just carried the body out, says to one of the machine operators: "We got some of our guys, the fire department got some of theirs, the city cops got one. Everybody tonight. It's crazy."

No one speaks of the civilians.

At 7:08, dawn streaks across the sky and the moon still hangs high. The morning crew begins to take control of the machinery. And Eddie Reinle turns off the lights.

Hard Hats and Soft Hands
at a Ground Zero Bar

JUNE 2, 2002

Taking a woman to a construction workers' party is like taking a steak to a dog run: nothing but panting and paws.

The more sophisticated of these wolves like to put lotion on their hands, and then gloves over those before they go to work, so that when they happen to meet a comely young woman on a chance occasion like this, they can take her fingers in their own and caress them as though they were a fat little partridge and say in a basso profundo, "Hello, I'm a construction worker." It seems to work. And woe to the man who took the woman to the party, because his only companions there will be his pint of beer and his roast beast sandwich.

That was the scene at Moran's Bar and Grill, on Washington Street just south of Ground Zero. It was a Thursday, an hour or two after the ceremony commemorating the end of the search for bodies at the wreck of the twin towers.

By anyone's account, the men were entitled to drink after eight and a half months of work in dust and asbestos. Before that Thursday, work at the Pit had stopped only on one other day: November 12, 2001, Veterans Day. That was when American Airlines flight 587 crashed in Far

Rockaway, killing 265 people. No one at Moran's considered that a day off.

So now they laughed, really laughed, and had a good time. In a little corner upstairs, they partook of pink drinks, because that's what the woman was drinking. They adopted a sensitive attitude and proper manners and, glancing at their watches, said coyly of their drinking habits, "Oh my! It's only three in the afternoon."

The woman felt the hands of one man, Frankie Hines, an operating engineer, and said, "They're so soft."

There was another man there, a tough-looking guy who was described by the others as a pit bull so committed to the rescue-and-recovery operation that he chewed the bolts off the columns. He never wore gloves on the job, it seems, and he was annoyed to hear of the lotion-and-glove trick.

The fine young lady with the dovish hands did not miss the opportunity to show that she was deserving of the attention when she took the pit bull's paw and stroked the pads. "Oh no," she smiled coquettishly. "They're very soft."

The pit bull blushed. "Thank you, thank you very much," he said. "I appreciate that."

The work at the Pit belongs to the politicians now, and that's okay with these men. They still have their brotherhood and the memories of what they accomplished here.

When someone lifted a glass for the fallen and for those in the bar whose honor it was to pick them up, the woman grew melancholy.

"I'll never forget you men," she said.

———————■———————

Hard Work in
Hostile Suburbs

When dusk comes, the streets empty and the *esquineros* hurry to the homes they share with fifteen, twenty and sometimes thirty others to drink beer and eat supper.

The *esquineros*—the men of the corner—used to walk home alone from the corners where they gather each morning to be hired out for yard work or other day jobs. Now they walk in groups. At one house, where the Guatemalans live, the door is punctured with bullet holes; a white man recently drove by and unloaded a pistol. The next block over, there is a white man who put his house up for sale after twenty Mexicans moved in next door. As he pulled into his driveway, he stared at his unwanted neighbors. He is a tough-looking guy, and he did not turn his eyes away. One of the Mexicans wore a secondhand shirt that read WE DON'T LIKE YOU EITHER.

Up until now, the cultural divide of the suburbs has been more a cold war than a hot one, an uneasy peace, with periodic clashes over public issues like limits on the number of boarders allowed in a house or a proposal in Suffolk County to sue the Immigration and Naturalization Service to enforce immigration laws more stringently.

But when two Hispanic men looking for work were lured to an abandoned building and attacked by two white men wielding a knife, a crowbar and a shovel, the assault was a sobering reminder of the half-lives of the unwanted strangers. The scenario out in New York towns like Brewster, Mount Kisco and Yonkers, and in Freehold, New Jersey.

But the emotions are rawest in Farmingville, where it is estimated that in the summertime, one in fifteen residents is a migrant worker. When October comes, a few men stay, but most follow their money home.

If the violence was a revelation to many whites, the hostility behind it was hardly news to the brown men in the Goodwill T-shirts and muddy jeans who come to the corner each morning looking for work.

Anger on Both Sides

Dionicio Urbina walked quickly through the white neighborhoods. He is twenty years old and was shocked when some white teenagers just a few years younger than he called him a Spic and squealed with cracking voices, "Speak English," and, "What are you doing here, Mexican?"

In the safety of his worn-down house, Mr. Urbina lay on his bedroll and listened to a light rain pelt his window—a bad omen for work in the morning.

"You don't know what it's like to be in a town where they hate you," he said in nearly perfect English. "The place is so weird to me. The suburbs. I never knew that word. In other parts of the country the Mexicans fight the Mexicans. Here, it's the white people who don't want us. It's not the country and it's not the city. It's strange, but, man, the money is here. I never dreamed about a hundred dollars a day."

There are plenty of jobs in this tree-lined hamlet in central Long Island that is home to fifteen thousand residents and acres of black-top and strip malls. Mostly the work consists of menial jobs, such as cleaning pools and landscaping, and, like a quarter of all jobs in the United States, it pays about eight dollars an hour.

The Latinos have come in great numbers to take the jobs locals are unwilling or unable to do. Most are here illegally, and it is their illegal status that most irritates local residents.

The people taunt each other. Some Americans picket the Latinos every Saturday as they stand on the corners waiting for work. The *esquineros* have become schooled in the ways of America. They picket back. And after the ambush of the two workers, more than five hundred of the illegal immigrants took to the streets demanding their civil rights.

Every morning a throng of Latinos stand on a small mound denuded of grass but choked with poison ivy. It is known as the *esquina,* or corner, and it is the best, most visible corner around. Some men walk two hours to get to this spot at Horseblock Road and North Ocean Avenue to be picked up for some work. It takes an hour if you run.

Farther back from the mound are some trees where men go in the sweltering mornings to relieve themselves or smoke a little mari-juana. Next to it is the 7-Eleven, and even though there is a sign in front of the store that says WELCOME TO FARMINGVILLE, the *esquineros* know that they are not welcome.

Here, three hundred brown men on the corner are as obvious as a herd of ostriches.

Before, they accepted their lot as unwanted outsiders. But the beating of the two men has made the *esquineros* angry. "Man, they want you here in the mornings to do their animal work and then at night they want you to disappear," said Carlos Antonio, nineteen. "If they want war, if they want Pancho Villa, then I can be Pancho Villa."

The American dream for the *esquineros* is to find a way off this corner. They tell the legend of the two brothers from Hidalgo who found their way to Farmingville twenty years ago. The brothers worked as stone masons and returned to Mexico with a fortune. Others followed, and now the *esquineros* come from all corners of Mexico and Central America.

Lalo Cervantes, thirty-seven, came. He is from Mexico City, He has gold in his teeth, and when he has no money in his pocket, he looks for a little work. Carlos Antonio came, too. And Gabriel Jimenez. Mr. Cervantes and Mr. Antonio speak good English. Mr. Jimenez, twenty-three, comes from the mountains. He is a peasant and understands little English beyond *push, pull, lift, over there, how much?* and *do you buy lunch?*

Often a carful of young white women drive by and whistle at the men. Sometimes they give the men the finger. Either way, the men shout back with dull agitation. They have grown used to it. White people have complained to the police about the men harassing white women.

"I wouldn't let my woman walk by here, either," Mr. Cervantes said. "To tell you the truth, the whole scene does look bad. But it all gets mixed up in racism. It's not because we're Mexicans. It's because we're construction workers, because we are men."

The morning traffic must make a right turn out of the 7-Eleven. And when the Americans make the turn, they look left to avoid looking at the *esquineros*.

When they do look, their cars are swarmed with workers. One American woman looked with purpose and lowered her power window. "I need only one," she said. She had some yard work. When a man jumped in, the ribaldry began.

"Big gringa in a big car," said Armando Perez, rubbing his palms together. "Thick and soft. That's your American girls. Their husbands go to work and I think they are lonely just like us."

The *esquineros* would like a woman of any kind. There are few

Mexican women out here, and their only female companionship arrives in vans on Friday and Saturday evenings from Queens. The price is twenty dollars.

A Day's Labor for One Hundred Dollars

A white man pulled up in a big white truck. He was new to the corner and had never hired *esquineros* before. Mr. Jimenez, Mr. Antonio and Mr. Cervantes piled in. The patron spoke loudly, as if the sheer volume of his voice would increase their understanding of English. "Boy, that's a zoo, huh? A free-for-all? You do that every day?"

He took the men to a chic neighborhood in Port Jefferson. You could smell the salt water first, then you could see the boats. Then over a slight hill was the patron's dream house. It had a pool, and it had cost twenty-five thousand dollars just to clear the trees. Where the trees used to be were twenty-four thousand square feet of bald earth where the men were to lay sod. Lalo Cervantes, with his nice English, became the crew chief. The boss's wife was very particular about her grass. But Mr. Cervantes was assiduous. He calmed the woman. The day was hot. The boss kept saying it wasn't too hot. Mr. Cervantes kept asking how much money he would be paid.

"I'll take care of you," the boss kept answering. The workers grew suspicious that they would not be paid.

Most workers will return with one hundred dollars in their pocket after long, dirty hours. A few will get nothing. They will get stiffed, and when they return home, all they will carry is malice in their hearts and a vague promise to get even with that gringo boss.

This boss had nice cars and two grown sons with Adonis-like bodies. They like to go to the gym, the wife kept saying. One son drove a Mercedes, the other a Porsche, and they lifted no sod.

"It's strange," Mr. Antonio said in Spanish. "These guys don't know the value of what they've got. Big bodies and no work. This must make the old man sad."

When the work was done, the boss handed two new fifty-dollar bills to each man and said, "You boys know anything about air-conditioning? I fired my whole crew because they're lazy. You guys like to work hard, I'll give you that."

He handed out his card and dropped the workers on the corner.

"Oh man," said Mr. Antonio, tapping the card with his nails. "It's my dream to get off the corner. Here's my ticket." He never did call the man.

Thirty Men, One House

The men walked down Horseblock Road to the Brewery, a cantina with gray walls that is one of the few places the cultures overlap: the American war veterans, the Portuguese-American contractors and the *esquineros.*

A man named Alex Martinez held his head in his hands, his elbows on the bar. He stared into his plate. He had problems with his American girlfriend, he said.

"She just doesn't understand," he told any stranger willing to listen. "All the things. The car. She wants more. I tell her, 'I work for these things. Do you know the value of work?' I don't think she does. We come from different places."

There is a ranch house off Horseblock Road. In the house are nine bicycles, thirteen toothbrushes, thirty men, a big bottle of bleach, a pot of boiling chicken and five lingerie catalogs. The rain began to fall again. Some men sat around the dirty kitchen, drinking beer and complaining about work.

"The boss, he tells me he's going to pay me only fifty dollars because he says I don't work."

"Fifty dollars? The garbage. So what did you do?"

"What could I do? I took the fifty."

In the morning, more rain fell and work was scarce. Across the street, white people picketed, as they do every Saturday, with signs that read GO HOME and STOP THE CRIME. A man drove back and forth taking photographs of the *esquineros*.

"I've got nothing against immigrants. Immigrants built this country," said the photographer, David Drew, forty-eight. "But these aren't immigrants. They're criminals taking advantage of a good thing. It's like putting bread out for the birds and the rats eat it."

The Mexicans understood his English. "This guy, he's not stable," Armando Perez said.

The *esquineros* have learned to stick up for themselves. Encouraged by men like Carlos Canales, an outreach worker for the Work Place Project, the *esquineros* have staged demonstrations at the county legislature when it considered passing laws aimed at them. They hold news conferences and picket the homes of contractors who do not pay their employees.

During one of these vigils, among taunts of "You make me sick" and "My father came here legally," a group of Latino men with varying shades of skin spoke with two white women, one old, the other young.

"Listen to me, please," the older woman said. "I've got nothing against you personally. But you are here illegally. There are too many of you. We're inundated. You take the money home and make no life here. You don't learn English."

A brown man responded in clumsy English, "But Spanish is the second language of the world."

"And guess what the first is," the woman said. "It's the language we speak in this country."

Pay the Rent or Else

When the white people showed up at the corner with signs on a wet Saturday morning a few weeks before the attacks, the *esquineros* pulled out their own banners and signs.

They crossed the street to confront the white people. The white people ran away to the taunts of *"fascistas!"*

By ten A.M., the rain was still falling and the men went home. At the ranch house on Horseblock Road, the landlord arrived wearing a dime-store badge. He had a siren in the window of his car. He was fond of telling the *esquineros* that he was a federal agent. He told them that if there was any trouble, if any man moved in without paying the $250 rent, then he had the power to arrest him, even to shoot him.

This made the Mexicans laugh. "It's really unbelievable, the life here," Mr. Urbina said. "These are the things the men go home to tell their families about America."

Brooklyn Poles and Jews Refashion Old World Ties

Stefanya, a doleful, aging Pole, sat on a milk crate early one morning in Brooklyn, vowing that she would work for no less than ten dollars an hour.

"I forgot tonight was Passover," Stefanya said through an interpreter, noticing that the bakery next door was closed. "I think they'll use their regular women today. They work you so hard for Passover that I won't do it for less than ten." The corner of Hooper Street and Lee Avenue in Williamsburg is where Polish women come to find work cleaning the houses of the ultra-Orthodox Satmar Jews.

The fortunate ones have stable jobs in Manhattan and Long Island paying twelve to fifteen dollars an hour. The desperate come to this corner to work for seven or eight dollars—if there is work at all.

The streets of south Brooklyn were decidedly unkosher yesterday morning. Bread loaves, crackers and cookies spilled from grocery bags after the Satmars and their cleaning women had purged the larders of all leavened products in anticipation of Passover, commemorating the exodus of the Jews from Egypt.

"The Jews are very, very particular," said Stefanya. "There must be no crumbs anywhere. That is why they prefer the Polish women. They think we are the best housekeepers in the world."

Soon, the corner began to fill with day laborers, and Stefanya's spirits lifted a bit. Perhaps there would be some work. Without rising from her crate, Stefanya had the other women agreeing to the ten-dollar minimum.

A man with a black hat came by with an offer of eight dollars.

"Ten," barked Stefanya, who knows little English beyond counting to twenty.

"Eight," he said.

"Ten. Ten. Ten," she said without looking at him, without rising from her crate, dignified-like.

He inquired among the other Poles, who had turned their backs to him. Then he went to the two Hispanic women, who shook their heads, and finally to the Haitian woman, who also waved him off. Finding no takers, he left.

"Passover, it's the worst time of the year to clean," a woman named Bogna said. "The Jewish ladies, they want you to boil the dishes. Wash the walls. Scrub the floors on your knees. Clean the corners with a matchstick. Wipe the tables five times over. They should at least pay ten dollars and give us lunch."

The irony of the Poles scrubbing the stoves and floors and toilets of Jews is lost on no one here. Millions of Jews were murdered in the concentration camps of Auschwitz and Treblinka in Poland. The survivors of the Holocaust came to America to practice their religion in peace. And now the Poles, whose homeland is nearly devoid of Jewish culture, have picked up its intricacies by picking up crumbs in Brooklyn.

"We did not kill the Jews," Bogna said. "The Nazis killed the Jews. The Nazis killed Poles, too."

In New York, Old World contempt breeds New World familiarity. In Queens, Pakistanis and Indians live side by side in Jackson Heights; Bosnians and Serbs in Astoria; Chinese and Taiwanese in Flushing. Poles and Jews in Brooklyn.

"Money talks," says Simon, a lean, silver-bearded Satmar, who watched the comings and goings with amused interest. "Three million Jews died in Poland. They deny it and we hire them. This corner is interesting. Everything happens for a reason."

Many of the Poles are divorced or have families back in the old country who are unable to get visas to the United States. The women live in spartan conditions and send their money home to their husbands and grown children.

Stefanya comes from Katowice, an industrial city in south Poland. She lives with four other cleaning women who are also somewhere in their fifties and sixties in a small apartment in Greenpoint, Brooklyn. Her share of the rent is $150 a month, plus $36 for utilities. She has relatives in Queens but refuses to live with them for reasons of pride and independence.

For the most part, the job is a decent one. The pay is good. She earned $105 for ten hours' work the other day, and the woman of the house fed her eggs, coffee and apple juice, and did not make her eat at the sink. Stefanya's hands are cracked and swollen from scrubbing with bleach and ammonia.

At the curb, Simon paced back and forth.

"We had a regular woman who worked for us," he said. "She always mixed up the meat and the milk. So we got rid of her. But if she comes here today, I'll hire her. You can't say no. Otherwise, I'll pay the extra two dollars. I'm not stingy and I give lunch."

A short time later, the man in the black hat returned.

"Okay, ten," he said.

—■—

Last Days
of the Baymen

The old trapper stopped a moment to wipe his hands, the blood staining fingerprints into his pants leg, spittle popping inside the wood-burning stove. He took up another muskrat, made two small incisions around its ankles and cut up under the tail, opening the vermin like a paper bag.

Nailing its tail to the rafter, he peeled the skin back, stretched it over a board and hung it on the shed ceiling to dry. The musk sacs were salted down and packed into jars. The sacs, used for such things as the base for ladies' perfumes, would fetch fifty dollars a quart. The skins would be sold at auction later in the spring to a dealer who would cure and resell them to various furriers. Soon, many fashionable women would wear the scent and skins of the trapper, Karl Kirchner II.

Mr. Kirchner made short work of the small pile of bodies, eviscerating them smoothly and cleanly. An experienced hunter wastes nothing and Mr. Kirchner laid the carcasses in a bucket of salt water that turned the dark flesh a smooth pink. A neighbor of Mr. Kirchner appreciates the flavor of muskrat meat, which he says tastes somewhat like rabbit.

Karl Kirchner II is a licensed trapper—most likely the only one still living and working in New York City. His breed of man, one who depends on the waters of Jamaica Bay to make a living, is nearing extinction.

The professional baymen: the trappers, eelers, clammers, draggers, gillnetters, lobstermen, baitmen, duck hunters and pinhookers are all but gone. They have either died off or migrated to fresher waters.

Development, pollution and overfishing are among the reasons, but Mr. Kirchner and some other baymen insist that government regulations passed to deal with those problems have also become problems. In the last twenty years, they say, tight controls on trapping and fishing have made life on the city's waters aggravating, hardly worth the while. Fathers no longer encourage their sons to take up the trades of the bay, pushing them instead toward the fire department or to college.

Mr. Kirchner said he bagged only thirty-five muskrats this season. Just seventeen years ago, he and his father took more than eight hundred. He has watched over the years as real-estate developers, home buyers and the Port Authority have filled in marshland, destroying precious habitat. He has seen how automobiles and their pollution kill bay life. It is called progress, he said.

"Progress stands still for no man, that's true enough," Mr. Kirchner said wistfully, "but that doesn't mean he has to like it."

New York was settled as a seafaring town, a port city that once measured time by the sun and tide. Now fishing has nearly disappeared and the last boats to visit Fulton Fish Market were more than fifteen years ago, two scallop draggers known as the *Felicia* and the *Pursuit*.

Once, thousands of baymen worked the urban bayou of Jamaica Bay, forty square miles of shoals and marshland stretching from the eastern reaches of Queens to the tip of Sheepshead Bay, Brooklyn, the Rockaway Peninsula and the southern bight of Brooklyn and Queens.

In 1997, by unofficial tally, there are Mr. Kirchner and his neighbors, Larry Seaman, his son, Lawrence Jr., and Mr. Seaman's brother, Bob. On the bay, they are regarded as the last of the eelers, although they augment their income by catching bait like bunkers, killifish and mudworms, which they sell to local bait shops. Bob Seaman also runs a bait shack outside his home on Hook Creek that reopened March 17, the first day of white flounder season.

At the northwest end of the bay, at Mill Basin in Marine Park, Brooklyn, where just thirty-five years ago there were more than forty full-time dragger boats, there are now just two: the sixty-foot *Rita*, skippered by two Polish immigrants, Joe Bielic and Miroslan Kazienko, and the *Jen Lissa*, owned by Donald Von Weken. There is also a lobsterman, Bobby Raduazzo, thirty-three, who bought the fifty-foot aluminum *Bridgette Ann* from Nick Rosa, who at sixty-seven still goes trawling occasionally when the mood strikes.

Just across the way, at Shell Bank Creek in Gerritsen Beach, is another full-time trawler, the forty-five-foot *Tammy Gale*, run by Frank Sabatino and his son, Michael, and the *Alfhild*, operated on a part-time basis by a city fireman, John Orloff.

In Sheepshead Bay, there is Richie Knauer, a lobsterman and the third generation of his family to run the old Stella Maris bait shop at the east end of the docks on Long Emmons Avenue. Then there is Joe Golemi, an eeler, fish packer, bait fisherman and general jack-of-all-trades.

In the Recent Past, a City Awash in Fish

It was only thirty-five years ago that the city was still considered something of a maritime hub. In the south of Brooklyn around Gerritsen Beach and Mill Basin were perhaps six dozen trawlers, twice as many lobstermen and crabbers and enough eel trappers to feed all the pubs of Berlin. Muskrat and duck hunters combed the marshes of Jamaica Bay.

The dragger boats worked the bay waters and ocean beds around

New York, scouring the Mud Hole, the upper part of the Hudson River Canyon, which was the river's bed during the Ice Age. In the Canyon's heyday, millions of tons of bluefish, blackfish, sea bass, striped bass, whiting, cod, porgy, black-back flounder, fluke and lobster were landed. They were packed out at Hunters Fish Packing House in Mill Basin, or AMC or Sciabara's in Gerritsen Beach, or the Fulton Fish Market in lower Manhattan.

But the Mud Hole corridor became nearly devoid of whiting in the sixties, after garbage barges filled it with acid, raw sewage and lead paint. And today, the numbers of the other species are greatly depleted.

"There was unbelievable fish out there," said Frankie Sabatino, who has been fishing out of Jamaica Bay for all but ten of his forty-five years. "There was so much fish, that it was going for twenty dollars a ton. When it was like that you could see the writing on the wall. It was all going to cave in."

The local crews were mostly mom-and-pop operations, small fifty-foot draggers that each fished with a three-hundred-foot net held open by wooden doors and anchored by a chain. The net scraped along the sea floor and the catch was hauled aboard. When the weather was inclement, people stayed home, and this kept the prices up and the fish stocks healthy. But soon, large factory trawlers armed with cameras on their nets and sonar capable of detecting schools of bottom fish pulled in hundreds of thousands of tons of seafood at a time, grinding up the seabed.

"It was a free-for-all," said Mr. Sabatino, who studied to be a marine biologist and is one of the few commercial fishermen who support the strict regulations on catch. "If it continued to go unchanged, we would have fished into extinction."

But in the late seventies, heavy state and federal regulations began. Controls on what could be taken from the waters were tightened, and the rules were extended to two hundred miles offshore. Still, the city's commercial fishing culture is hanging by its nails.

Waterfront development is at a premium. What's left of the old docks along Jamaica Bay is just a few crumbling feet of blacktop. Old pilings pock the water like stray whiskers. On the north side of Mill Basin is a large shopping center, and all around are expensive sport-fishing boats and million-dollar homes with satellite dishes and indoor basketball courts.

There are few docks and ice houses to service the remaining fishermen. Jimmy Hunter's fish-packing house is still open but does little business. Mr. Hunter recently sold his commercial license back to the federal government, because "there's no money in it anymore."

Byron Young, a marine resource specialist with the State Department of Environmental Conservation, says: "Something has to give. There are more mouths than fish. You can't just go let them catch the last of these species."

Mr. Sabatino agrees in theory, but even he cheated the rules. Two summers ago, he was caught pirating striped bass, a prized game fish. Commercial fishermen are strictly limited in the amount of striped bass they can take from local waters. Mr. Sabatino was fined two thousand dollars by the state. The federal fines, which he is appealing, may amount to thirty-seven thousand and the loss of his license. It could mean total ruin. "What can I say?" Mr. Sabatino said. "I didn't think I was going to get caught. Not then, at least."

Light Catch, Heavy Scrutiny

Donald Von Weken skippered the *Jen Lissa* back into the Mill Basin docks about five P.M. one Tuesday evening, the sun setting a dull gold. The burly skipper was annoyed. The sea had been flat and easy for the first time this spring, but the catch was light, and the Coast Guard had boarded his steel-hulled dragger early in the morning to check his permits and net size with a pocket ruler. "It's like you're the only show in town and they just wait for you," he complained. "You get to know them sea Nazis on a first-name basis."

Mr. Von Weken and Mr. Sabatino—indeed, all the baymen who are left—know that overfishing has depleted stocks, but they say the authorities should not be so quick to point the finger at commercial fishermen. They insist that sport fishermen, whom they refer to as "doctors and lawyers," take a greater share than anyone. Statistics back them up. Sport anglers take approximately ten times as many striped bass from state waters as commercial fishermen.

"I'm not saying there wasn't a problem," Mr. Von Weken said while clearing his net of flounder. "The point is, though, that the fish are coming back and we shouldn't have to pay for all the past sins."

The regulations—federal and state—are complex, and fishermen complain that when jurisdictions overlap, they are expected to follow the more stringent guidelines, making it all the tougher to keep a business afloat. A commercial fisherman may take only two hundred pounds of flounder a day, and the net mesh must have five-and-a-half-inch gaps. "That's like putting a hose in your pocket and trying to catch water," one draggerman complained.

That Tuesday, Mr. Von Weken landed his limit of flounder, for which he would be paid a dollar twenty-five a pound, and fifty pounds of fluke, which would fetch two dollars a pound. Subtracting for fuel, insurance, wages and incidentals, he found the net total for twelve hours work equaled one angry wife.

"A fisherman is only happy twice in his life," said Nick Rosa, sixty-seven, standing on the docks helping Bobby Raduazzo mend his lobster pots as Mr. Von Weken unloaded. "Once when he buys his boat and once when he sells it."

The previous year was a lean one for lobster. And men like Mr. Raduazzo had to take their small boats farther out to sea, where they set pots baited with ground fish and chicken parts. Going sixty miles out is desperate and dangerous. Still, Mr. Raduazzo said, "I could never give it up. It's a special kind of life."

At the Dock of the Bay, a Bounty of Fish Stories

Larry Seaman, the eeler, understands. He has lived that life for most of his fifty-three years, has heard most of the baymen's stories and can tell a good one himself:

It used to be said that the water of Jamaica Bay was so spoiled it could be bottled and sold for poison. The bay has been closed for clamming since 1916.

During Prohibition, Broad Channel, an island that lies between Howard Beach and the Rockaway Peninsula, was known as Little Cuba because so many rumrunners lived there. There were speakeasies and casinos there and on the Raunt and Ruffle Bar islands, in the bay. Local legend has it that they were the favored spots of Al Capone.

An old doctor from the Boer War lived alone on one of the islands. He had a peg leg and a kept a pack of wild dogs. One year during the Depression, so it goes, the bay froze over, he was cut off from the world and forced to eat his pets.

One of Mr. Seaman's favorite personalities was a "sea hag named Killi Mary" who trolled the bay in a barge, mining the waters for killi-fish bait and bunkers. She is remembered for her sizable chest, her salty mouth and the few teeth that kept her company in the last years of her life.

Finally, there was Artie Bertram, who ran an old ale house and din-ing room off Hook Creek on Rockaway Boulevard that, Mr. Seaman said, was a magnet for every rummy, wine-soaked wretch and human piece of flotsam that drifted up from the marshlands.

"The façade was a large false windmill, and the building sat on the highest point in the neighborhood," he said. "Bertram's Mill was the sort of place where a crooked, knob-kneed fisherman would get so drunk, he could walk home straight. Artie was proprietor for sixty years, and his father owned it before him.

"Artie kept a room there and hardly went home to his wife on the island," he went on. "He loaned money freely, had the first television in town and always dreamed of fishing. Finally, in the late sixties, Artie sold out to the International House of Pancakes, for a dime. He bought himself a small boat and said, 'Boys, I got it made. I'm finally going fishing.' A week later, he was found dead of a stroke, lying on the dock next to his boat."

Making Preparations for the Last Eel Season

One Sunday, Mr. Seaman and his brother, Bob, fifty-one, replaced the rotting planks in their boat, preparing for their last eel season. When it ends in the fall, Larry plans to move to Virginia.

"There's just no money in it," he said. "People don't eat eels like they used to, and you need a permit just to breathe. You have to be a lawyer to fish these days. In the meantime, the government is mucking everything up."

Mr. Seaman's house sits directly below the western approach to Kennedy International Airport, and the big jets often fly directly overhead. But on that Sunday, the winds were blowing from the south and the planes were landing from the north. The fog was thick and erased the sky, and the planes could not be heard.

Suddenly gunshots echoed across the bay. Then the squeal of waterfowl. It was agents from the Department of Agriculture, shooting at the wild birds that occasionally get caught in the jet engines. "Some days," Mr. Seaman said, "you find bagfuls of them floating out there."

Fading into the Sunset

A group of men in Mike's Tackle Shop stared out at the gloom and doom of an Atlantic storm that had blown in from the south. The rain was warm and the men sat on crates tying hooks to nylon line, preparing for the blackfish that will soon come.

It has been this way for fifty-one years on Emmons Avenue in the small brick shop just across from Pier 8 in Sheepshead Bay, Brooklyn—as predictable as a full moon. Then the men in suits started coming around, poking at the walls and measuring the floors with a yardstick.

The men were developers, interested in turning this waterfront property and the adjoining lot into a walking mall and flea market. That's when the men in the bait shop began to understand that their era had ebbed.

"I haven't taken inventory in two years, because I figure this is our last season," said Edward Maffai, thirty, who, along with his brothers John and Charlie, owns the business but not the deed. The stock-room upstairs is empty. "I don't know what I'm going to do. I just don't know."

The property is in litigation now. The bank and the owners are squabbling over the mortgage, Mr. Maffai said. He expects it to be settled by the end of the summer, and then bulldozers should arrive.

The shop was built in 1946 by Mr. Maffai's grandfather, Michael, who was looking to escape the congested, postwar streets of Hell's Kitchen. In those days, tree-lined Emmons Avenue was considered one of New York's most beautiful waterfront thoroughfares. Seventy party ships docked along the piers to take fathers and children to fish off the shipwrecks in the lower bay. There were a string of top seafood restaurants in Sheepshead Bay, like Gene's, Pappas, Tappan's and Lundy's.

The family and the bait shop prospered. There was plenty of fish and plenty of money, and there were enough weekend anglers that the family did not worry when Mike Maffai sold the property to the Lundy brothers for some quick cash and then leased it back on a handshake. The father passed the shop on to his son, who in turn passed it to his sons.

Then the fish supply dried up. The cold-weather stocks like whiting, ling and cod were gone, and so went the cold-weather business. People sold their property or lost it when they defaulted on their bank loans. Lots emptied along the avenue, and Sheepshead Bay became a shell of its former self.

"The whole place is finished," said John Kliwalczik, sixty-five, as he sat on a stool twisting hooks. "Real estate is the worst enemy for the coast."

New strip development has come to town, and a large tri-level women's discount shop now abuts Mike's. For years there had been talk of a renaissance, about a possible tourist village with a seafaring flavor to rival South Street Seaport. It was never to be.

"There were a lot of promises a few years ago," Mr. Kliwalczik said. "It used to be that a handshake was good enough."

Springtime for the Harbor Police

The men of the harbor police "Charlie" unit have the grisly task of fishing cadavers from the water. They sat in the station house listening to the gurgle of the scanner the other day while eating their lunch.

"Bodies always float facedown," said Sergeant Larry DiGiamo, explaining that this quirk of nature makes it easy for the police to rope the body under the arms and extricate it. "We got four in the second part of April," the sergeant said, speaking matter-of-factly through a ham sandwich. "We try to handle the remains as humanely as possible. You don't want to treat the body like fish." The few weeks at the end of spring are usually the busiest time of year for the harbor police. Almost without exception, people who drown in New York Harbor during the winter sink and stay down. A corpse will linger on the river bottom until spring when the temperature warms and gases form in the body, making it buoyant. This usually occurs from the middle of April through May.

Normally, the police will collect perhaps a dozen bodies in these six weeks. Among them are Christmas season suicides, wise guys and drunken students.

The Charlie unit is situated near Gowanus Bay at 33rd Street in

Sunset Park, Brooklyn. Stationed there are seven boats, thirty-four officers and twenty-three scuba divers, who attend to water emergencies in the upper and lower bays and the Harlem and East rivers. The police remove bodies with a contraption of chains and rope that works like a lasso. It was developed in the 1950s by a police department blacksmith and has never been patented.

The bodies that don't float are hauled out by the scuba team. Visibility in the city waters is usually zero, but on a sunny day a diver may see his hand. Most times, however, a body is found by bumping into it.

Some 95 percent of people who drown will submerge, according to Dr. Charles Hirsch, the chief medical examiner of New York City. Bodies begin to rise when the air temperature reaches a regular seventy degrees. "It happens this time of year, but it's not a huge event," Dr. Hirsch said. "It's not like the swallows returning to Capistrano."

The season peaked in the sixties, when hundreds of bodies were removed from the river each year, the police said. Just thirty-one bodies were recovered in 1996, a macabre barometer of the declining importance of the city's waterways.

There are particular spots where bodies tend to congregate, rivermen say. In between the Manhattan and Williamsburg bridges, there is a channel called Wallabout Creek. At ebb tide, an eddy effect occurs, creating a backflow. All matter of debris suck into the mouth of the channel: logs, plastic and bodies.

Captain Aldo Anderson, sixty-nine, a drift collector for the Army Corps of Engineers, saw a corpse recently. "It was high moon tide," he recalled from the deck of the *Gelberman,* his tugboat. "It was ten in the morning and we were collecting debris off the Sixty-ninth Street Pier in Bay Ridge. The water was easy so we could see a hump I thought was a dog."

It was the body of a Fordham University student whose disappearance had triggered a nationwide search months ago.

Once a body is identified, it is returned to the family. For paupers and vagrants who have no relatives, the bodies are packed into cheap coffins provided by taxpayers and ferried to Hart Island, the city's potter's field in Long Island Sound. When a boating accident occurs or someone goes missing near the water, the Charlie unit is notified. Sooner or later, they will get their man.

"We just pulled a guy out of the water on Tuesday who must have been down a long time," said Officer John Girani. "He was covered with barnacles."

The Man to See
for Raccoon Pie

There are a hundred ways to cook a raccoon, and only one way to skin it.

There is coon fricassee with walnuts; baked coon soaked in brine and basted in onion, garlic and wine. Raccoon mincemeat pie with lard crust is a favorite among outdoorsmen, as are coon stew, broiled coon, braised coon, pan-fried coon, chicken-fried coon, coon chop suey and browned coon in Creole sauce served over fluffy rice. For the curious and coon connoisseur alike, one of the few places to procure this meat, which tastes something like a mix of pork and mutton, is from Hank Dam, the trapper man who lives about an hour and fifteen minutes from the city on the dewy shores of the Huntington Peninsula on Long Island.

The coon trapping season, which runs from November 1 to February 28, is short and the window of opportunity for the small-game gourmet is closing. What's more, the noose is tightening on the trapper himself, pushed out and penned up by sprawling development, the vagaries of the fur market and increasing prohibitions on his method of earning a livelihood.

"With the bunny-huggers making a squawk about the business and the destruction of natural habitat, I'm about what's left," says the seventy-seven-year-old Mr. Dam, who now earns most of his income removing nuisance critters from attics and chimneys. "Can't make a living off the land if it's covered in blacktop."

Nestled among the million-dollar homes of this old Victorian whaling village is Mr. Dam's suburban Appalachia, filled to the gunwales of its four acres with motors, mounted animals, whale oil lamps, wine casks, beehives and berry bushes.

On most afternoons during the raccoon season, this wiry bantam of a man, who looks as though he stepped out of a nineteenth-century seaside daguerreotype, can be found on his property dressed in rubber boots and a woolen cap, peeling the gray and white pelts from their carcasses and hanging them on boards to dry.

Trapping, like chamber music, is a dying art, and with animal-rights advocates lobbying to do away with the practice, the requiem for the wild fur harvester on Long Island can be heard in the distance. Trapping is no longer permitted on state land on Long Island or in the township of Huntington.

"It don't make a lick of sense," Mr. Dam said as he wiped blood into his pants leg. "The species is beginning to overpopulate the island. More coons get hit by cars than get taken by trappers and I want to use them, not throw them over a fence."

Though Long Island is no longer an open, pristine woodland, it is still a nice place to be a raccoon. Paradoxically, with the loss of habitat, the nocturnal, solitary animal has flourished. In the Adirondack Mountains, for instance, there is less than one coon per square mile. In the Catskill range, the ratio is fifteen coons per square mile, and in Long Island they number more than one hundred per square mile.

"There is a lot more food and a lot more garbage cans in the suburbs than there is in the wilds," said Mark Lowery, a spokesman for the New York State Department of Environmental Conservation. "What these guys do has become a necessity in managing the species."

But animal-rights advocates believe there is a better way to control the coon population. "Put straps over your garbage cans," said Gerald Lauber, a director of the Suffolk County Society for the Prevention of Cruelty to Animals. "Trapping is inhumane. The whole concept of killing animals for their fur is a concept whose time has passed."

But men like Mr. Dam ask how you can treat a raccoon inhumanely. "They're animals," he said. "I'm a conservationist and I believe in reality, not fantasy. When I take an animal, I use the whole animal."

The son of Danish immigrants, Hank Dam moved out to Cold Spring Harbor from Brooklyn about 1945 and began to make his living off the land. He worked as a game warden, bay constable, fisherman and shipbuilder. During those years he could set six hundred traps from Roslyn through Smithtown.

But with the suburban development that has cleared over 85 percent of the island's thirteen hundred square miles, most of it since 1950, Mr. Dam works a meager territory of fifteen hundred acres on the North Shore.

"There used to be so much room out here that you could fall asleep walking the open spaces," Mr. Dam said while laying traps on his postage-stamp-size hunting grounds, the location of which he wishes not to divulge for fear of other predatory trappers and militant animal-rightists.

Like the rat and the pigeon in the city, the mature *Procyon lotor* does well among human beings in the suburbs. It measures more than three feet long and weighs up to forty pounds. It can chew through gutters, peel shingles from a roof and eat through wire fencing. In the wild, raccoons nest in hollow logs and burrows, but in the suburbs a chimney or attic or storm drain will do. Their teeth are serrated on both sides and they will eat most any organic matter, including house pets, and may carry diseases like trichinosis, distemper and rabies.

In 1998 on Long Island there were 1,510 reported cases of dog bites, 206 cat bites, fifty-three rat bites, twenty-one bat bites and twenty raccoon bites. Statistics on human bites are not kept. And because the coon continues to multiply, the Department of Environmental Conservation now licenses 360 wildlife nuisance trappers in New York City and on Long Island who work year-round from the Bronx to Staten Island to Montauk.

Unlike Mr. Dam, most other nuisance trappers are not outdoorsmen but pest exterminators and chimney sweeps, and many kill the coons with poison and dump the beasts in trash bins.

Wild animals supply only 10 percent of the world fur market, said Pete Bartholomew, secretary of the Upper Mohawk Fur Harvesters, a group that sponsors fur auctions where people like Mr. Dam sell their wares. Most raccoon pelts go to Russia and China, where hats and coats are made for export.

When the ruble tanked, so did the market. Since then, in less than twelve months, the price for a raccoon pelt has dropped from twenty-seven to sixteen dollars. Then factor in the unseasonably warm weather.

"You can't sell a fur to a guy standing there in a T-shirt," Mr. Bartholomew said.

Mr. Dam also supplements his Social Security check with the sale of coon meat. A fresh carcass goes for three dollars and transactions are done strictly on a drop-in basis. His clientele ranges from bristle-faced outdoorsmen to transplanted Southerners who consider the meat something of a delicacy.

To feed and clothe these hungry masses, Mr. Dam rises every morning before dawn, straps his revolver to his hip and sets out for his trapline with a steaming mug of coffee in his hand. He is a time-piece among the blue-haired ladies at the espresso bars and the dress shops, and occasionally he still runs a stoplight that wasn't there the month before. When that happens, Hank Dam rails against the sprawling development and remembers the horse wagons that used to work in town.

The morning is crisp and fine, and fog steams out from Mr. Dam's beard as he stops to study some roadkill. With less and less space, and thirty-five seasonal trappers combing the island, a man has to work the margins, even though Mr. Dam is usually responsible for about 20 percent of the year's harvested coons.

"Waste not, want not," his credo goes, but he wants not, since this unlucky coon has tread marks across his back. It is a bright day and Mr. Dam inspects his traps hidden among the golf course. He keeps his eyes up and his head down because though his trade is legal, the elderly golfers "get upset when they see Rocky the Raccoon laid out stiff with rigor mortis."

He uses two types of traps. The box is used around inhabited areas to capture the animal live in a wire cage. These coons are taken out to the woods and shot in the head.

The other type of trap is called a Conibear, a loaded snap-spring hidden in a small box and baited with doughnuts. When the animal crawls in for a snack, its windpipe is shut closed by the trap, leaving it with the milky expression of a drunk who has fallen asleep with his eyes open.

Sometimes, like today, Mr. Dam will unintentionally snare a smaller animal, and this upsets him for a moment.

"Goshdarnit," he growls as he shakes an old tom from his trap. "Just goes to prove, curiosity kills the cat."

So It's a Lighthouse.
Now Leave Me Alone.

On the westerly point of Coney Island is a spit of land known as Nortons Point. On that sliver of rock are a cottage and a lighthouse with peeling paint that are defended by a wizened old man who prefers the roar of the tide to the ring of the phone.

The old man is Frank Schubert, eighty-five, the last civilian lighthouse keeper in the country, and until a few weeks ago, very few people knew that he or his lighthouse existed. Then a national radio program found him. In the interview, Mr. Schubert sounded put-out and prickly; as charming as an ex-husband. Now everybody wants to talk to him. Television reporters. Documentary makers. Newspaper writers. Curiosity seekers. Lighthouse buffs. Romantics. Kooks. All want an audience with the hermit of the harbor. "My head's going to explode," Mr. Schubert says, blaming his telephone, which bleats as endlessly as a colicky sheep. "I don't have anything interesting to tell."

But his bosses at the Coast Guard keep sending everybody by. "I tell the boss, 'Why don't I just quit?'" Mr. Schubert continues, having worked up a good lather now. "'Why don't you just fire me? Why don't you stop these people from calling me?' The boss says we can use the publicity. What does the Coast Guard need with publicity? Who doesn't know who the hell the Coast Guard is?"

Fame is not the issue. As the last civilian lighthouse keeper—in Brooklyn, no less—Mr. Schubert occasionally surfaces in the news pages and on the airwaves, and in a normal year he gets a few hundred visitors.

But the magnitude of this year's attention is inexplicable to him. Perhaps it is a post–September 11 nostalgia for the old, simple days. Perhaps fifteen minutes of fame these days means fifteen minutes of fame on every cable channel. Whatever it is, he doesn't like it.

"*Bang, bang, bang;* they knock on the door," he complains. "I've gotten discovered and now people won't leave me alone. People think there's something romantic about a lighthouse. It's just a lighthouse. I don't understand it, really."

So, in defense of his peace of mind and insular way of life, Mr. Schubert has contrived a brilliant scheme. If someone rings with a voice he does not recognize, Mr. Schubert will say that nobody by the name of Schubert is there, and he will set the telephone on a side table for the remainder of the morning. If the caller remains on the line, he will get an earful of the morning talk shows and the comings and goings of the man not-named-Schubert.

If a person reaches him in person on his doorstep, Mr. Schubert will excuse himself and say that he is waiting for an important call from Boston despite the fact that his phone is off the hook.

"Come back in five weeks," he says. Five weeks later, Mr. Schubert will tell the guards of the gated community to turn away outsiders since he will not be accepting visitors that week.

"Sorry," says the sergeant of the Sea Gate police department, an armed private security force that patrols the sand-blown cul-de-sac that includes Nortons Point. "He's an old man with particular tastes. He just really likes to be left alone."

So, in this game of gotcha, some members of the news media have come up with foxy ways to corner him. They pretend to be relatives. They present themselves as handymen. They call and call and call. Even his bosses at the Coast Guard can't reach him.

"I'm the last civilian manning a lighthouse in the country; so what?" Mr. Schubert says on his porch on a beautiful windswept afternoon, a tanker moving past the property and up the harbor while his companion, Blaze, an overweight cocker spaniel, snarls at unannounced visitors.

"Does that mean I can't be left alone?" he asks. "I've got reporters coming around at night, on Sundays when I have visitors over for dinner, all times of the day.

"They shoot film for four hours and then call me back and say they want to shoot some more, that they got more questions to ask. How many questions can you ask about a lighthouse? They want me to climb up so they can film me. That's eighty-seven steps. I've been up there so many times I've got vertigo."

His superiors at the Coast Guard say they have received three to five calls a day requesting interviews with the old sea dog since he was featured on *All Things Considered* on National Public Radio in early February.

"They're like: 'Tell us about Frank at the lighthouse; tell us about Frank at the lighthouse,'" said Petty Officer Frank Bari, a spokesman for the Coast Guard. "The guy can't sit and have a cup of coffee without being bothered. The man's not talking out of his head. He's sane and sensible. He's just an old salt lighthouse keeper. He doesn't mind talking now and then. But how would you feel?"

When Mr. Schubert does talk, he delivers a quick and well-practiced litany of the Coney Island Lighthouse.

Built in 1890, he says in a timbre of irritation. About eighty-five feet high. Cast iron. Owned and operated by the Coast Guard. He has been tending lighthouses since 1937, when he joined the Coast Guard as a civilian, and has been at the Coney Island house since 1960.

The light is an automated 150-watt bulb now. Back when, the lights were fueled by whale oil, lard or kerosene floating on mercury and lit by hand. If you weren't wearing the proper eye protection, the flash would blind you. It was an isolated occupation. Some men found companionship in drink, some went rabid with loneliness. They are all gone now. Technology has done away with them, and the last one standing is Mr. Schubert.

These days, Mr. Schubert serves as steward to the light, does some painting, grass mowing and tour guiding.

"I'm eighty-five and sometimes I say I should just chuck it," he says, still holding on to his screen door, the cocker spaniel still yelping. "I've got a son in New Mexico. He wants me to come out there to live with him. But there's no water there. I've spent my whole life around water."

He stops for a moment and his blue eyes settle on the horizon toward Gravesend Bay. The wind snaps like a sail. "That's why they keep me around," he says flatly. "Publicity."

With that, the interview is over. He turns and closes the door behind him.

THE
SLAUGHTERHOUSE

THIS STORY WAS NOT written from New York. It was written in Lumberton, North Carolina, and it is included here because it took me a long time to write it, and I think it says something about who we are. It was part of a series of articles that won the Pulitzer Prize.

I went to Lumberton in 1999 to write about work—race and work. I got a job butchering hogs in the world's largest slaughterhouse.

Up at a quarter to four in the morning, home by six in the evening. They were long, mulish days full of runny noses and cramped hands. That's what work is in the real world. I had almost forgotten.

After the story ran in the *Times* in June 2000, there were the inevitable follow-up articles. The local papers had their questions. Nothing came from any of it. Wages remain low. Illegal immigrants still do most of the work. The company makes big profits. America— a nation of Louis the Sixteenths—gets its breakfast sausages.

In one of these follow-up stories, a representative from the factory told a local reporter that I had come to the South with an agenda and that the agenda entailed smearing the reputation of the South and ridiculing its fine ladies and gentlemen.

For the record: I lived among the working-class Southerners. I worked with them. I ate with them. I worshiped with them. They are my friends, and they thanked me for taking an interest in their lives. I learned that Southerners in certain ways live more honestly than Northerners.

The company should pay them better.

At a Slaughterhouse,
Some Things Never Die

It must have been one o'clock. That's when the white man usually comes out of his glass office and stands on the scaffolding above the factory floor. He stood with his palms on the rails, his elbows out. He looked like a tower guard up there or a border-patrol agent. He stood with his head cocked.

One o'clock means it is getting near the end of the workday. Quota has to be met and the workload doubles. The conveyor belt always overflows with meat around one o'clock. So the workers double their pace, hacking pork from shoulder bones with a driven single-mindedness. They stare blankly, like mules in wooden blinders, as the butchered slabs pass by. It is called the picnic line: eighteen workers lined up on both sides of a belt, carving meat from bone. Up to 16 million shoulders a year come down that line here at the Smithfield Packing Company, the largest pork production plant in the world. That works out to about 32,000 a shift, 63 a minute, one every 17 seconds for each worker for eight and a half hours a day. The first time you stare down at that belt you know your body is going to give in way before the machine ever will.

On this day the boss saw something he didn't like. He climbed down and approached the picnic line from behind. He leaned into the ear of a broad-shouldered black man. He had been riding him all day, and the day before. The boss bawled him out good this time, but no one heard what was said. The roar of the machinery was too ferocious for that. Still, everyone knew what was expected. They worked harder.

The white man stood and watched for the next two hours as the blacks worked in their groups and the Mexicans in theirs. He stood there with his head cocked.

At shift change the black man walked away, hosed himself down and turned in his knives. Then he let go. He threatened to murder the boss. He promised to quit. He said he was losing his mind, which made for good comedy since he was standing near a conveyor chain of severed hogs heads, their mouths yoked open.

"Who that cracker think he is?" the black man wanted to know. There were enough hogs, he said, "not to worry about no fleck of meat being left on the bone. Keep treating me like a Mexican and I'll beat him."

The boss walked by just then and the black man lowered his head.

Who Gets the Dirty Jobs

The first thing you learn in the hog plant is the value of a sharp knife. The second thing you learn is that you don't want to work with a knife. Finally you learn that not everyone has to work with a knife. Whites, blacks, American Indians and Mexicans, they all have their separate stations.

The few whites on the payroll tend to be mechanics or supervisors. As for the Indians, a handful are supervisors; others tend to get clean menial jobs like warehouse work. With few exceptions, that leaves the blacks and Mexicans with the dirty jobs at the factory, one of the only places within a fifty-mile radius in this muddy corner of North Carolina where a person might make more than eight dollars an hour.

While Smithfield's profits nearly doubled in the past year, wages have remained flat. So a lot of Americans here have quit and a lot of Mexicans have been hired to take their places. But more than management, the workers see one another as the problem, and they see the competition in skin tones.

The locker rooms are self-segregated and so is the cafeteria. The enmity spills out into the towns. The races generally keep to themselves. Along Interstate 95 there are four tumbledown bars, one for each color: white, black, red and brown.

Language is also a divider. There are English and Spanish lines at the Social Security office and in the waiting rooms of the county health clinics. This means different groups don't really understand one another and tend to be suspicious of what they do know.

You begin to understand these things the minute you apply for the job.

Blood and Burnout

"Treat the meat like you going to eat it yourself," the hiring manager told the thirty applicants, most of them down on their luck and hungry for work. The Smithfield plant will take just about any man or woman with a pulse and a sparkling urine sample, with few questions asked. This reporter was hired using his own name and acknowledged that he was currently employed, but was not asked where and did not say.

Slaughtering swine is repetitive, brutish work, so grueling that three weeks on the factory floor leave no doubt in your mind about why the turnover is 100 percent. Five thousand quit and five thousand are hired every year. You hear people say, they don't kill pigs in the plant, they kill people. So desperate is the company for workers, its recruiters comb the streets of New York's immigrant communities, personnel staff members say, and word of mouth has reached Mexico and beyond.

The company even procures criminals. Several at the morning orientation were inmates on work release in green uniforms, bused in from the county prison.

The new workers were given a safety speech and tax papers, shown a promotional video and informed that there was enough methane, ammonia and chlorine at the plant to kill every living thing here in Bladen County. Of the thirty new employees, the black women were assigned to the chitterlings room, where they would scrape feces and worms from intestines. The black men were sent to the butchering floor. Two free white men and the Indian were given jobs making boxes. This reporter declined a box job and ended up with most of the Mexicans, doing knife work, cutting sides of pork into smaller and smaller products.

Standing in the hiring hall that morning, two women chatted in Spanish about their pregnancies. A young black man had heard enough. His small town the next county over was crowded with Mexicans. They just started showing up three years ago—drawn to rural Robeson County by the plant—and never left. They stood in groups on the street corners, and the young black man never knew what they were saying. They took the jobs and did them for less. Some had houses in Mexico, while he lived in a trailer with his mother.

Now here he was, trying for the only job around, and he had to listen to Spanish, had to compete with peasants. The world was going to hell.

"This is America and I want to start hearing some English, now!" he screamed.

One of the women, a Puerto Rican, told him where to stick his head and listen for the echo. "Then you'll hear some English," she said.

An old white man with a face as pinched and lined as a pot roast complained, "The tacos are worse than the niggers," and the Indian leaned against the wall and laughed. In the doorway, the prisoners shifted from foot to foot, watching the spectacle unfold from behind a cloud of cigarette smoke.

The hiring manager came out of his office and broke it up just before things degenerated into a brawl. Then he handed out the employment stubs. "I don't want no problems," he warned. He told them to report to the plant on Monday morning to collect their carving knives.

$7.70 an Hour, Pain All Day

Monday. The mist rose from the swamps and by four forty-five A.M. thousands of headlamps snaked along the old country roads. Cars carried people from the backwoods, from the single and doublewide trailers, from the cinder-block houses and wooden shacks: whites from Lumberton and Elizabethtown; blacks from Fairmont and Fayetteville; Indians from Pembroke; the Mexicans from Red Springs and St. Pauls.

They converge at the Smithfield plant, a 973,000-square-foot leviathan of pipe and steel near the Cape Fear River. The factory towers over the tobacco and cotton fields, surrounded by pine trees and a few of the old whitewashed plantation houses. Built seven years ago, it is by far the biggest employer in this region, seventy-five miles west of the Atlantic and ninety miles south of the booming Research Triangle around Chapel Hill.

The workers filed in, their faces stiffened by sleep and the cold, like saucers of milk gone hard. They punched the clock at five A.M., waiting for the knives to be handed out, the chlorine freshly applied by the cleaning crew burning their eyes and throats. Nobody spoke.

The hallway was a river of brown-skinned Mexicans. The six prisoners who were starting that day looked confused.

"What the hell's going on?" the only white inmate, Billy Harwood, asked an older black worker named Wade Baker.

"Oh," Mr. Baker said, seeing that the prisoner was talking about the Mexicans. "I see you been away for a while."

Billy Harwood had been away—nearly seven years, for writing phony payroll checks from the family pizza business to buy crack. He was Rip Van Winkle standing there.

Everywhere he looked there were Mexicans. What he didn't know was that one out of three newborns at the nearby Robeson County Health Clinic was a Latino; that the county's Roman Catholic church had a special Sunday Mass for Mexicans said by a Honduran priest; that the schools needed Spanish speakers to teach English.

With less than a month to go on his sentence, Mr. Harwood took the pork job to save a few dollars. The word in the can was that the job was a cakewalk for a white man.

But this wasn't looking like any cakewalk. He wasn't going to get a boxing job, like a lot of other whites. Apparently inmates were on the bottom rung, just like Mexicans.

Billy Harwood and the other prisoners were put on the picnic line. Knife work pays $7.70 an hour to start. It is money unimaginable in Mexico, where the average wage is four dollars a day. But the American money comes at a price. The work burns your muscles and dulls your mind. Staring down into the meat for hours strains your neck. After thousands of cuts a day your fingers no longer open freely. Standing in the damp forty-two-degree air causes your knees to lock, your nose to run, your teeth to throb.

The whistle blows at three, you get home by four, pour peroxide on your nicks by five. You take pills for your pains and stand in a hot shower trying to wash it all away. You hurt. And by eight o'clock you're in bed, exhausted, thinking of work.

The convict said he felt cheated. He wasn't supposed to be doing Mexican work. After his second day he was already talking of quitting. "Man, this can't be for real," he said, rubbing his wrists as if they'd been in handcuffs. "This job's for an ass. They treat you like an animal."

He just might have quit after the third day had it not been for

Mercedes Fernandez, a Mexican woman. Mr. Harwood took a place next to her by the conveyor belt. She smiled at him, showed him how to make incisions. That was the extent of his on-the-job training. He was peep-eyed, missing a tooth and squat from the starchy prison food, but he acted as if this tiny woman had taken a fancy to him. In truth, she was more fascinated than infatuated, she later confided. In her year at the plant, he was the first white person she had ever worked with.

The other workers noticed her helping the white man, so unusual was it for a Mexican and a white to work shoulder to shoulder, to try to talk or even to make eye contact.

As for blacks, she avoided them. She was scared of them. "Blacks don't want to work," Mrs. Fernandez said when the new batch of prisoners came on the line. "They're lazy."

Everything about the factory cuts people off from one another. If it's not the language barrier, it's the noise—the hammering of compressors, the screeching of pulleys, the grinding of the lines. You can hardly make your voice heard. To get another's attention on the cut line, you bang the butt of your knife on the steel railings, or you lob a chunk of meat. Mrs. Fernandez would sometimes throw a piece of shoulder at a friend across the conveyor and wave good morning.

The Kill Floor

The kill floor sets the pace of the work, and for those jobs they pick strong men and pay a top wage, as high as twelve dollars an hour. If the men fail to make quota, plenty of others are willing to try. It is mostly the blacks who work the kill floor, the stone-hearted jobs that pay more and appear out-of-bounds for all but a few Mexicans. Plant workers gave various reasons for this: The Mexicans are too small; they don't like blood; they don't like heavy lifting; or just plain "We built this country and we ain't going to hand them everything," as one black man put it.

Kill-floor work is hot, quick and bloody. The hog is herded in from the stockyard, then stunned with an electric gun. It is lifted onto a conveyor belt, dazed but not dead, and passed to a waiting group of men wearing bloodstained smocks and blank faces. They slit the neck, shackle the hind legs and watch a machine lift the carcass into the air, letting its life flow out in a purple gush, into a steaming collection trough.

The carcass is run through a scalding bath, trolleyed over the factory floor and then dumped onto a table with all the force of a quarter-ton water balloon. In the misty-red room, men slit along its hind tendons and skewer the beast with hooks. It is again lifted and shot across the room on a pulley and bar, where it hangs with hundreds of others as if in some kind of horrific dry-cleaning shop. It is then pulled through a wall of flames and met on the other side by more black men who, stripped to the waist beneath their smocks, scrape away any straggling bristles.

The place reeks of sweat and scared animal, steam and blood. Nothing is wasted from these beasts, not the plasma, not the glands, not the bones. Everything is used, and the kill men say that even the squeal is sold to the toy companies.

The carcasses sit in the freezer overnight and are then rolled out to the cut floor. The cut floor is opposite to the kill floor in nearly every way. The workers are mostly brown—Mexicans—not black; the lighting yellow, not red. The vapor comes from cold breath, not hot water. It is here that the hog is quartered. The pieces are parceled out and sent along the disassembly lines to be cut into ribs, hams, bellies, loins and chops.

People on the cut lines work with a mindless fury. There is tremendous pressure to keep the conveyor belts moving, to pack orders, to put bacon and ham and sausage on the public's breakfast table. There is no clock, no window, no fragment of the world outside. Everything is pork. If the line fails to keep pace, the kill men must slow down, backing up the slaughter. The boxing line will have little to do, costing the company payroll hours. The blacks who kill will become angry with the Mexicans who cut, who in turn will become angry with the white superintendents who push them.

Ten Thousand Unwelcome Mexicans

The Mexicans never push back. They cannot. Some have legitimate work papers, but more, like Mercedes Fernandez, do not.

Even worse, Mrs. Fernandez was several thousand dollars in debt to the smugglers who had sneaked her and her family into the United States and owed a thousand more for the authentic-looking birth certificate and Social Security card that are needed to get hired. She and her husband, Armando, expected to be in debt for years. They had mouths to feed back home.

The Mexicans are so frightened about being singled out that they do not even tell one another their real names. They have their given names, their work-paper names and "Hey you," as their American supervisors call them. In the telling of their stories, Mercedes and Armando Fernandez insisted that their real names be used, to protect their identities. It was their work names they did not want used, names bought in a back alley in Barstow, Texas.

Rarely are the newcomers welcomed with open arms. Long before the Mexicans arrived, Robeson County, one of the poorest in North Carolina, was an uneasy racial mix. In the 1990 census, of the hundred thousand people living in Robeson, nearly 40 percent were Lumbee Indian, 35 percent white and 25 percent black. Until a dozen years ago the county schools were de facto segregated, and no person of color held any meaningful county job from sheriff to court clerk to judge.

At one point in 1988, two armed Indian men occupied the local newspaper office, taking hostages and demanding that the sheriff's department be investigated for corruption and its treatment of minorities. A prominent Indian lawyer, Julian Pierce, was killed that same year, and the suspect turned up dead in a broom closet before he could be charged. The hierarchy of power was summed up on a plaque that hangs in the courthouse commemorating the dead of World War I. It lists the veterans by color: "white" on top, "Indian" in the middle and "colored" on the bottom.

That hierarchy mirrors the pecking order at the hog plant. The Lumbees—who have fought their way up in the county apparatus and have built their own construction businesses—are fond of saying they are too smart to work in the factory. And the few who do work there seem to end up with the cleaner jobs.

But as reds and blacks began to make progress in the 1990s—for the first time an Indian sheriff was elected, and a black man is now the public defender—the Latinos began arriving. The United States Census Bureau estimated that one thousand Latinos were living in Robeson County last year. People only laugh at that number.

"A thousand? Hell, there's more than that in the Wal-Mart on a Saturday afternoon," said Bill Smith, director of county health services. He and other officials guess that there are at least ten thousand Latinos in Robeson, most having arrived in the past three years.

"When they built that factory in Bladen, they promised a trickle-down effect," Mr. Smith said. "But the money ain't trickling down this way. Bladen got the money and Robeson got the social problems."

In Robeson there is the strain on public resources. There is the substandard housing. There is the violence. In 1999, twenty-seven killings were committed in Robeson, mostly in the countryside, giving it a higher murder rate than Detroit or Newark. Three Mexicans were robbed and killed in the fall of 1999. Latinos have also been the victims of highway stickups.

In the yellow-walled break room at the plant, Mexicans talked among themselves about their three slain men, about the midnight visitors with obscured faces and guns, men who knew that the illegal workers used mattresses rather than banks. Mercedes Fernandez, like many Mexicans, would not venture out at night. "Blacks have a problem," she said. "They live in the past. They are angry about slavery, so instead of working, they steal from us."

She and her husband never lingered in the parking lot at shift change. That is when the anger of a long day comes seeping out. Cars get kicked and faces slapped over parking spots or fender benders. The traffic is a serpent. Cars jockey for a spot in line to make the quarter-mile crawl along the plant's one-lane exit road to the highway. Usually no one will let you in. A lot of the scuffling is between blacks and Mexicans.

Black and Bleak

The meat was backing up on the conveyor and spilling onto the floor. The supervisor climbed down off the scaffolding and chewed out a group of black women. Something about skin being left on the meat. There was a new skinner on the job, and the cutting line was expected to take up his slack. The whole line groaned. First looks flew, then people began hurling slurs at one another in Spanish and English, words they could hardly hear over the factory's roar. The black women started waving their knives at the Mexicans. The Mexicans waved theirs back. The blades got close. One Mexican spit at the blacks and was fired.

After watching the knife scene, Wade Baker went home and sagged in his recliner. CNN played. Good news on Wall Street, the television said. Wages remained stable. "Since when is the fact that a man doesn't get paid good news?" he asked the TV. The TV told him that money was everywhere—everywhere but here.

Still lean at fifty-one, Mr. Baker has seen life improve since his youth in the Jim Crow South. You can say things. You can ride in a car with a white woman. You can stay in the motels, eat in the restaurants. The black man got off the white man's field.

"Socially, things are much better," Mr. Baker said wearily over the droning television. "But we're going backwards as black people economically. For every one of us doing better, there's two of us doing worse."

His town, Chadbourn, is a dreary strip of peeling paint and warped porches and houses as run-down as rotting teeth. Young men drift from the cinder-block pool hall to the empty streets and back. In the center of town is a bank, a gas station, a chicken shack and a motel. As you drive out, the lights get dimmer and the homes older until eventually you're in a flat void of tobacco fields.

Mr. Baker was standing on the main street with his grandson Monte watching the Christmas parade march by when a scruffy man approached. It was Mr. Baker's cousin, and he smelled of kerosene and had dust in his hair as if he lived in a vacant building and warmed himself with a portable heater. He asked for two dollars.

"It's ironic isn't it?" Mr. Baker said as his cousin walked away only eight bits richer. "He was asking me the same thing ten years ago."

A group of Mexicans stood across the street hanging around the gas station watching them.

"People around here always want to blame the system," he said. "And it is true that the system is antiblack and antipoor. It's true that things are run by the whites. But being angry only means you failed in life. Instead of complaining, you got to work twice as hard and make do."

He stood quietly with his hands in his pockets watching the parade go by. He watched the Mexicans across the street, laughing in their new clothes. Then he said, almost as an afterthought, "There's a day coming soon where the Mexicans are going to catch hell from the blacks, the way the blacks caught it from the whites."

Wade Baker used to work in the post office, until he lost his job over drugs. When he came out of his haze a few years ago, there wasn't much else for him but the plant. He took the job, he said, "because I don't have a 401(k)." He took it because he had learned from his mother that you don't stand around with your head down and your hand out waiting for another man to drop you a dime.

Evelyn Baker, bent and gray now, grew up a sharecropper, the granddaughter of slaves. She was raised up in a tar-paper shack, picking cotton and hoeing tobacco for a white family. She supported her three boys alone by cleaning white people's homes.

In the late sixties something good started happening. There was a labor shortage, just as there is now. The managers at the textile plants started giving machine jobs to black people.

Mrs. Baker was forty then. "I started at a dollar and sixty cents an hour, and honey, that was a lot of money then," she said.

The work was plentiful through the seventies and eighties, and she was able to save money and add on to her home. By the early nineties the textile factories started moving away, to Mexico. Robeson County has lost about a quarter of its jobs since that time: unemployment in Robeson hovers around 8 percent, twice the national average. In neighboring Columbus County it is 10.8 percent. In Bladen County it is 5 percent, and Bladen has the pork factory.

Still, Mr. Baker believes that people who want to work can find work. As far as he's concerned, there are too many shiftless young men who ought to be working, even if it's in the pork plant. His son-in-law once worked there, quit and now hangs around the gas station where other young men sell dope.

The son-in-law came over one day last fall and threatened to cause trouble if the Bakers didn't let him borrow the car. This could have turned messy; the seventy-one-year-old Mrs. Baker keeps a .38 tucked in her bosom.

When Wade Baker got home from the plant and heard from his mother what had happened, he took up his pistol and went down to the corner, looking for his son-in-law. He chased a couple of the young men around the dark dusty lot, waving the gun. "Hold still so I can shoot one of you!" he bellowed. "That would make the world a better place!"

He scattered the men without firing. Later, sitting in his car with his pistol on the seat and his hands between his knees, he said, staring into the night, "There's got to be more than this. White people drive by and look at this and laugh."

Living It, Hating It

Billy Harwood had been working at the plant ten days when he was released from the Robeson County Correctional Facility. He stood at the prison gates in his work clothes with his belongings in a plastic bag, waiting. A friend dropped him at the Salvation Army shelter, but he decided it was too much like prison. Full of black people. No leaving after ten P.M. No smoking indoors. "What you doing here, white boy?" they asked him.

He fumbled with a cigarette outside the shelter. He wanted to quit the plant. The work stinks, he said, "but at least I ain't a nigger. I'll find other work soon. I'm a white man."

He had hopes of landing a roofing job through a friend. The way he saw it, white society looks out for itself.

On the cut line he worked slowly and allowed Mercedes Fernandez and the others to pick up his slack. He would cut only the left shoulders; it was easier on his hands. Sometimes it would be three minutes before a left shoulder came down the line. When he did cut, he didn't clean the bone; he left chunks of meat on it.

Mrs. Fernandez was disappointed by her first experience with a white person. After a week she tried to avoid standing by Billy Harwood. She decided it wasn't just the blacks who were lazy.

Even so, the supervisor came by one morning, took a look at one of

Mr. Harwood's badly cut pork shoulders and threw it at Mrs. Fernandez, blaming her. He said obscene things about her family. She didn't understand exactly what he said, but it scared her. She couldn't wipe the tears from her eyes because her gloves were covered with greasy shreds of swine. The other cutters kept their heads down, embarrassed.

Her life was falling apart. She and her husband both worked the cut floor. They never saw their daughter. They were twenty-six but rarely made love anymore. All they wanted was to save enough money to put plumbing in their house in Mexico and start a business there. They come from the town of Tehuacan, in a rural area about one hundred fifty miles southeast of Mexico City. His mother owns a bar there and a home but gives nothing to them. Mother must look out for her old age.

"We came here to work so we have a chance to grow old in Mexico," Mrs. Fernandez said one evening while cooking pork and potatoes. Now they were into a smuggler for thousands. Her hands swelled into claws in the evenings and stung while she worked. She felt trapped. But she kept at it for the money, for the nine dollars and sixty cents an hour. The smuggler still had to be paid.

They explained their story this way: The coyote drove her and her family from Barstow a year ago and left them in Robeson. They knew no one. They did not even know they were in the state of North Carolina. They found shelter in a trailer park that had once been exclusively black but was rapidly filling with Mexicans. There was a lot of drug dealing there and a lot of tension. One evening, Mr. Fernandez said, he asked a black neighbor to move his business inside and the man pulled a pistol on him.

"I hate the blacks," Mr. Fernandez said in Spanish, sitting in the break room not ten feet from Mr. Baker and his black friends. Mr. Harwood was sitting two tables away with the whites who were trying to make a pretty Indian woman.

After the gun incident, Mr. Fernandez packed up his family and moved to the country, to a prefabricated number sitting on a brick foundation off in the woods alone. Their only contact with people is through the satellite dish. Except for the coyote. The coyote knows where they live and comes for his money every other month.

Their five-year-old daughter has no playmates in the backcountry and few at school. That is the way her parents want it. "We don't want her to be American," her mother said.

"We Need a Union"

The steel bars holding a row of butchered hogs gave way as a woman stood below them. Hog after hog fell around her with a sickening thud, knocking her senseless, the connecting bars barely missing her face. As coworkers rushed to help the woman, the supervisor spun his hands in the air, a signal to keep working. Wade Baker saw this and shook his head in disgust. Nothing stops the disassembly lines.

"We need a union," he said later in the break room. It was payday, and he stared at his check: 288 dollars. He spoke softly to the black workers sitting near him. Everyone is convinced that talk of a union will get you fired. After two years at the factory, Mr. Baker makes slightly more than nine dollars an hour toting meat away from the cut line, slightly less than twenty thousand a year, forty-five cents an hour less than Mrs. Fernandez.

"I don't want to get racial about the Mexicans," he whispered to the black workers. "But they're dragging down the pay. It's pure economics. They say Americans don't want to do the job. That ain't exactly true. We don't want to do it for eight dollars. Pay fifteen and we'll do it."

These men knew that in the late seventies, when the meatpacking industry was centered in northern cities like Chicago and Omaha, people had a union getting them eighteen dollars an hour. But by the mid-eighties, to cut costs, many of the packing houses had moved to small towns where they could pay a lower, nonunion wage.

The black men sitting around the table also felt sure that the Mexicans pay almost nothing in income tax, claiming eight, nine, even ten exemptions. The men believed that the illegal workers should be rooted out of the factory. "It's all about money," Mr. Baker said.

His coworkers shook their heads. "A plantation with a roof on it," one said.

For their part, many of the Mexicans in Tar Heel fear that a union would place their illegal status under scrutiny and force them out. The United Food and Commercial Workers Union tried organizing the plant, but the idea was voted down nearly two to one.

One reason Americans refused to vote for the union was because it refuses to take a stand on illegal laborers. Another reason was the intimidation. When workers arrived at the plant the morning of the vote, they were met by Bladen County deputy sheriffs in riot gear. NIGGER LOVER had been scrawled on the union trailer.

Five years ago the workforce at the plant was 50 percent black, 20 percent white and Indian, and 30 percent Latino, according to union statistics. Company officials say those numbers are about the same today. But from inside the plant, the breakdown appears to be more like 60 percent Latino, 30 percent black, and 10 percent white and red.

Sherri Buffkin, a white woman and the former director of purchasing who testified before the National Labor Relations Board in an unfair-labor-practice suit brought by the union in 1998, said in an interview that the company assigns workers by race. She also said that management had kept lists of union sympathizers during the '97 election, firing blacks and replacing them with Latinos. "I know because I fired at least fifteen of them myself," she said.

The company denies those accusations. Michael H. Cole, a lawyer for Smithfield who would respond to questions about the company's labor practices only in writing, said that jobs at the Tar

Heel plant were awarded through a bidding process and not assigned by race. The company also denies ever having kept lists of union sympathizers or singled out blacks to be fired.

The hog business is important to North Carolina. It is a multibillion-dollar-a-year industry in the state, with nearly two pigs for every one of its 7.5 million people. And Smithfield Foods, a publicly traded company based in Smithfield, Virginia, has become the number-one producer and processor of pork in the world. It slaughters more than 20 percent of the nation's swine, more than 19 million animals a year.

The company, which has acquired a network of factory farms and slaughterhouses, worries federal agriculture officials and legislators, who see it siphoning business from smaller farmers. And environmentalists contend that Smithfield's operations contaminate local water supplies. (The Environmental Protection Agency fined the company $12.6 million in 1996 after its processing plants in Virginia discharged pollutants into the Pagan River.) The chairman and chief executive, Joseph W. Luter III, declined to be interviewed.

Smithfield's employment practices have not been so closely scrutinized. And so every year, more Mexicans get hired. "An illegal alien isn't going to complain all that much," said Ed Tomlinson, acting supervisor of the Immigration and Naturalization Service bureau in Charlotte.

But the company says it does not knowingly hire illegal aliens. Smithfield's lawyer, Mr. Cole, said all new employees must present papers showing that they can legally work in the United States. "If any employee's documentation appears to be genuine and to belong to the person presenting it," he said in his written response, "Smithfield is required by law to take it at face value."

The naturalization service—which has only eighteen agents in North Carolina—has not investigated Smithfield because no one has filed a complaint, Mr. Tomlinson said. "There are more jobs than people," he said, "and a lot of Americans will do the dirty work for a while and then return to their couches and eat bonbons and watch *Oprah*."

Not Fit for a Convict

When Billy Harwood was in solitary confinement, he liked a book to get him through. A guard would come around with a cartful. But when the prisoner asked for a new book, the guard, before handing it to him, liked to tear out the last fifty pages. The guard was a real funny guy.

"I got good at making up my own endings," Billy Harwood said during a break. "And my book don't end standing here. I ought to be on that roof any day now."

But a few days later, he found out that the white contractor he was counting on already had a full roofing crew. They were Mexicans who were working for less than he was making at the plant.

During his third week cutting hogs, he got a new supervisor—a black woman. Right away she didn't like his work ethic. He went too slow. He cut out to the bathroom too much.

"Got a bladder infection?" she asked, standing in his spot when he returned. She forbade him to use the toilet.

He boiled. Mercedes Fernandez kept her head down. She was certain of it: he was the laziest man she had ever met. She stood next to a black man now, a prisoner from the north. They called him K.T. and he was nice to her. He tried Spanish, and he worked hard.

When the paychecks were brought around at lunchtime on Friday, Billy Harwood got paid for five hours less than everyone else, even though everyone punched out on the same clock. The supervisor had docked him.

The prisoners mocked him. "You might be white," K.T. said, "but you came in wearing prison greens and that makes you good as a nigger."

The ending wasn't turning out the way Billy Harwood had written it: no place to live and a job not fit for a donkey. He quit and took the Greyhound back to his parents' trailer in the hills.

When Mrs. Fernandez came to work the next day, a Mexican guy going by the name of Alfredo was standing in Billy Harwood's spot.

JOINTS

I WAS TALKING with Eddie Keating, the photographer whose work has often accompanied mine, about the regular people in New York, the small people and small places and small moments that newspapers have no room for. A lot of these moments take place in bars.

The bar is one place where New York overlaps and meets itself. Even churchgoers go to bars. There are eleven thousand drinking establishments in the five boroughs and millions of sinners who swear by them.

The dark, oily places keep the best secrets, but you are required to drink in order to hear them. Nobody trusts a teetotaler, and Eddie doesn't drink. The chore was left to me. After two or three weeks of writing the drinking column "Bending Elbows," I began to worry that my brain was turning to boiled beef.

Nobody seemed to notice.

At This Bar,
Everything Is on the Table

She is a champion of social drinking, an unapologetic gossip who believes that everything—everything—should be discussed at her bar.

Monica Constantinides is the owner of Cafe Bar in Astoria, Queens, at Thirty-fourth Avenue and Thirty-fifth Street, across from the Kaufman sound stages. Alcohol sows hard seeds, and if you've never been angry with this woman, you're probably not her friend. Lou the Landlord likes to drink, and he used to like to drink with her. Then she remodeled the kitchen and laughed too many times at him.

"Lou, you're here so much," she said, "you paid for my kitchen."

This made Lou mad, so he stopped drinking there. Now he drinks down the block at Tupelo, a new place owned by the Roumeliotis brothers. Evangelos Roumeliotis used to work for Monica. His brother Fotios was a marble cutter.

Monica and the Roumeliotis brothers and two other bartenders live in Lou the Landlord's building, which is on a third corner between the two bars. The residents of his building can't help mucking up one another's lives. That's how the bar business is.

In the bar business, your life becomes the bar, Monica says. And it is easy to tell when she feels sad or happy or bloated. She strips the walls, papers them with foil or paints them orange.

She can be imperious, and though the waiters and waitresses at her establishment are notoriously slow, she expects them to keep her evening glass filled.

She is thirty-four, and pampers herself. The lifestyle has added a few pounds to her tall frame, and this makes her sad. She has taken to fad dieting. As Oprah says, the hardest beauty to appreciate is your own.

She is known to have had two serious men, both of whom she met at her bar. One and a half of those men did not work out. This may seem a private matter, but little is private in her bar.

There is a little old man in the neighborhood who has nothing but old photographs and sad memories. He wandered into the bar one morning and she fed this stray tea and milk. Now he has companionship and a Scrabble game some mornings.

"She saved my life," he said of her. "If she wasn't here, this beautiful girl, I would have killed myself."

Another patron, who long ago became a friend of Monica's, had a sister. When his sister died, the patron cried on her neck all night.

She got him good and drunk and listened closely, which is not her nature. She sent him home in a car and then talked about him and his grief at the bar. This was fine, because it saved the patron the pain of having to tell everybody himself. He was grateful.

She lends money to customers in need, gives unearned bonuses to employees with troubles in the old country. She cooks Thanksgiving dinners for lonely old men.

A bar is a bar regardless of what hangs on the walls, and a drink is a drink, more or less. The finest places are made up of the finest people, and hers is a fine place to drink.

Schlitz on Draft

It has been said that drink is the curse of the working class. It has also been said that work is the curse of the drinking class. And so it stands to reason that a carpenter taking lunch at the neighborhood tavern usually dines with the damned.

Jimmy Williams sits at the wood trying to get a third one down his neck before the foreman notices he is missing. "Better lemme get a corned beef sandwich to go," he barks to the barman. "Don't want the boss smelling vodka on my breath again. And if my wife gets a whiff of it . . ."

"You want it to go?" asks Tommy Cornish, warming up the same gag he uses every working day. "Where you want it to go?"

The Schlitz Inn is the kind of bar that reminds you of a time when you weren't around, a garish place with plastic flowers, dusty plants, checkered tablecloths, stag heads, jugs of Paul Masson rose wine and rye whiskey. It is in a two-toned painted brick building at 137th Street and Willow Avenue in Port Morris, the Bronx, and it can safely be called the last remaining German restaurant and bar in the area.

There used to be others, says the sinewy Maria Wechsler, who is listed on the business cards as the "prop." She is also cook, waitress, pit bull and historian. Mrs. Wechsler shows off pictures of factory workers in fedoras and superintendents in suspenders to prove that people actually used to come to this part of town. But the once vibrant neighborhood fell under a shadow when Robert Moses decided to jam the Bruckner Expressway right down its throat in 1953.

The neighborhood became so decrepit that the Schlitz was used as the bar in the 1981 film *Fort Apache, the Bronx,* starring Paul Newman.

Madam Wechsler comes out of the kitchen for the after-lunch lull and sits at a back table for a smoke. "Newman, he wasn't my type," she says, coughing like a goose. "He was too short. I wasn't impressed."

Mr. Newman is long gone and has never returned. But the good news is that the neighborhood is making a comeback. Nearly all of the commercial buildings in this urban pile along the East River are full. The *New York Post* is constructing a printing plant a few blocks away. That means a lot of new paychecks going toward gravy and pickles and other homemade foods not likely to be found at home anymore.

And of course, there's Schlitz beer on draft.

But the new business also brings its own brand of gentrification. The place used to be strictly word-of-mouth. Now suits are coming to the neighborhood, as well as ham-fisted workers from the suburbs who don't understand that in these kinds of bars, class distinctions trump racial and ethnic ones.

Two Hispanic men come in for a shot and two burgers to go. They leave without saying hello. "You figure these guys come to this country and can at least learn the language," says one road worker to the bar, lined with blacks and whites.

"Take it easy, bud," Jimmy Williams tells him. "Didn't you see their hands? They were working men. One of us."

A Bar on Rails

The 6:07 to New Canaan was sitting empty on track 25. Empty except for the barkeep, who was preparing the bar car for the commuter rush. He was crushing ice. Sounds of *The Nutcracker Suite* echoed down the tracks from Grand Central Terminal.

"This is Vinny's train," he said. "But Vinny's on vacation, so I got it tonight. It's a player type of crowd. It should be pretty good." The first player came aboard at 5:45. He was wearing a nice coat and ordered a gin and tonic. A second player arrived a moment later, wearing a tangerine tie. It was a daring accessory. Currency makes men courageous. Scotch and rocks for him. Next, the Romantic in a purple scarf requested a Scotch and soda with a twist.

The Connecticut contingent of Wall Street and Park Avenue arrived in waves of cologne. They were bond traders and advertising executives, lawyers and radio personalities, the blue bloods and blue shirts. The men wore tasseled loafers, suede loafers, wing tips. They sported gold watches and legal briefs. The woman wore a power suit.

By 5:56 they were fifteen deep at the bar and there was a certain esprit de corps among them. The market had gone to the moon that day, registering a record.

"The economy's going to come down for a soft landing," one jowly advertising executive said. "It has to. You know how much freaking work I'm having done to my house?"

"Doesn't matter to me," said the Nasdaq trader, who had the charming habit of picking at his nails while his pinky finger was stuck out in the Emily Post position. "My bonus is going to be bigger than last year's. Volatility is my friend. Volatility is my children's friend."

The Metro-North bar cars are hermetically sealed tubes of linoleum in which million-dollar deals are made over plastic-cup cocktails, and golf matches and dinners with the wives are arranged.

But some teetotaling commuters want to take this all away. The evening trains are crowded and to make room for the bar, eighty seats have been removed. This is an unfair advantage for the lovers of libations, the dry commuters contend.

"They're just jealous," said Michael Danforth, a bar car regular and an advertising sales manager. "They can't stand to see a guy have a good time."

And the evening was nothing but good times. There were no laptops or cell phones, no reading of the serious broadsheets. Just liquor and the gossip pages. The riders stood with their backs to the window as Harlem at 125th Street passed below and the people on the streets stood in groups drinking from paper bags, bracing themselves against the wind.

Meanwhile, there is a poster in the bar car of James Bond, who tells the commuters what kind of watch they should wear.

The train passed over the Mianus River at 6:46 and the revelers could feel the bridge rumble beneath their feet. The last stop is New Canaan at 7:15. THE STATION NEXT TO HEAVEN, the sign says. And the wives are waiting in their new Mercedeses.

Smile for the Camera

There is a video surveillance camera on top of a light post in Harlem at 141st Street and Adam Clayton Powell Jr. Boulevard.

It is meant to deter bad people from doing bad things. The trouble is, most people who spend time at the corner resent the mechanical snooping. Who asked to have the camera put up? One suspects the decision was made by a white man in a downtown office. This small metallic spy box contributes little toward racial brotherhood in a city that prides itself on tolerance.

So when a person of light pigmentation is found north of 125th Street, people assume that he is either lost, looking for drugs, an undercover cop or a hayseed. It is explained to him—as if he knows the white man responsible for this outrage—that the camera gives a person a bad feeling to be standing in its unblinking eye, being scrutinized on a warm summer evening while trying to have an alcoholic beverage with your friends after a long, dull day of work.

"That's life in the 'hood, son," he is told.

The drinks on this corner must be surreptitiously poured into plastic-foam cups bought from the bodega. The cups come with a plastic top, straw and ice cubes, and the disguise is a neat one, as rum and Coke is indistinguishable from chocolate milk.

A group of men stood under an awning for a spell. One had a face heavily fatigued by the fists of one J. Black, a boxer who didn't like the way this lesser man had talked to his sister. Another, Sherrod Brown, was wearing Curve cologne, and it was agreed that women prefer this scent to Joop!, the previous favorite, which fell out of favor when the Jamaicans caught on to it.

Rain fell heavily, and the men decided to drive two blocks north to Danny and Mel's Barbershop for a haircut and some privacy. Danny and Mel's is a center of social life. Drinking is permitted as long as the patron behaves himself. The establishment is so popular that traffic is routinely double-parked out front.

Dax Church is a welfare-fraud investigator. His is a thankless, dangerous job that ranks down there with the prison guard and surveillance-camera installer. "There's a lot of hostility directed toward you," he said. "And you can understand it. I mean, I'm not leaving your living room until you can tell me how you're affording eight hundred dollars rent."

After days like this, Mr. Church said, he needs a cocktail.

The drinks at the barbershop were muscular and, as is often the case in mixed company, the talk veered to the racial. It was a friendly conversation until a woman screamed, "White man!"

A cramped, nervous silence fell over the barbershop until she repeated herself.

"White van," she said. "The police are out there ticketing a white van."

A Beer Hall with
Homegrown Czech Nostalgia

Absinthe, as described by Oscar Wilde to Mrs. Leverson, his hairdresser: "After the first glass, you see things as you wish they were. After the second, you see things as they are not. Finally, you see things as they really are and that is the most horrible thing in the world!"

According to the books, absinthe is a pernicious green liquor that is distilled from wormwood, tastes like licorice and is 160 proof. It is said to turn your brain to lard after prolonged use, and it has inspired poets to reflect on the warm cheeks of fresh corpses. Though it was outlawed in most countries after World War I, two countries still manufacture the stuff: Spain and the Czech Republic.

Last summer at the Bohemian Hall and Park in Astoria, Queens, a beer garden that Eastern European immigrants affectionately call Little Prague, a large-knuckled man with an egglike head raised a green bottle and proudly proclaimed it absinthe. Some in the crowd stared longingly, as though it were a photograph of home.

The Bohemian Hall and Park, at Twenty-ninth Street and Twenty-fourth Avenue, a block off the elevated line, is a good summertime place to socialize. Built on a cow pasture nearly a century ago, the hall is the last European-style beer garden in the city. It can seat one thousand drinkers and a tuba band, and outside there are picnic tables under a cooling canopy of sycamore and oak trees.

When the wet winds blow, the adjacent Czech Hall is filled mainly with Czechs and the sweet smell of beef dumplings. So before the skies warm and the place becomes diluted with Midwesterners and dogmen and Bowzer, it seemed a prime time to return and research the legend of the bottled green ruin.

The hall is run by John Bartunek, a lugubrious man who walks the dark corridors with a perpetual pint of Pilsner as if it were a lantern and he the ghost of Christmas future.

In a monotone gloom, he will list the year's events: the pork fest, the New Year's fest, Oktoberfest, Easter fest, the Czech-Slovak fest. He will list the menu: Wiener schnitzel, kielbasa, meat loaf. No absinthe. "Absinthe," he declares, "is absolutely illegal."

Jadga the architect is one of two men who wear a suit to the hall. He drinks beer greedily, like a nursing kitten. "Absinthe? I don't know so much about that," he says. "But the breweries in Pilsen have open lagoons of fermenting beer. They are as large as Olympic pools. How nice it would be to jump in and stay drunk all the time."

In the spring, when the clouds open up, the place begins to steam. Some of the Czech women are picturesque, tall and square-jawed. The problem is, beauty doesn't buy you a green card.

"Who built America?" asks the ravishing Daniela. "Europeans, that's who. Now, why in America do they allow so many Spanish and Indians and no more white people? We need help, too. In my country, the Russian gangsters control everything."

And what about absinthe? She frowned. "It's for old men and pigs."

The Harbor Light
Stays On

The stranger walked into the Harbor Light Pub and was met with stares. Gloomy, downcast eyes dressed in black.

The stares themselves were not an odd thing. Most strangers who walk through the doors are usually given the once-over. This is not a bar strangers find by chance. It is at Beach 129th Street and Newport Avenue on the Rockaway Peninsula, twelve miles and a world away from Manhattan. The men who grow up on the peninsula's western tip lean toward two careers: finance or the fire department. Those who pick finance are often the sons of firefighters, whose fathers have discouraged them from the job, thinking Wall Street would be safer.

Two weeks ago, on September 11, when the first jet plowed into the offices of Cantor Fitzgerald, an international bond firm in the World Trade Center, people found out just how dangerous the world of high finance could be.

About ninety people from the west end of the peninsula died in the attacks, both stockbrokers and men from the fire brigade. Most of the bodies have not been recovered.

In the Harbor Light, the quality of the eyes was noticeable. They were hard, almost hostile stones belonging to people who had just returned from a memorial or a wake or the couch of a widow.

Hardly a word was spoken there the other afternoon, though the place was doing a brisk business. There was no Champagne or expensive wine. Just beer and liquor chased with the silence of human companionship. Photographs from the owner's days in the fire department hung on the stucco walls. Food was frying on the grill. An unwelcome light poured in through the large plate-glass window.

The owner's name is Bernie Heeran. His son Charlie worked on the trading desk at Cantor Fitzgerald. "I lost my son, and I've got fifty funerals to go to," Mr. Heeran said. "I don't feel anything."

The bar fell back into soundlessness except for the television, which broadcast, among other things, a commercial for the good American life. It was an ad about sailboats and blondes in bikinis and surefire methods to stop hair loss.

If it were only hair loss. They figure forty people from the immediate neighborhood died, and if you trace a finger along the web of friendship, the losses multiply into the hundreds. Perhaps thousands.

The stranger eventually spoke. "Excuse me, sir," he asked a morose-looking man who stared into his glass. "Can you tell me where the church is?"

The man raised his head without taking his eyes from the glass.

"Right out there," he said, and motioned toward the window with his chin. "Just look for the priest."

The Lights Are Bright,
the Hours Always Happy

The Great White Way is no longer the stomping ground for dancing girls and streetwalkers, prizefighters and gangsters. The old bawdy spots are mostly a memory cemented over with theme bars and pricey hotels.

But Times Square is still an electric forest fire more splendid at midnight than noon, and there is still a shabby little bar in the back of a shabby restaurant, a relic of other days.

Howard Johnson's lights up the corner of Forty-sixth Street and Broadway, as it has for the last forty-two years. The paper sign in the window advertises happy hour from four to seven, and all drinks are $3.25. But read the small print on the sign: EXCEPT PREMIUM BRANDS.

Nine o'clock is a good time. Olga is the bartender, and though the bar is nearly empty, the waiters have a hard time finding enough space to negotiate around the pretty Russian without pawing or manhandling her. The cook wears enormous shoes coated in grease, and the waiters are such an international group that they have to say things twice to one another because their English, the only common language, is incomprehensible.

Joseph, the manager for thirty-five years, would not reveal the identity of the owner, and kept his own last name confidential, too. Despite numerous offers to buy, there are no plans to sell, he said.

"We went through a lot of hard times here," he said. "I would stare out the window and watch muggers slit open the back of people's pants and steal their wallets, or sometimes they would spray ketchup on a tourist's back, and while they were apologizing and wiping it off, they would pick the poor guy's pocket."

Joseph explained that the place is now making money, but even so, it has not been remodeled since the sixties, because the clientele favor the nostalgic look of the cheap paneling, brass chandeliers and orange banquettes.

"It's like we haven't aged," the manager said.

The battery in the bar clock has never been changed, so the clock says 10:45 permanently.

"To have a clock at the bar is a bad idea," Joseph said. "They should come to drink, not to read the time. Our regulars like to feel like it's their dining room."

There was an obese couple who sat by the bar. He ordered a shell steak and baked potato smothered in gravy, Texas chili to start, a strawberry shortcake to finish and a light beer.

His wife asked him if the beer wasn't too much, and he told her to shut up. She asked him why she was supposed to shut up.

"Because you talk too much," he said. "So zip it."

She did, and when the platters arrived, he speared one of her fries and ordered another beer.

Stars, Stripes and Insults

Inside Lafayette American Legion Post 1906, at Nineteenth Street and Bath Avenue in Bensonhurst, a stained American flag hangs on one paneled wall.

There is a pool table, a television set on top of an old refrigerator, and three men at the bar. The bartender's name is Mikey. The front and back doors are propped open, letting in the dying sunlight and a scent of curry from the street.

Bobby Hair has dabs of paint on his face. He turns to the man sitting next to him. He's known him forever.

"What's your name again?"

"Noel."

"Like Merry X-mas Noel?"

"No. Like Noel Parking."

"Boy, that's something," says Bobby Hair.

"You bet that's something."

"Something I never heard of," says Bobby Hair. "Your mother must not have liked you much."

"Speak for yourself. She breast-fed me," Noel informs him.

"Ah," says Bobby Hair with a wave of the hand. "She breast-fed everybody."

"Hey, give me some respect," says Noel. He's an older guy with white hair. "I'm a hardworking man."

"Hardworking man?" repeats Bobby Hair.

"Yeah. I'm a workaholic."

"You work in Harlem?"

"You know, I'm not feeling comfortable in here yet," says Noel.

"Try your home," says Bobby Hair.

Mikey the barman puts a couple of Heinekens on ice for Noel.

Then the light above the pool table goes out. Mikey puts Bobby Hair up on his shoulder and waltzes him around the pool table like he was his bride. Bobby Hair replaces the bulb, and Mikey lets him down.

"You're incredible, Mikey," says Bobby Hair, full of admiration for the stamina of the older man.

"Yeah, Bobby. And you're dimmer than that forty-watt bulb."

Mikey goes to close the door. When he does, the television turns to static.

"Hey, you're killing the TV," screams Bobby Hair.

Mikey opens the door. There is a sign on it that reads MEMBERS ONLY.

A man called Dino shoots pool. He's going to jail in the morning.

Lulu walks in. She's tall, in her forties, and has a curly bush of red hair. She wears blue lenses and her lips are wrinkled. She sits next to Bobby Hair.

"Pssst," Bobby Hair says, leaning into her. "I used to have hair like that. Except it was blond. Then I cut it because I started losing it. That's why they call me Bobby Hair. Even if I don't got it no more."

"This hair's real, honey," Lulu tells him. She has a boyfriend.

Bobby Hair walks to the other side of the bar.

"I've got to get out," he says after a silence.

He is drunk now. He's figured it out.

"I don't know what I'm doing here: thirty-nine and nothing," he says. "I got no dreams. I got no future. I'm not even a vet. I missed that boat. Guess I'm gonna finish this beer and head west."

No Ferns, Please

"There ain't no Mr. Wonderful in here," says Lou the barman. "You've got to go over to P.J. Clarke's if you're looking for the million-dollar crowd."

The midtown drinking scene is mostly effete and clean. But the Subway Inn, at Sixtieth Street and Lexington Avenue, remains a regular bar. Weekdays belong to the working class: doormen, cabbies, Average Eddie and Nice Guy Nick. They pour into the bar from the subway tunnel out front and the shipping docks at Bloomingdale's, across the street. They stand around listening to the jukebox, waiting for the vodka to work. At the Subway, they pour the liquor with a generous hand, filling the glass more than three fingers high. That's the way they've been pouring since the place opened in 1933, when the actual subway cost a nickel and a nickel bought a drink.

Some claim that the Subway Inn was the first bar in New York to get its liquor license after the repeal of Prohibition, that it was the first bar in the city to have a television set and that nothing's been changed in the place since it was built: not the mahogany bar, not the spotted mirrors.

The first two assertions are unverifiable and the third is a lie.

There has been one change since the Great Depression: the cracked-leatherette banquettes from 1955. That's when the Third Avenue El was razed and the rum houses and dive bars began closing down as part of the neighborhood's rejuvenation. Naugahyde and Formica were the Subway's nod to class and progress.

Charlie Ackerman, the owner, is a puckered, saggy-bottomed crank. Salty as a pickled fish. Warm as a furnace without oil. This is according to the prank caller who phones regularly in the early evenings to wake him. Charlie will be ninety on March 28 and he spends the afternoons in the back booth with his arms to his sides and his forehead on the table. He looks inebriated, but he's just old.

Charlie is closemouthed, and if you ask him questions, he is likely to scream something like: *"I can't hear you. It's dark in here."* But there are two things he will let you know about himself: He was in World War II, and he drank with Marilyn Monroe.

Charlie served in the Air Force. The Pacific. Papua New Guinea. He likes to tell the mods and hipsters who crowd his bar on weekend nights, "I fought the big war so you can sit on your soft tush and drink all night."

Ms. Monroe used to come to the Subway to drink while she was shooting *The Seven Year Itch*. "She drank Champagne," Lou says, like he slept with her or something. "She always drank Champagne." There are pictures of her everywhere and dusty figurines. If you bring a picture of yourself they will gladly hang it on the wall.

The barmen are well aware that the drinking life will strangle your ambition. But they say loneliness can be worse. "I'm a social drinker, maybe four days a week, and I'm stuck," says Lou to a patron. "Now, you look at a guy like Pete Hamill. First thirty years of his career, he writes two books. Then he quits the bottle and writes eight books in five years."

The patron thinks a moment, takes a sip, then says, "Yeah, but those first two books were his best."

A Real Fireman's Bar

Bernie Heeran knew something was going to happen. He just knew it, and had been saying so for the last few weeks.

It is important to say a few things here about Bernie, whose son Charlie died in the World Trade Center massacre. He lost many old friends from the fire department there. He lost many friends from the neighborhood there. The cooks at his bar, Harbor Light, lost their brother there. Their brother lived above the bar. Nine weeks after the attack, Bernie was not convinced that dawn had broken on his nightmare. Then, last Monday morning, American Airlines Flight 587 fell out of the sky and crashed catercorner from his bar on Newport Avenue near Beach 130th Street in Belle Harbor, Queens.

As one side of the block burned, people on the other watched in horror.

A retired fireman, Bernie made his place available for the rescuers who were pulling charred bodies from the wreckage. Drinks were on the house, and Bernie had plenty himself. No one passed judgment on him but to say, "Bernie Heeran is one of the best damned men to ever have walked the shores of Rockaway."

The bar grew full as the day wore on, as the firefighters were dismissed and the fire dissipated to smoke and smoke became dust and the dust became particles. They drank by candlelight and a lamp lit by a generator, and somehow the beer stayed cold. A haze of cigarette smoke and fuel vapors hung like stiffened laundry.

The chief walked in with his white helmet and started barking orders.

"I thought I told you men wearing bunker gear to get the hell out of this bar," the chief growled. "I don't want to see men in uniform drinking. Now, clear out!"

His timing and his tone struck the firemen as extravagant and overdone. And though the men were aflame in adrenaline, they were obedient to the chief, who was a small but intimidating man.

"All this job is anymore is pulling bodies," said a fireman in bunker gear as he filed out the door. "Any more and I'm going to crack up."

A small, trenchant man, a firefighter who was not in uniform, shouted unpleasant things about the chief's mother, and at this point Bernie Heeran, the fine man from Rockaway, stepped in the middle.

"Come on, this is a fireman's bar," he told the chief. "Take it easy."

"Bernie," the chief said, "I love you, but stay out of this." Looking into Bernie's tormented eyes, the chief hugged him with his hands and walked out.

"Life will go on, we'll be okay," Bernie said to the fireman. "Now, finish your drink."

How Diplomats Drown
the Sorrows of the World

The crush at the delegates' bar in the United Nations comes around six o'clock in the evening, when the diplomats have pushed their last papers of the day, disposed of their last dossiers. This cuts against the widely held belief that the diplomats at the United Nations do not work at all.

It may be the most complicated drink in New York, as the discussion can veer from the violence in the Middle East to the lapdog nature of the American news media to the libido of North African women. The weight of the conversation does not smother the mood but seems to fuel it. One globe-trotter laughed at how he was nearly assassinated in East Timor. Richard Lato, a mail-room clerk, from the Central African Republic, sipped Grand Marnier and shrugged when asked about letter bombs and anthrax packages. "It's a living," he said.

The bar itself is a dreary cubicle in the rear of the building, but it comes in handy when an emissary is in need of one. It is set off from a main lobby by a wooden partition. The only artwork on the walls are two metal signs that read SMOKING AREA. The cantina is not open to the general public, and one must clear three checkpoints before entering. No taxes are charged. The beauty of the bar is not derived from its aesthetics, said Emilia Chelminska, the bartender, but its cocoonlike character.

"It's a nice place, because you don't have to worry what's happening in the outside world," she said without irony.

It is difficult to impress people here. The patrons speak as many as five languages each. They wear dark, modern suits and they have good haircuts.

Mrs. Chelminska offers table service, and some of the patrons believe that if the United States would pay its dues in full, then perhaps she could afford to hire a cocktail waitress.

Mrs. Chelminska has tended bar her whole adult life, stretching back to her youth in Communist Poland. She is a short, round-faced woman, who pours without arrogance and adheres to the golden rule practiced among the finest bartenders and international spooks: Hear nothing, know nothing, repeat nothing.

She was born in Warsaw on May 9, 1945, the day the Germans capitulated. This, she said, makes her the peace child and, so, suited to pour drinks for the legislature of humankind.

The day of her birth happened this way: "My father ran into our home and yelled, 'It's over, finished, no more war!'" Mrs. Chelminska said. "My mother said: 'I'm ready! The baby is coming!'" She was born in her parents' bed.

Last call came at seven-thirty. Mrs. Chelminska peeked around the partition. "And Iraq?" she said, scanning the lobby. "No, no Iraq today."

A Steak Pub Missing
a Central Ingredient: Steak

If you are dying for a good steak, and you are thinking about Denny's Steak Pub in Kensington, Brooklyn, you might as well come in a hearse.

"We got your clams and scampi, scungilli, veal," Tom DeRosa says. "My chili's good, but we don' got no steak."

Mr. DeRosa, fifty-five, is the chef de cuisine, whose résumé includes Joe's Bar on Avenue U in Gravesend and Vitale's on Avenue P. "We ought to have steaks, though, that's a fact," says Tommy, mulling it over as he smokes a battered cigar. "The place is called a steak pub. We ought to have steaks."

Denny's, at Church and McDonald avenues, is the only bar in Kensington. It is a boozy little grotto with soft lighting where a pint goes for two and a quarter. The bartender is quiet because the patrons here are put off by overassiduousness. The air-conditioning is kept low because it makes the old-timers cold.

They used to serve beef, and the twenty-six-ounce prime rib was known from Coney Island to Bensonhurst. But in 1992 the kitchen was closed.

"The cook started drinking a lot," explains Rich Shoemaker, the barman. "The food got pretty bad. And then the neighborhood changed."

Denny's grand reopening was July 1. On weekends they put cloths on the tables to lend an air of regalness to the place. But they forgot to put steaks back on the menu.

Outside the window, a hundred Bengali laborers mill about the street, eating seeds and spitting the shells on the sidewalk. All along McDonald Avenue there are Bengali hair salons, Bengali restaurants, Bengali clothing stores and, word has it, a Bengali nightclub open only on weekends.

"Those people don't eat steak or pasta," says John Ryan, forty-five, a meaty man with ham fists and a long memory. "They stick to their own and they don't buy anything from anyone but their own kind."

This is not a xenophobic rant, John Ryan wants people to know. It is simply the bald, naked truth, and if the truth offends, he says, then so be it, because it's left to people like him to teach the immigrants about being American.

A mechanic by trade, he is something of an amateur cartographer. He will draw an ethnographic map of the neighborhood as quickly as some can draw directions to their homes.

The Albanians and Italians on Dahill Road. The Bengalis on McDonald Avenue. The Chinese on East Second Street. The Italians and Irish have East Third Street. Ocean Parkway belongs to the Russian Jews.

"The neighborhood went down when the kitchen went down, but it's starting to pick back up again," Mr. Ryan says.

"You're getting the new type of immigrant now," he says. "Europeans who want to mix and the people from Park Slope who can't afford the prices anymore."

These people eat pasta, Mr. Ryan says. These people eat steak.

But if anyone would bother to ask the Bengalis, it would become apparent that many of them like a good steak, too. There's just one problem.

"Steak?" A Bengali man on the street said with a laugh. "They don't have steak in there."

Join the Navy
and See the Light

Two young sailors walked into the cool darkness and took off their caps. The quiet saloon grew quieter. Two men hunched over their bottles squinted toward the light of the door and nodded to the sailors.

As though by prearrangement, an old Miles Davis standard began to fill the cramped little bar. When you walk into Jimmy's Corner, you realize just how dead old-time shore leave is, and how the only thing left with any style in Times Square is Jimmy's cracker-box bar and, perhaps, a couple of streetwalkers on Eighth Avenue. Looking at the fresh-faced sailors, one cannot help feeling nostalgic for the gutter.

The fleet sailed into New York Harbor last week, and the sailors will be here for a week more. Given that many of them were aboard the first ships to deploy after September 11, sailing blindly into a new, unknown world, it seems only right that the civilians of this city should lift a glass and thank them for their service.

There are a few things one should know, however, before drinking with a sailor. First, never try to drink him under the table. He knows a shortcut. Second, remember this story:

There once was a sailor who accidentally cut his finger off, and for forty years he could feel the nagging ghost of the extended finger still there. He was afraid to drink, scratch his nose or even rub his eye, for whenever he brought his hand near his face, he was certain that the phantom finger would poke his eye out.

He was only cured of his phobia when his whole hand went numb from diabetes, and only then did the feeling of the missing finger disappear.

So, unless the sailor is an amputee, chances are he will drink until your money is gone. If he claims to have no money, ask to look inside his shoes.

Conan Morgan, twenty-two, and Joe Sherman, twenty-three, are petty officers third-class aboard the frigate *Elrod,* two men from opposite coasts who grew to respect each other during these past months while on duty in the Mediterranean.

Theirs are similar stories. High school was over and one day they woke up and looked out the window. Seeing no options standing on the front lawn, they joined the Navy.

"Best thing I ever did in my life," Mr. Morgan said. He checked his hair in the mirror. "I've seen the world."

"That's true," Mr. Sherman said. "We were in Bulgaria. That's a well-kept secret, Bulgarian chicks."

Swannee the barmaid snorted at this. "You haven't seen much of the world, then," she said. "The most beautiful women are the Polish women. They've been conquered so many times the mix is beautiful."

One suspected that Swannee was a Pole. "Poland, huh?" Mr. Sherman said. "I got to get there."

———■———

Looking for Mr. Dreamy

The singles scene can be depressing, and most New York women know a good man is hard to find.

This may be more true for a woman who is fifty-four than one who is thirty-four. "An older woman can't go into a bar alone, because she appears desperate and lonely," says Diane, a handsome blond professional of a certain age. "Especially in New York," says Claire, her friend and coworker, who is blessed with shapely legs, wears a red silk blouse and feels funny about the whole thing.

"The best bars for a mature woman are in Venice," she says. "There they put you in a window on display. They're proud of your presence and call you *bella*. It's quite charming, really. They understand the grace of a good woman."

The problem is, this is New York, not Italy. From the perspective of these women in their fifties, New York is about meat. And most people like their meat fresh.

Claire and Diane, who asked that their last names not be used for fear of appearing pitiful, recently decided to have an after-work aperitif. But where to go for a classy drink, where classy men will pay a bit of attention?

The ladies choose some spots near the office in midtown: the Blue Bar at the Algonquin Hotel on West Forty-fourth Street, the new M Bar at the Mansfield Hotel across the way and the Campbell Apartment, in the west wing of Grand Central Terminal.

At the Campbell Apartment, the crowd is young and arrogant in that new-money-smell-my-cigar sort of way, and the place reeks of stale tobacco and old socks.

But the Algonquin Hotel is a winner. The Blue Bar is frequented by widows and well-traveled gentlemen with a predilection for theater.

Christian is the bartender there, "but the name don't fit the character," he says. He is more than willing to match a lonely heart with a ringless finger.

Diane approaches a handsome, well-dressed Wall Street type. Mr. Dreamy lets it be known he is a self-made man who worked his way out of Levittown, New York, to Upper Montclair, New Jersey. He studies law at night, minds portfolios by day and has a passion for music and art. Most important, he seems to understand a good woman.

"There is a lot of advantage to age," Mr. Dreamy says sympathetically.

"Youth comes and then it's gone," Diane says. "Who wants to try to relive it?"

"Men, unfortunately," Mr. Dreamy confides. "Men can be dense. A good one is hard to find."

Bingo! Diane giggles, touching his arm.

Mr. Dreamy accompanies the women to the M Bar for a nightcap. The place feels like a dreary mix between a Roman bathhouse and a law library. But Mr. Dreamy is a shining light. He asks the ladies their favorite New York memories. He laughs at the right moments, and looks them in the eyes.

The ladies are charmed until he looks at his watch and excuses himself. He has another engagement.

As he leaves, they study his posterior and quickly do the calculus: personable, handsome, witty and he bought the drinks. Too good to be true.

"Do you think he was gay?" Claire asks.

Diane studies his credit card carbons. "I don't think so," she says. "He left less than fifteen percent."

A Life off the Books

The bar was dark and the piano man played. Tony Love sat propped against the leather banquette, the candlelight dancing across his face like the passing frames of a motion picture. He mouthed the words to an old tune he knew: "I only have eyes for you."

He took nuts from a bowl, but before he ate them, he thoroughly wiped the salt away. No more salt, no more cigars, the occasional beer. "I got to watch it, high blood pressure," said Mr. Love, every bit of seventy-five. He has a mane of white hair, a fading retina, bad knees, a brittle shoulder and a pig's valve implanted in his heart.

"I don't eat pork no more," Mr. Love said. "Pigs are family now."

Tony Love has lived a life off the books. He drove a truck for seven weeks in Alabama some four decades ago, but beyond that, he characterized his existence as "a little of this, a little of that." It was a life, he said, where "nobody got hurt, although a few should have."

Among his endeavors, Mr. Love is a New York bit actor. He has driven Robert De Niro and sold a newspaper to Michael Douglas, but mostly his work has not made it past the cutting-room floor. That's not because he's a bad actor, he insisted. It's quite the opposite. "These big names don't like you to look better than them, nope."

Mr. Love is currently working on a slip-and-fall lawsuit and other undecided projects. He has had no acting gigs for a while and there are none scheduled. If there are any directors or producers in need of his services, Mr. Love would like them to know that he owns his own car and is reachable by pager twenty-four hours a day: (917) 393-3745.

But this evening at Bemelmans Bar in the Carlyle Hotel on Madison Avenue was not a sad occasion, it was a happy one. Mr. Love, born Tony Joe Rossi and raised in SoHo, and his lawyer, John Ciafone, had something to celebrate. Finally, after forty-five years of marriage, Mr. Love got his divorce.

He explained that the first half-dozen years of matrimony were a relative dream; the next half-dozen were a living nightmare; and the next thirty were spent begging his wife to sign the papers.

"She ruined me," he said. "Hey, I know she heard things on the streets, but I never got caught. So I'm not to blame here."

And so Mr. Love watched the young crowd drink Champagne, watched the piano man play and sipped his drink. He was free now, free to perfect his greatest role, that of the geriatric Don Juan.

"I like young broads," he said. "Who the hell doesn't?"

Manners, Morals and
Money at a Room Salon

Most evenings, a blue sandwich board stands on the sidewalk at Thirty-sixth Street and Broadway. It reads, in Korean characters, ROOM SALON.

The building's elevator opens into a chromium parlor with a divan and a bar in the corner. A patron sat there the other evening with a consort. He had paid $125 for a bottle of Scotch and the privilege of saying lascivious things to the woman. The establishment's madam, looking like a Laura Ashley girl gone wrong, exchanged a few words with the patron, Mr. K., a Korean journalist, and ushered an international group accompanying him into a side room.

The men took their places around the glass table. "Two hundred fifty each," Mr. K. whispered to the Americans in his group. "No sex."

The door opened and five women entered. Each took a seat next to a man. They were pleasant-looking young women with round, painted faces and little command of English.

The city's Korean salons differ from its Japanese geisha houses. The Japanese houses, found around the United Nations, are almost imperial in their atmosphere. The men must wear slippers and kimonos, and the women are courtly and quiet and schooled in the art of traditional dance. Touching is absolutely forbidden.

In the Korean salons, you may grope. The women did not dance, but they slurred through Beach Boys and Beatles tunes on the karaoke machine with the sweet chirping voices of house sparrows. They lighted the men's cigarettes and hand-fed them fruit and, periodically, blew at their ears as though there were piles of dandruff on their suit shoulders. The whole point, it seemed, was to make the men feel special and powerful and to get them to spend money.

One woman seemed skeptical and bored with the whole business and refilled the glasses before they were empty. She crinkled her nose at the odd, nervous behavior of the Americans. Mr. K. disappeared for twenty minutes. He came back to the room flushed and red. He took up his jacket, had a few words with the remaining Korean man, Mr. S., and skipped out on the bill. Mr. S. threw his hands up and gave a "Who me?" look. The Americans suspected something was amiss.

"The king has left and so should you," said one woman who spoke a bit of English. The room salon scene works on a need-to-know-you basis, it was explained.

The bill arrived: $1,250, gratuity included. Mr. S. had no cash. Mr. M., an American reporter, pulled out his Visa, leaving him with the sick taste of dried squid that no amount of Johnnie Walker could wash away. As the men found themselves deposited on the street, Mr. M. asked, "What just happened in there?"

Never Trust a Man
Who Kisses His Own Fingers

There is a certain class of drinking man who is both the finder of good occasions and the wrecker of them.

He is the sort who will take a lady's hand firmly in his own, kiss his top knuckles and order himself a cabernet. He will then raise the hand he has just kissed and announce to his drinking pals that she has promised to be his and his alone. "And why not?" he will exclaim in west Irish cadence. "I, sirs, am a splendid specimen!"

One will notice that the woman wipes her hand on her slacks, because the mere thought of his lips touching her makes the flesh creep.

The specimen will also notice her defiant gesture. He will turn to the boys and proudly announce, "A friend of mine is an enemy of hers! She will make a terrific little wife, and we shall live miserably ever after."

The men will laugh and the piano will begin to play. The piano player, if he is any sort of human being, will have noticed this ungracious scene and will strike out a sympathetic and teary-eyed rendition of "The Wedding March." Everyone will laugh except the prospective bride, who will sit at the end of the bar with her palms pressed to it until her liquor takes effect.

The piano player will be an overweight, smooth-skulled man. He will play with a steady hand and sing with a Southern lisp even as an elderly woman in fur falls to the floor and is carried out by paramedics. When she goes, the piano man will segue into "Camp Town Races," and everyone will laugh some more and order fresh drinks.

Such is the scene at Mimi's. And it can be seen as regularly as a Broadway show, five nights a week, on the northeast corner of Fifty-second Street and Second Avenue. Hunter Blue is the piano man, nine o'clock is the hour. There is no ticket booth, no reserved seating.

The crowd is an inscrutable one: uptown, downtown, out of town, down in the mouth and mouths that won't quit. The place has stained-glass panels and checked tablecloths and dark corners.

The name sounds sexy, but Mimi is Neapolitan shorthand for Dominick. There are no busty sirens here except when Mr. Blue invites the occasional hairy-armed cross-dresser to perform. Dominick, who founded the establishment in 1956, died some time ago.

It is a lively scene, not without its imbroglios. Mike O'Hara, a dissolute man with silver hair, sits at the cramped bar drinking with Raphael Santa Rosa, who has a phlegmy cough as thick as a steak. There is a seat next to Mr. O'Hara, and a peculiar gentleman in a woolly sweater takes it.

"Why are you sitting so close to me?" the peculiar man asks.

"What are you talking about?" Mr. O'Hara says. "I've been here for three hours. Go sit by the piano player if you don't like it."

"The music's too loud."

"Then get lost," Mr. O'Hara says with a thumb. "There. Go over there by my fiancée." The man takes a seat next to the woman with her palms on the bar. The music stops. "What a nut," Mr. O'Hara says. "Maybe he's an aristocrat."

The Life of the Party

Thank God!" the teenagers shout out in unison, like congregants in the Church of the Perpetual Recreationist. The keg has arrived. Now they will have some booze to help wash down the pills.

Another Friday night in Long Beach. An island surrounded by Long Island. A geographic cul-de-sac with three roads in and none out. Two bridges and twenty miles to Manhattan. Forget Manhattan. For these high school seniors standing on the porch of adulthood, the neighborhood is still the best place in the world and there is no reason to go anywhere else. It's pointless even to think of anywhere else. It is ten o'clock and things are cooking pretty good. More chicks than guys, plenty of weed and now ice-cold suds. "Good ol' C.J.!" They slap his back and pull crumpled bills from their pockets as he makes his way around with the cups. C.J. is nineteen and out of school. Among boys he is the man, the man with the beer connection.

Fifty white suburban teenagers and two black ones. A keg and enough smoke to kill a coal miner. White tablets and a hundred tattoos and a thousand questions. Conversations about the future. Graduation looms like a dark cloud.

"Man, don't you know it's illegal in the Army not to get up for work?" asks a stumpy kid named Billy. "Why don't you just take classes at Nassau Community College?"

"I don't know," shrugs the future Private No Name. "I'm trying not to think about it." He's busy concentrating on the group of girls standing in the dark recesses of the patio, who are busy concentrating on him, with his arms bulging out of a shirt that is as tight and thin as a sausage skin. There is a cold breeze blowing in off the ocean.

The point of the party is nothing, really. Just a place to get wasted. It was supposed to be at Vinny's new place but Vinny never moved in. He got busted for speeding. Again. Vinny drives fast. He was supposed to be moving up and out of his mother's house to an apartment in Cedarhurst, the Long Island Shangri-la where the rich kids live an almost utopian existence of Polo and Porsches. But Vinny got caught. And now he has to save his money for the judge.

"You knew he wasn't moving anywhere," says Doo Doo, seventeen, to her clique of girls. "He's not going anywhere but jail." She says it as a compliment. Doo Doo is getting a lot of attention from the boys filing by toward the keg, because she's built and she's bombed and it's only eleven o'clock. The attention paid to her makes her friends unhappy.

The party ended up here at Sara's house by happenstance. Just like that, the way a circus pulls up stakes and pitches its big top in the next town. Vinny has no place. Sara's parents are away for the weekend. Her house looks like a Swiss chalet with its two peaks and wood trim.

All night long they come and go. They drink and vomit in the bushes and fall into the picket fence and urinate on the house. They listen to rap and alternative on a boom box while they watch television with the sound turned down. The pills make them feel good, and they grope each other in poorly lighted corners of the yard to be sure it's true that they feel so good. These aren't bad kids or good kids, just typical ones. Some are children of divorced mothers who live with a man they call by his first name. Some have metal studs embedded in their faces and stapled to their ears and skewered through their tongues. They reek of sweat and cologne and lust. They smoke drugs. Some ride skateboards. Others drive cars with outrageous sound systems.

Out on the street, Ronnie, eighteen, shows off his stereo to a group of guys who work at the gas stations and electronic stores during the week. It's loud enough to drown out a civil-defense siren.

"It's the baddest system in town," Ronnie gloats.

"Word," says one of the counter clerks.

The old woman across the street complains that the speakers are making her windows shake. The clerk spews unpleasantries toward her. He mocks her appearance and she goes back into her house.

Sara paces the street like a nervous hen.

It is around midnight when he arrives. Vinny. Vinny, the shuck-and-jive hipster who prowls the mean streets of Long Beach. Vinny with the summons. For the blunt-smoking, slack-shouldered teenagers of suburbia, having a court case is a nearly heroic thing. It gives you street cred. Makes you the real deal. It's better than having nude Polaroids of your girlfriend in your wallet.

This was supposed to be his party, his apartment-warming in Cedarhurst. He was supposed to be illuminated under the bright porch lights of Friday night. The girl passed out on the couch, she was supposed to be sleeping on his couch next to him.

But Vinny messed it up. Another mess-up in a long line of mess-ups. Truth is, he doesn't even have a couch. All he has is that court date.

"I learned my lesson," he tells a group of feminine admirers from underneath a hood that casts shadows over his eyes. An awesome plume of marijuana smoke belches out after his words. The seventeen-year-old girls, giddy from the alcohol and pills, find him exotic. Vinny lists his life like a rap sheet. Eighteen. Suspended license. No insurance. No registration. A reputation. Caucasian. A police record. A connection in "black Harlem," he says. A tether to Long Beach. A court date.

Vinny smiles. The girls smile. There are no worries tonight. No future to consider. No other place to go but this narrow alley lined by the aluminum siding next to another alley lined by aluminum siding and so on down the block. They're buying the line, so Vinny reverses field with impeccable timing.

"No, I haven't learned my lesson," he says. "When I get my car back, I'll take you for a ride." The bit is going over. He might not need the girl on the couch after all. How wonderful it would be if life never changed, if you never had to grow up.

Poor Angie. She's swaying on a rough sea of beer. She speaks too loudly and she's bringing everyone down. They step around her on the way to the keg. Only M—— listens to her opinions about suburban life. These kids, they're all so normal and predictable, Angie complains. There are no surprises and everyone seems to want it that way.

"I'd like to see things, you know?" she says. "I'd like to go out into the world and swim in another ocean besides the Atlantic. I'd like to go to Paris and speak French and stuff. I'd like to find a good man who wants to work and have a house."

She says she would also like to have bigger breasts because all things being equal, most boys will pass on a small chest. Even the good ones.

The guys who are her own age disappoint her. "You can read it all over these boys. Who's going to be a loser. Who's going to go someplace and who's going to show up at the reunion fifty pounds heavier. It's kind of sad to watch, you know?"

M—— drinks more than Angie. M——, eighteen, has a date in New York with an overweight, balding thirty-year-old man the following night. She's not enthusiastic about this specimen. He thinks she's older and lives somewhere else. "I think he has money," she says in a slur.

The cops drive by around one-thirty A.M. They roll down their windows and tell the skateboarders to get out of the street. The old biddy is standing in her window. One of the black kids ducks into the house where he is met with a chorus of "Hey, Oreo!" The black kid smirks. "Man, I'm your savior," he tells the party. "Once you step into the city you're gonna be glad you knew a black dude like me."

"Manhattan might as well be a million miles away for all I care," says Brendan, an eighteen-year-old who is a dead ringer for Mickey Rooney. He talks out of the side of his mouth as he speaks with a scrum of other short white kids. "There are two kinds of black people," he says. You know the line. Some of his best friends are black.

A white kid can't buy a break in the city, Brendan says. You always feel afraid. Afraid that you're not cool enough. Afraid they will make fun of your dancing. Afraid that what you say gets blown out of proportion and then someone kicks your head in. "Call us whatever you want," he says to a chorus of baying boy-men, a pack of howling dogs. "This is our town and no one touches that."

More than one guy from the city has limped home from Long Beach, says a barrel-shaped kid with a bad haircut. He suggests they go find some interlopers now and beat them like alley cats. But the pull of the keg holds sway over their impulses, and when it taps out around two A.M. everyone is thinking more about french fries than fighting.

The party is clearing out now, save a few stragglers checking behind the cheese for stray beer bottles and wine coolers. The floor is littered with cigarette butts and plastic cups. The drunk girl sleeps on the couch. Vinny hits the toilet. On his way out the door, Vinny stops. He looks at the girl on the couch and covers her with a blanket.

Shimmering Beauty in
a Sweltering City

She.

She comes with her friends, of course. Women never come alone. Her group stands in the shade with drinks in their hands. But the sun seems to find her. They talk, whisper almost. The friends seem uninterested, and their eyes wander about, searching in that way. She, on the other hand, is a statue. Tall and confident. She is solid. Enamel. Lacquer. Hair the color of wine.

She has no need to look around. She does not seem to wonder if the men have found her. Of course they have.

She makes a small gesture. A hand on the hip. She plays with her hair. Fingers brushing softly across her forehead. The men have followed her, along with the sun.

She laughs at something, and they yelp like puppies. These panting American boy-men. Ball-chasers. Shoe-fetchers. It will be years before they will understand her. And then it will be too late. By then, they will be gray beneath their snouts.

She flatters the surroundings. And they flatter her. Cocktail hour on the granite rooftop of the Metropolitan Museum. A portrait of line and form and functionality. The greenery of Central Park. The canopy of oak and spruce and elm. Modigliani could do no better.

She has bashful eyes. They are at her feet now. Her fingers are on her neck. Her glass perspires. A maddening image for the men who have no means to leave this sweltering city. And in this moment, it seems, they have no desire. No desire but her.

She has come here a thousand times before. They will see her a thousand times again. Perhaps her hair will be up; perhaps she'll wear a hat, a bag from a Fifth Avenue store on her arm, heels to hold her high. She will have another name. Her eyes will be another color.

She will be alone but surrounded by people, as she is today. You would like to ask her something, but that would ruin it, turning the moment into memory. It would be like the lover who has come and gone and left you only dead flowers and a few photographs. So you let her be. And life is young today and the day is long and the sky is slate gray.

She laughs and her breasts heave. The strings play in the Great Hall and you may wish to take her in your arms and dance her all the way to Spain, or some other great place of romance.

She is beautiful, and her back is the most beautiful thing. The spine and blades. The least object of her vanity. The self she cannot see. A secret just for you.

She is not perfect. She is woman, after all.

She is everything you have seen before, and she is different, somehow, this time.

A Valentine's Story:
Take out Your Handkerchiefs

In a city notorious for broken hearts, this may be one of the saddest St. Valentine's Day stories of all: a real massacre.

The evening takes place at Rao's, the tiny 105-year-old restaurant and bar in East Harlem known for its exclusivity. No table available till July. The food is family-style Neapolitan. The clientele is Italian and well dressed. Our group sat at the table closest to the bar, between the autographed photos of Robert Goulet and Dick Clark. Among us was a local tough who had made something of a name for himself as a Hollywood stuntman. There was the Hollywood actor who plays tough guys and writes poetry in his spare time. There was the actor's wife. There was the man with the keen hearing. There were two Russian girls from Brooklyn who looked as though they were dressed for the roller disco. There was our man Tommy Noodles, who asked that his last name not be used because among his circle of acquaintances, vulnerability is a contemptible thing.

Tommy's heartbreak began a dozen years ago as he was chasing a Brazilian model around the world. He pursued her to Paris, Rome and Buenos Aires. It was in Brazil that he finally caught her, and she agreed to be his wife. It was also in Brazil that he caught a tropical virus, a nasty bug that gnawed at the well-being of his heart. Within six months, he had a heart transplant.

"It was true love, you know," he told the Russian girls, whom he had brought along as valentine companions. "True love. Really."

Only nineteen, the girls seemed as unimpressed with his reminiscences of *amore* as they were with the privileged surroundings.

"He's told this story a hundred times," Ilyana said in English. "He's even shown us photos."

"On gloopy," the other said distractedly, in Russian. "He's stupid."

The girls smoked incessantly. They smoked through their medium-rare steaks and they smoked over their glasses of pink zinfandel. Tommy's lungs labored.

"I left my first wife for her," he told the table, clearing the cloud with a wave of his hand. And to prove this, he showed a portrait of the Brazilian woman that was tattooed on his right bicep, above the name of his first wife, which was tattooed on his wrist. The Brazilian was indeed beautiful, if the tattoo is to be believed.

"Anyway, that was twelve years ago and now my heart's wearing out," Tommy said between sips of Chianti and forkfuls of chicken parmigiana. "My arteries are a hundred percent closed. I got two months left if I got a day."

Tommy said his Brazilian beauty left him a few months ago. By his account, she is modeling for a new man in Miami. This seems to have crushed his second and ruined heart.

"Anyhow, she's nothing to me now," he said rather unconvincingly.

The girls were smoking like a pile of burning leaves by the time the coffee arrived, and Tommy wheezed like a kazoo.

"Listen, can't you cut the smoking out for just fifteen freaking minutes?" he snapped. His teeth were showing. His chest was heaving. "I'm dying over here."

He stepped outside to calm his lungs.

The girls lit another one and asked for the steak to be put in a doggie bag.

REGULARS

SOME of the blokes in here are older than the wallpaper, and less interesting.

—STEVE DUNLEAVY

If Glasses Are Half Full,
Wallets Are Half Empty

Everybody in here looks like Dick Tracy or something," said a woman as she navigated between the ironworkers, cops and actors, and the steam table loaded with roast brisket, roast turkey and pot roast.

Smith's Bar and Grill, at Forty-fourth Street and Eighth Avenue, is one of those old-school places where if they've seen you twice, your drink will be sitting on the bar before you're sitting on the stool. They talk about all the old things here, like Vietnam, $2.50 pastrami sandwiches and "Fast" Harry Zeller the riveter, who died at ninety and predicted the day of his own death. The other evening, there were two Vinnys bartending; three guys on one corner of the bar named Bobby, Bobby and Bob; and three guys on the other side named Jimmy, Jimmy and Jimmy. The punch line?

"We're not very original around here," one of the Vinnys said.

It was tough along Eighth Avenue when Bobby Coach, a very heavy man, first stepped into this bar twenty-five years ago and watched a guy get knifed outside.

"Now you wouldn't find a knife sharp enough around here to cut butter," he said. "New York's become so phony baloney."

He stopped and took a laborious breath and then continued. "But still, you'll catch the real New York walking by this stool."

Rick Morrison, the last of the true bohemians, does walk by the stool a few hours later. And when he's done telling his tale—a morose little riddle as to whether his glass of life is half empty or completely empty—a listener makes a reminder note to himself to go home and make love to his sofa.

A couple of months ago, Mr. Morrison, a photographer who once had a little gallery in Alphabet City, lost his apartment in Brooklyn. It was a convoluted story about a roommate who drank the rent. The artist admitted that he too was bitten by the bottle and the barbiturates, and soon embarked on an eight-week journey that spanned seven couches. He slept on love seats, eight-foot leathers, a comfy pink number; he even insinuated himself onto the couch of a woman who was nine months pregnant.

"You cad," someone interrupted. He shook his head as if to say, "I know."

The newspapers said last week that rents were coming down in Manhattan, but the apartments more in keeping with his budget, in the ten-dollar flophouses, were full. So first he spent a warm evening in Bellevue's emergency room and finally found refuge in the storage cage where he keeps his photo equipment.

"It felt good to be around my stuff," he said over a sympathy beer. "Reassuring."

As it turns out, the security guards at the storage place tried to shake him down for rent. Not having the twenty-five dollars they demanded, and preferring to drink what little money he did have, Mr. Morrison was homeless again.

"It's pretty weird fantasizing not about beautiful women but about grocery shopping," he said. "I try to be bitter, but it's not in me."

He borrowed a cigarette and tried to light it, but his lighter had run out of fluid.

"Can I get a match, too?"

A Merry, If Pensive,
Old Soul at Just the Right Bar

It was the end of the business day and the bike messenger had one last package to deliver to the St. Regis Hotel.

He seemed impressed with the high-backed chairs and the rigid guests sitting in them. He admired the crystal chandeliers and the car call booth outside, which he mistook for a shower. He was sweating profusely. He delivered his package, then ducked into the King Cole Bar for a beer. The bar is a polished one; a mix of blue bloods, society skeletons, cigar zealots and well-dressed businessmen who spend 80 percent of their time putting out fires and 20 percent building them.

The oak bar at Fifty-fifth Street and Fifth Avenue is lit like a stage and is best known for the mural "Old King Cole" (1894), painted by Maxfield Parrish, that hangs behind it.

The bottled beer cost eight dollars, which made the bike messenger raise his eyebrows. He produced a ten-dollar bill, left a dollar for the barman and began wandering around the lobby with his drink.

"Ha-him," the concierge cleared his throat. The dark-skinned messenger turned around on his heels. "Ha-him. Sir, sir. If the gentleman would like to take his drink to the bar. If the gentleman would like to take his drink to the bar."

The messenger swallowed his drink whole, set the empty glass on the desk and left by the side entrance.

Watching from the bar was Thomas Scott, a lonesome business-man, who turned to his glass as if something might be determined from the ice cubes.

He is a man of a certain sophistication. His watch is expensive, and he was smoking a Cuban cigar that he brought from out of the country because cigars here are, well—and he wrinkled his nose at this—"gamy."

"Racism, you know, I just hate that," Mr. Scott, a white man, said about the bike-messenger incident. "What people don't realize is education is the root of it.

"If you're educated, then racism doesn't exist!" he said. "Poor people need to educate themselves."

Then he was on to other things.

"Hey, Bill, another Johnnie Black on the rocks."

Mr. Scott is in the consulting game. He travels half the year, and he knows every hotel bar in New York from Seventy-sixth Street to Gramercy Park. The Four Seasons? "Worse than the lunch room at General Motors." The Waldorf-Astoria? "Shabby, like a garage sale."

The King Cole, on the other hand, is discreet and dark and the drinks are generous. And this is preferable to a man with a wife and a baby back home. Mr. Scott was expecting an old girlfriend who happened to be in town from Los Angeles.

"You know traveling used to be fun, now it's just lonely," he said. "It's like being in the Army. It sounds really great to be in the Army. Then once you're in the Army, you think, 'Oh man, what am I doing in the Army?'"

He has never been in the Army, just the consulting game. But when the woman arrived, he stood, saluted the barman and they slipped off into the evening.

Big Shoes to Fill
with Wine and Whiskey

Big Foot needs a coat.

It's like that every autumn for him, because he spends his time drinking instead of obsessing about the frivolities of life. He also needs gloves and boots. His hands are thin and shaky. His feet are size fifteen and a half and hang over the sides of his sandals. He walks with a cane and sleeps where he pleases.

Big Foot is sitting on a plastic milk crate on the corner of St. Marks Place and First Avenue and is joined by Hambone Tommy, the pie-eyed orator, and David Russell, the professor of garbology.

On the north side of St. Marks is the Holiday Cocktail Lounge, owned by Stephan Lutak, an old, silver-haired Ukrainian. When the rains are especially cold, like tonight, Big Foot will wander into the dark saloon and, without a word, Stephan will pour him a shot of the hard stuff, no charge. But the Ukrainian has just banned Big Foot tonight, accusing him of stealing a lightbulb from the toilet.

"What the hell am I going to do with a lightbulb?" Big Foot would really like to know. "I'm a chief, not a thief."

Big Foot's true name is Merrith Stops at Pretty Places. He is a forty-three-year-old Crow Indian from the Wyola reservation in Montana, and has been a popular totem on this East Village corner for the past twenty years. He has the long, elegant face of a wolf. He wears his hair pulled back and tied down and a large, chrome-plated Buffalo nickel on his chest.

He will drink a gallon of fortified wine if it suits him. He keeps his bottle in a brown paper bag tucked in his milk crate.

"The stuff's destroying him," Mr. Russell says in a sad Glaswegian brogue. "Alcohol is no laughing matter, me boy. It'll eat you up."

Big Foot is anemic. He has a bum leg, a bad liver and a faulty bladder. He recently spent a month in Cabrini Medical Center after checking in with a distended stomach. They pumped twelve liters of fluid from his guts and put in two pints of blood.

"It was warm in the hospital," Big Foot remembers.

The topic of conversation turns to morose tales of hypothermia and gangrene, stories of men passing out under bridges and losing their limbs or stumbling along the highways and falling into snowdrifts. To a man, they talk about faulty fathers and battered mothers and larders stocked with whiskey.

"Jeez, I'm getting cold out here," Big Foot says before taking a swallow. The wine makes him warm and satisfied, and at moments like this he is one of the friendliest men on the block. People give him bills.

Mr. Russell would rather pick trash than panhandle. He knows you can move a woman to tears by permitting her to see you eating grass in her front yard, but he just doesn't have it in him. "I've found everything I need in these bins, you name it, I've found it," the hobo says.

"How 'bout size fifteen and a half boots?" Big Foot asks somewhat hopefully.

"Nope, come to think of it, I've never found that."

Wheels of Fire,
Beards of Gray

There is a big man who belongs to the Black Falcons Motorcycle Club on East 180th Street at Third Avenue in the Bronx who says to call him Johnny X.

"Oh, are you a member of the Nation of Islam?" asks a visitor who has been given a bottled beer by the club's president. "No, I ain't no member of the Nation of Islam," he smolders, knocking back a shot of Scotch, belching.

"Well, that's an interesting last name you've got there. X, I mean."

"It ain't none of your damn bid-ness what my last name is. You call me X. You write that in your notebook. Johnny X. My name is Johnny X and yours is mother-effing cop."

Sensing that X must be short for Excuse Me, the visitor moves a little closer to the other end of the bar, toward the pool table.

All and all, Johnny is not a bad man, but he does have the bad habit of pouring himself drinks from other people's bottles. The Black Falcons is not a bar but a clubhouse, founded in 1968 and named after a local liquor store. Each man is assigned his own bottle, Wild West style. Smoky, Stretch, Claw, D-Lite, Hard Drive. Johnny drinks from them all.

No one tells him no.

Johnny is unpredictable the more he drinks. After one, he's admiring your boots. After four, he's ridiculing your haircut. He is an older man, a boiler mechanic and a former truck driver. He is tall and well built and shows off a tattoo on his arm of two skulls and the scales of justice balancing a Bible and a gun. *God Forgives. I Don't,* it says. Johnny rides a Harley.

"Been all over the place," he says after his third one. "There ain't no town I haven't spent a night in."

Gary, Indiana? "Shoot, buy five chicken dinners, get one free," he says of that steel town.

Portland, Maine? "Good mashed potatoes. Big pork chops. They don't like serving colored people up there, but they know we like our mashed potatoes."

Kansas City? "Which one? You come out of Kansas and you in Kansas."

He knocks another down.

The Black Falcons is a club—not a gang—of aging men who, if they don't find some young, dues-paying bikers soon, may have to close their doors, says the club president, known as the Whit.

"But the biggest thing after money that will bust up a club is Big Mama," he says. Big Mama is shorthand for your woman.

"I seen Big Mama bust up more biker clubs than the police ever did."

The Whit says the Falcons are a peaceable lot, but Johnny, who is on his sixth or seventh drink, starts to menace the visitor.

"Do I look like I'm from Inny-anna, boy?" he slurs. "I ain't from Inny-anna, and I ain't laughing."

The evening ended early.

"The Saloon Priest"

There is a crowd sitting at a table near the window at Elaine's. One man is the Porta Potti prince of New York, the other is a nightclub owner. The club owner's wife is sitting there with him and she looks good. At the adjoining table is the Reverend Peter Colapietro, the saloon priest who, at 275 pounds, fills a chair.

It's still early in the evening, and already their eyes are glistening. The titan of toilets tells the one about the priest and the rabbi. Then there's the one about the three men looking for a cheap drink. And then the one about the three construction workers who throw themselves to their deaths. Father Pete hears this one and snorts into his bourbon.

"Jesus, Father, I'm rotten," the toilet titan says.

"No, you're a good man," Father Pete reassures. "You just have to change."

The toilet titan wrinkles his nose as if the booze has gone bad. "I'm talking to a priest and I'm getting sober."

Father Pete claims that he has never had a bad time in the twenty years that he has visited Elaine's, the famous bar, restaurant and gossip stand at Eighty-eighth Street and Second Avenue that is favored by the city's literati and some celebrities.

Most recognize Father Pete even when he's out of uniform and dressed in slacks and a blue oxford shirt. When Catholics walk past his table, they promise him they'll return to church.

"What they make of the scene here is baloney," Father Pete says. "It's just a bar and restaurant. You can bring your mom, you can bring your wife. I suggest, though, that you don't come with your mistress."

Father Pete, fifty-two, is the pastor of the Holy Cross Church on West Forty-second Street, across from the Port Authority Bus Terminal, and his community includes addicts, prostitutes, newspaper photographers, struggling actors, immigrants and the elderly. He is also chaplain for the Manhattan Restaurant and Liquor Association, the transit police, the Sanitation Department and the state parole officers.

Raised in the Castle Hill section of the Bronx, this son of an Italian-born saloon owner is as comfortable in the company of the wicked as he is with the wealthy. When Elaine Kaufman, the restaurant's owner, comes by the table, Father Pete swears he loves her with all his heart and half his liver. "We're all flawed," he says from beneath a cloud of tobacco smoke. "God loves us all, but maybe he loves some more than others."

That's when Tommy Carney walks into the bar to a standing ovation. He takes a chair at Father Pete's table. Tommy's been a barman here for twenty-six years, and it's his first night out since having a heart attack. It happened on a farm upstate at a wedding in a big tent in a big field.

He's having his first drink in three weeks.

"I didn't think 'Oh my Lord' or anything like that while it was happening," Tommy says. "But I'm thinking it now. I know the gift of life, I'll tell you."

"Yes, Tommy," Father Pete says.

"And boy, does this drink taste good."

Geeks and Freaks

He's only three-foot-eleven and still he doesn't believe it.

Koko the Killer Clown waddled with menace around the bar, a miniature baseball bat in his hand. His tiny fists clenched and unclenched its shaft, and his greasepaint smile turned to a frown. Another midget stood in the open-air entrance staring stupidly at Koko. "That guy gives little people a bad name," Koko announced to the bar, pointing a sausage-size finger at the interloper. "He has his nose in the air and besides he can't dance."

The midget in the entrance began a mocking, little soft-shoe accompanied by a whistle blown in sharp, shrill bursts. A little girl looking down on the scene from her bar stool began to cry.

It was appalling. It was shocking. It was, for the money, entertaining.

Step right up to the last freak show in America. Once there were hundreds of them, flame swallowers, bearded ladies and two-headed babies. Now there is just Sideshows by the Seashore on the Coney Island Peninsula at Surf Avenue and West Twelfth Street.

The freak show features the man who puts screwdrivers up his nose and hums little melodies, the snake-charming ladies who from a distance are of an indiscernible sex, the tattooed man, the Killer Clown and sundry other attractions.

But best of all in this Empire to the Nickel is the little plywood-topped bar littered with grapes, the Racing Form and a newspaper horoscope page. The clock above is stuck at 12 and one second and the sign below it reads IT'S TIME TO BUY A FREAK A DRINK.

The freak bar is among the most democratic in the city. From one P.M. to midnight, Friday through Sunday, it is lined with feeble ancients, frightened children, new immigrants, outdated suits and people with holes in their shoes who have paid two or three dollars to watch the revolving show. One of the finest ways to see the show is never to see it at all. A better plan is to simply sit at the bar and watch this carousel of outcasts swirl past as you nurse a beer.

As a rule, freaks don't drink while on the job. This, they explain, is because of a certain professionalism and respect for the occupation. "Besides," says Frank Hartman, twenty-eight, the purple-haired barker, sword swallower and escape artist, who began his career on the strange stage at the age of twelve, "you don't want to be drunk while you're locked in an iron maiden."

Eke the Geek is one of the few men in the city who lists his occupation as "showman" on his tax forms. He has a tattooed head and is electrocuted on the hour. The Prince of Wales regards his station in life with no less pride than Eke the Geek. "I'm the doorkeeper of a dying art," he explains with all earnestness.

It is no wonder, then, that this giant of a man chases Koko around the lobby after the little clown has interrupted his show to curse the audience into making room for the standing customers.

"I'm an artist!" the Geek says. "How dare you!"

Koko, a clown from the projects, must be restrained from breaking the Geek's knees with the bat.

The girl begins to cry again.

Absolute Dunleavy

These days were made for a guy like Steve Dunleavy. The big-talking, big-drinking columnist for the *New York Post*, the unblinking defender of smokers and gun owners and cops.

"The bombs of righteousness are falling on Afghanistan," he said, plagiarizing his own column. "And I'm here, listening to my answering machine." He was sitting in his office having lunch with Tex McCrary, ninety-one, the newspaperman who got to Tokyo before MacArthur. The men drank vodka-and-tonics, Dunleavy chain-smoked Parliaments. The bread rolls went untouched, as always; Dunleavy does not take food with his meals.

Dunleavy has a desk at the *Post*, but his real office is just down the street at Langan's, a restaurant and pub on West Forty-seventh Street. The barman knows his schedule, the waitress acts as a secretary: "Steve. It's the *Post* on line one."

Dunleavy will take the phone. Regardless of the number of drinks he has ingested, no matter how slurred his speech, he has the curious ability to pan nuggets of gold from the pond of his intellect and extemporaneously recite them to his editor.

"It's amazing how liberals, whom I regard as traitors in this time of crisis, quote the Constitution," one column read recently.

Dunleavy is sixty-four, the photo above his column fifteen years out of date. Until last Thursday night—when he shaved his head to win a thousand-dollar bet to benefit a fallen firefighter—he had a silver pompadour that mocked gravity and a face that had succumbed to it. He is thin; a slight cough has set in. He wore a checked jacket, a blue shirt and a gold pinkie ring.

He has circled the globe in his career, which began fifty years ago in Australia as a copy boy at *The Sydney Sun*. Since then, he has gone from Hong Kong to Calcutta to Los Angeles to Bosnia. He has covered war. While he never won a Pulitzer Prize, he did write the first tell-all Elvis book.

That's history. What Dunleavy wants now is permission to pack his writing foot and wrap his flask and head off to the Middle East. But the boss—whom he is quick to compliment—has not given him the green light. Is it age, he was asked?

Perhaps, Dunleavy said. More likely, he's not worth the money. "I've been to wars, and I've been to heavyweight fights," he told Mr. McCrary. "I'm sure someone from the *Post* will end up in Afghanistan, but it probably won't be me. It makes you come to terms that your days are over."

Look on the bright side, he was told. It's doubtful that his liver could clear customs, anyway.

"You might have a point, mate," he said. "You might have a point!"

The Roar of the Beer Suds, the Smell of the Fish

The bars in the Fulton Fish Market bring to mind the drinking establishments of the Alaskan Panhandle. The men are coarse and rough. The language is salty and blasphemous. And when the fish are in, pockets are filled with money.

The best time in the fish market is Friday, because Friday is payday; and eight A.M. is happy hour. It is then that the sun breaks through riverbank fog and the men drift to the saloons as predictably as the tide. Some men sit bare-chested, others with gaffs on their shoulders, all with fish entrails on their boots. The company stinks.

They are journeymen: the filleters, box men, freezer workers and carters. They work like oxen and drink like camels, and they come from exotic-sounding places like Babylon and the Ivory Coast and Sierra Madre.

David Reid comes from uptown. "Every man on these slips works himself into a hump," says Mr. Reid, forty-six, a thick man made thicker each day by the forty-five thousand pounds of tuna and swordfish he moves. "And you got to water the hump."

His eyes are reddened like coals from the cigarettes he smokes and the early-morning hours he works. His arms are big and blistered because rubbing against swordfish will burn the skin like poison oak.

There are two bars in the fish market where the journeymen like to drink: the Market Bar at Peck Slip and Front Street, and Jeremy's Ale House at Front and Dover streets. Like most of the older buildings in the district, the Market Bar is made of hand-molded brick, stuck together with mortar as thick as cake icing.

Mr. Reid will not drink here, because he has a beef with the owner. The cause of the beef is forgotten, but the grudge is not. But he likes to walk by the Market Bar on paydays anyway and watch the rough-looking women who dress in lace and sit on the bench in front of the plate-glass window.

Among them is a dissipated woman who is reviled by some, loved by others and known by all as the Kook of South Street.

"Annie been here least forty years, probably more," Mr. Reid says. When asked her age, Ms. Annie lifts her shirt. She wears no bra and says with no humility: "Two!"

"Oooooeeeeeeh!" hoot the journeymen. Mr. Reid wanders on and says nothing until he reaches Jeremy's, where he takes a stool and orders a quart of beer.

Jeremy's is a converted garage and the kegs are stacked in the corner like bowling pins. The walls are lined with knickknacks and bras. The skylight provides good sunshine to drink by.

"Annie hasn't changed, but plenty of other things around here have," Mr. Reid says. "It ain't so tough around here for one. Used to be loan-sharking, dope, you name it. Once I saw 'em put a forklift through a car and move it cause it was parked in the wrong spot.

"Then there's less fish. Like sturgeon. It's the most incredible fish. It has lips like human beings. I can't get over that. Like human beings. It's illegal to sell now." He orders a second quart.

"Yep. 'Bout the only thing that hasn't changed is Annie. Annie, and this fish stink. I ain't never been able to wash it off."

An Actor Awash
in Ambition and Merlot

He stood in the portico awash in light cast by a flickering gas lamp. It was raining, and his jacket did not quite fit. He had come from an audition. He had already had a few glasses of wine and apologized for them as though they were high-strung pets.

"There's nothing more important than Europe," he said for the first time that evening. He would say it many more times before the night was over. He would say it for the last time when the club closed and the doorman asked him out, into the rain. The meaning of this opaque phrase would grow murkier over the course of many drinks, but one must make allowances. George Demas is a stage actor after all, a man whose motivations and appetites lie at the bottom of a dark well.

He has appeared in the short-lived *The Escape Artist* by Michael Lawrence and *Master of Monstrosities* by Edgar Oliver, the East Village Poe. He is considered more than respectable at his craft, but acting has yet to pay his rent.

What his years in alternative theater have earned him is a candidacy at Players, a club in Gramercy Park that was founded in 1888 by Edwin Booth, the brother of Lincoln's assassin, for men of the stage, the letters and the arts. Its hallowed halls have been graced by the presence of notables like Mark Twain, Lauren Bacall and Paul Huber, a character actor and great-uncle of Mr. Demas.

He is hoping that along with admission to the club will come all its privileges, hobnobbing with directors and producers who might change his business address from Off Off Broadway to On.

But there is a predicament here. The greatest role played by Mr. Demas is that of a lover of wine and song. And in the stodgy environs of the Players Club, allowances are few and respectability is paramount, and Mr. Demas finds his candidacy under subtle scrutiny.

The good pledge does make an effort at decorum. The other evening, he spent his more sober moments in the downstairs parlor, expounding on the greatness of ancient Greece, the philosophy of psychosis and this canned peach: "Theater is infinitely more powerful than film."

But soon the ghosts stole up on Mr. Demas and he found himself standing in the drizzle of the second-floor balcony, a glass of merlot in hand. His father, it seems, was a top midshipman at the naval academy who, as a young man, shook the hand of President John F. Kennedy. After a term in the Navy, the father went to Harvard, and then became a successful economist, businessman, inventor and husband.

The genius the son pursues is much less mensurable.

"I would just for once like to make my father proud," Mr. Demas said into the long cold evening. "If I ever win the Oscar."

And then it was back to the parlor for a game of billiards, another glass of wine and a splintering rendition of "I've Got to Be Me," which is an honorable sentiment for an actor but a questionable one for an aspirant.

Frankie and Johnnie,
Together Again

Frankie and Johnnie are sweethearts. It's true. Just like the song. Their driver's licenses said so. Frank and John.

The two lovers sat on two stools at the marble bar in Monster, a place in the West Village. It was decorated with balloons, streamers and paper lamps. Some people wore cocktail dresses. A piano man played near the window. Frankie held his long arm around Johnnie. Johnnie was someplace else, looking up at the wall where the red ruby slippers hung. The shoes were encased in a glass box with the heels mounted together.

Johnnie was dreaming of an easy way home, a way to tell her. He had been drinking kind of heavily. Steadily and heavily. He had that lost-boy look to him. Big sad searching eyes. He looked that way because that's what he is. A lost boy. Sad and searching.

"I don't know what to do, Frankie," he told his lover. "I really don't."

"I told you what to do," Frankie said. "You finish your drink and you order another and you try to enjoy the evening, because the Lord knows, there may not be another tomorrow."

"It's not funny, Frankie. I'm in pain. My wife and kids are clueless."

"I know sweetheart. I know," Frankie said with real sympathy. "Now, finish your drink." Johnnie did.

Theirs is not a young love. Frankie has lived a lot of life. He has been divorced, been widowed and now, he said, he is a mistress. He is fifty-two, blond, blue-eyed, tall. He wore white shoes and bifocals and had a mustache.

"I understand him," Frankie said about Johnnie. "I hid behind a woman for nineteen years. I've had other things happen in my life. I had a lover die in my arms. Those were dark, dark days. That was until Johnnie came along."

There are certain virtues in this man, Frankie said: passion, gentleness, understanding. Frankie gets sick with headaches sometimes and Johnnie brings him soup and cigarettes.

Johnnie has a set of keys to Frankie's apartment. His wife doesn't know what those keys are for.

Johnnie is forty-three. He is short, with dark hair and dark eyes. "Opposites attract," Johnnie said. "I guess that's why I married a woman, because opposites attract."

He laughed into his ice cubes. His two lives. His tortured, married lie and his happy, secret nights. He ordered himself another drink, swallowed that and ordered another.

The clock said 9:15, and Frankie got one of his headaches. The men decided to leave, even though the dancing boys would not be dancing for another two hours. The piano man played on.

A Tasteful Mix of Blood,
Beer and Dirty Pictures

The telephone rang.

"I'm at the corner of Thirty-fifth and Eighth, where a man was shot earlier this afternoon," the newspaperman called to say. This particular reporter is known for his macabre tastes and Weegee-esque photographs of suicide jumpers, murder scenes and other theaters of misadventure. He sounded happy. "There's a puddle of blood and a pile of bloody clothes outside," he went on. Some men in the background were arguing about bullet calibers. The conversation had an exhilarated ring to it, as if the man who lay between the curb and the grating had deserved what he got.

"I was forced to step into a working-class greasy spoon where they sell Budweiser sixteen-ounce bottles for a dollar-sixty a pop," the reporter said. "I was so overjoyed, I had to call someone."

This tip sounded like it deserved investigation, as though there could be news fit to print. The greasy spoon is called Quick Tasty Food, which is a half-truth. It is a run-down joint underneath a sweatshop, and at five o'clock the workers come to wash down the lint with a dollar-sixty beer. The eating room toward the back is smoky and stained. There is a sign that asks patrons to refrain from spitting on the floor and a framed print of "Nude in the Bath," by the French painter Pierre Bonnard.

At one of the front tables sat the newspaperman and the sergeant, a Vietnam veteran. The Sarge is a bundle of whiskers and stick limbs who grew up in these precincts, as his father was the warden of the old Alimony Jail on West Thirty-seventh Street.

"They called it that because a man would rather go there than pay alimony," the Sarge said. "It usually worked to his advantage. Since he was in jail, the ex-wife figured it was better to ask the judge for a lesser amount than getting nothing at all."

The Sarge wore a cap that testified to his service in the 101st Airborne, along with a brown Army shirt with staff sergeant stripes and purple braiding, long shaggy hair, a pencil behind his ear and his mother's silver wedding band on his left hand. And always with him is a leather satchel. The newspaperman, eternally curious, asked to see its contents.

There was a death card with the ace of spades and Vietnamese writing on it that loosely translates to "the 101st Airborne was here." There were yellowed newspaper clippings about his father's career. Photographs of his brother and tasteful eight-by-tens of a nude woman wearing an open robe on a mahogany staircase. The Sarge, it seems, is something of an amateur photographer.

As it turns out, the newspaperman also served in the Army, also enjoys photographs of nude women and enjoys drinking in dirty dives. The men got on splendidly.

By eight o'clock the rain had washed the blood away, and the only memento of the shooting was a bullet hole in the nearby phone booth.

The Piers, a Blind Man
and an Old Seaman's Eyes

The blind man walked out of the bar. He said nothing until he bumped into a garbage can. Then he said into the cold Brooklyn evening, "Hey?"

"Yes, sir," the answer eventually came. He turned toward the voice. "Where's Clinton Street?"

"Over there," the stranger said, and pointed.

"Where the hell is over there? I can't see nothing."

"Sorry," the stranger said. "To your right about two blocks down."

"Well, I'm going there," the blind man said. He waited for a reply that did not come. His tone softened. "Could you walk me?" he asked. The stranger did.

The blind man smelled like booze. "I don't drink much. Just two beers now." He said his name was Francis. "I used to drink more, but I got diabetes. You drink too much with diabetes and you'll have a stroke. And drinking's not too good for you if you're blind."

The wind was blowing down Atlantic Avenue through the shipyard, through the pilings of Piers 5, 6 and 7, through the stooped and brittle bones of Francis. He lives nearby in Red Hook, although he couldn't tell you the difference between a red hook and a blue hook. He's been blind since birth. His eyes are a milky swirl of glue. He was going to the grocery store to buy a loaf of bread with his Social Security money, bread for sandwiches that he was going to eat by himself. He had dropped another seven dollars of it for two bottles of beer in Montero's Bar and Grill.

"That's a good bar over there, Montero's," Francis said. He whispered here. "They got hookers in there."

But there weren't any hookers in Montero's. Just a few old neighborhood types, who refuse to be pushed out by the money.

Pilar Montero, who opened the place in 1947 with her husband, sat in the far corner of the glass-block bar. There was also her cousin Salvado Rivas, seventy-one, a retired merchant mariner, and Rosario, a local hard-luck case.

Death swirled around Rosario. His mother lay with cancer in the hospital across the street. His teeth had died a long time ago. He kept his head on the wood blubbering non sequiturs to himself.

The place is a rough-hewn monument to the mariner with its ships-in-a-bottle, life preservers from the old ocean freighters, and the toilet that smells like a cargo hold. They say the King of Denmark once had a drink in here, and so did the prostitutes but they're not allowed in anymore.

"That old blind buzzard, he wouldn't know a hooker if he saw one," Captain Rivas barked in his Galicia-stained English. "And he can't see nothing anyhow. He's blind."

The captain is older than most of the memorabilia, and when he gets wound up he is a boil of opinions on everything from Truman to the loss of the seafaring way of life to Medicare.

"Old people built this country," he said while strangling the stranger's arm. "Now I got to pay fifty dollars for eye drops. What they want? For me to go blind? It's terrible to be blind."

Rosario got up then from the bar wiping tears from his eyes. He crossed himself as he walked out the door. It was a full moon.

Fifteen Minutes of Fame
Where Black Is the Color

W ho's that?"
  The question percolated through the Fashion Week crowd at Lotus, one of Manhattan's fancy new nightclubs. It went from the waitress to the Frenchwoman to her husband the wine connoisseur to the German model to a bald man in a suit and to the Europeans sitting on the divan. It wended its way to the back of the lounge, bounced off the mirror and returned like this:

"I think the Indian was the actor in *One Flew Over the Cuckoo's Nest,* and the midget is a Gucci model."

They were talking about Big Foot and Koko the Killer Clown.

Big Foot is six feet five inches tall. Koko the Killer Clown is three feet eleven. Big Foot has size fifteen and a half feet. Koko's are five and a half.

Big Foot is a conscious objector to the nine-to-five work world. Koko is a featured performer in the Coney Island attraction "Sideshow by the Seashore."

Big Foot has slept where he pleases for the last twenty years. Koko lives in the attic of his parents' apartment in Brighton Beach, Brooklyn.

Both men know their way around New York, and for that reason they were invited by a reporter to sample the nectar at Lotus, on West Fourteenth Street in the Meatpacking District.

Lotus is a place where you can see that there is a certain comfort in money. Those who have it are insulated from the unpredictability of poor grammar and strong body smells. In this ten-dollar martini set, the rabble is generally left behind the velveteen ropes, ensuring a safe and self-assured feeling of respectability inside.

But once on the other side of the ropes, the giant Indian and the Puerto Rican dwarf transmogrify into something more spectacular. Almost instantly, they have become men to know, men to see. The doorman, a white man who uses black slang as easily as a blind man rides a bicycle through Midtown traffic, ignored the ragtag retinue until he saw that their names were indeed on the guest list.

"Awright," the doorman said. "Tear it up, yo!"

It is an up-to-the-moment crowd wearing many shades of black. Satin black, dull black, dark black and black on black.

"Technically speaking, black is not a color," lectured Big Foot, who is something of a Fifth Avenue fashion plate; that is, whenever he decides to panhandle on Fifth Avenue.

"Black is a way of life," Big Foot explained as he limped upstairs to the lounge in his tattered jeans and secondhand shoes.

Big Foot ordered a White Russian. Koko drank vodka and cranberry. The lighting was sleek and dark, the drinks strong and tall.

The flashbulbs went off and the leather-clad owner made his way to the table for a photo with the visitors. *"Hoka-hey ko-la!"* Big Foot whooped in Lakota, his mother tongue.

And that does it. The crowd is sure he is a movie actor, a medicine man or something, despite his protestations that he is neither. The Frenchwoman, the wife of the wine connoisseur, does not know that the phrase means "Today is a good day to die." She cozied up to Big Foot and they kissed.

Koko, the model, is now on the divan with two women. "Yo! This place is fly!" He gave it two small thumbs-up. He is famous for the evening.

MR. AND MRS. NOBODY

THE HARDEST thing to be in the New York is a nobody, and the town is full of them. The blind, the broke and the beaten. Nobodies. They count, too.

The Pair of Bickering Brothers
Who Made Coney Island Hot

On suffocating days when the horizon cannot be seen, a good place to clear the lungs is the Coney Island boardwalk.

There, lost among the salt air and the bikinis, the airborne paper plates and the smell of corn on the cob, is Ruby's, the surfside bar, a dark, unwholesome place. The other day, everything looked and smelled as it should. The open-air bar reeked of the sea, onions and cheap cigars. The wall was lined with stereoscopes, hundreds of postcards, and photographs of Coney Island in its early days. A prostitute was on the job. There were lovers, fuddy-duddies and musclemen.

But there was something lonesome about the saloon, and drinking there felt like a dismal duty.

"Hey, where's Phil?" a customer wanted to know.

"Dead," came the answer.

"Oh, yeah?" the customer said. "First Ruby, now Phil. You couldn't have a Ruby without Phil."

Ruby and Phil Jacobs were the owners of Ruby's. They were brothers who were raised on Twenty-seventh Street in Coney Island, and only once in their lives were they separated from each other or the beach. That was in World War II.

Ruby died in April, of an infection, at seventy-six. Phil went in November, at eighty-four. They both died in the off-season.

Phil and Ruby always argued. If Ruby saw the sun, Phil saw a cloud. If Ruby offered money, Phil refused it. Ruby mumbled. Phil hissed. Ruby's name was on the deed, but Phil was the personality, and most people thought Phil was Ruby. They both wore liver spots and caps and pants hitched around their navels.

Their friends at the bar surmised that after Ruby died, Phil died of a broken heart. You couldn't have a Ruby without a Phil. Loneliness. That's one theory.

There is another.

"Man, those guys were like a bad marriage," said a tattooed man named Scotty who was drinking under a parasol. "I think it was like Cain and Abel. I think Phil killed Ruby and then died from the sheer joy of it."

The brothers grew up poor and earned their money during the Depression combing the sands for valuables. Ruby left behind a collection of more than a thousand gold rings, dentures, knickknacks and curios. They hustled ice cream on the boardwalk and paid the police to let them do it.

After the war the Jacobs brothers became the bathhouse barons of the boardwalk. They owned four bathhouses, including the last, Stauch's. They bickered even then.

Now, the brothers lie next to each other in a cemetery near the Belmont Race Track. Ruby's tombstone reads CONEY ISLAND, THE ELIXIR OF LIFE.

"Hero" Label Lifts a Life

Just back from an extended alcoholiday, John Byrnes is rebuilding his life from the bottom.

Recently, Mr. Byrnes was walking by a wooden two-family house on 123rd Street in College Point when he noticed flames coming out of the bottom window. It was about eleven-ten A.M., fire officials said, or somewhere between a quarter-past and half-past a pint, according to colleagues of Mr. Byrnes who said they were drinking with him that day at College Point Park.

Mr. Byrnes said he began pounding on the door and a woman appeared in the upstairs window, screaming hysterically. "Throw the baby," he pleaded. She did, Mr. Byrnes caught the two-year-old, the assembled crowd cheered and the next day Mr. Byrnes made local and national headlines. HOMELESS HERO, one newspaper called him. DRUNKEN BUM RESCUES TWO-YEAR-OLD, declared another. (A local merchant with a ladder rescued the mother. The family's pit bull died.)

Mr. Byrnes, forty-two, a former autobody man, described himself at the time as a drunken, homeless bum. His brother James said Mr. Byrnes had returned to Queens after his fiancée had died of an aneurysm in Florida. Her death shattered him, his brother said, and

John Byrnes began to look for the pieces of his life at the bottom of the bottle.

"I ain't no hero," Mr. Byrnes said the day after the rescue. "I'm just a drunk bum, but I knew the right thing right then and there."

Still, the news media insisted on making him a hero—at least for fifteen minutes. He was written up in the city's tabloids and in *The National Enquirer.* Michael Palumbo, sixty-two, who said he used to pass the bottle with Mr. Byrnes, put it this way: "John Byrnes is no hero but he is the greatest man I ever met—in this park at least."

Throughout the next week, Mr. Byrnes, a ruddy man with a red beard and a solid six-foot-two-inch frame, insisted he'd done nothing special. It almost went to fists at the Russia Bar on College Point Boulevard when, after a couple of congratulatory cocktails, he grew agitated at the attention, said one friend, Bob Doti. "After enough backslapping he got real angry," said Mr. Doti, sixty, who is a well-worn fixture on College Point Boulevard. "He said, 'I told you I ain't no hero. Anybody would have done the same thing in my spot.' He said that but I don't think it's so. There were a lot of people standing around watching." On the other hand, he added, "You're supposed to help a kid in a burning house."

James Byrnes said he had allowed his brother to stay at his College Point home until his drinking habits became unbearable. "Johnnie knew it was just a good newspaper story," James Byrnes said. His brother, he said, thought that "no one was going to remember him or what would become of him."

But a reporter said she felt sorry for Mr. Byrnes and called the New York Hospital Medical Center of Queens to see if he could be admitted to a detoxification program. Mr. Byrnes was sent to a residential drug treatment center in Long Island. If he can get himself out of the drinking life, his brother said, "then he'll be a hero."

Society's Throwaways,
with Booze and Attitude

Twenty-four cans of malt liquor. A ten-dollar bottle of rum. A cheap room. An extension cord bringing stolen electricity to the TV and tape player. A needle.

It was a punk party in Bushwick, Brooklyn. The solitary lamp cast a tilted mood. Moonlight poured into the empty kitchen. The shadows of the trees came knocking at the window. "Is someone at the door, white boy?" a paranoid white boy asked.

"Go look," said Hatred, the oldest. Puke went to look.

"Is it those crackheads? The black guy with the dreads?"

"Nobody," Puke said at the peephole. "But turn down the radio."

Puke went back to his can of malt liquor. He's sixteen and, like the rest, is from the West. "My mom smokes crack," Puke said. "She sits on her butt, plays solitaire and beats my dog." A kid named Chris sat against the wall in a half nod, holding a frying pan and a fork.

They were a group of young people confessing their ancestry, their social yearnings, their street status. Getting high. They do what they want, when they want, how they want. What they can't get, what they're not given, they take. If someone is receiving mommy money, he doesn't admit to it.

You hear most of them tell stories about divorce and the wasteland suburbs and parents who do drugs. By the earnestness in their voices, you're likely to believe them when they say they hurt. Their stories are consistent.

They talk about being kicked around in life. Though they run in a pack, they are not stray animals. It is an impromptu family made up of damaged citizens nobody seems to want. They are gentle to one another, and what one has they all have.

There are longings beneath the leather and tattoos, and listening to them, it seems as if half of them will come out of this somehow. They all talk about kicking the dope. Then there are the ones like Nate, who says he doesn't worry about sharing a needle. He's got strong Nordic blood.

Puke has dreams. He wants a farm somewhere in Nebraska. He heard they give land free out there if you squat on it long enough. He would like a piece somewhere far away from everybody where he can grow his vegetables and play his music and have mad parties.

"Being a dumb teenager dude, it was just meant to be this way," he said. "It's a good life, though. I just want to have a good time."

Outside on the street the bass of hip-hop thumped from somewhere. In the apartment the grind of punk rock guitars and the evening news. Pictures of dogs and movies and beauty pageants.

"Man, that's lame," Laura said. "Everything that's going on in the world, and that's it?"

Saluting the Fourth

A sign in the veterans hospital in Brooklyn reads THE PRICE OF FREEDOM IS VISIBLE HERE.

Yesterday, the first Fourth of July of the twenty-first century, Americans were supposed to remember. Yesterday, hundreds of thousands of people celebrated on the shores of New York Harbor as they watched one of the largest armadas ever assembled. Meanwhile, fewer than two dozen people went to see the men of war and military service who sat silently in the beds and halls and doorways of the Veterans Administration Hospital, unable to see the flotilla from their windows as it passed underneath the Verrazano-Narrows Bridge just a quarter-mile away. These men passed the morning inhaling the smell of antiseptic and the stench of bedpans, listening to the mumblings of the dying, lying in bed watching the beautiful boats on their televisions.

Ward 8 is the cancer precinct, and the men here wait for disease to do what fighting wars could not. To a man, they said they were disappointed that their sacrifices—some fought, some served, none regretted any of it—were not appreciated more yesterday, that there was no band playing, that there was no child's hand to hold.

They said they were lonely.

"The Star-Spangled Banner" played on a television and its melody drifted down the hall. The music came from the room of Frank Pardal, fifty-four, who held his eyes closed. He breathed from a tube while his lips mouthed the words. When the music was over, he opened his eyes. He was alone. There was footage of the boats sailing by on his screen.

"Holy mackerel, that's big holiday stuff," he said. "They look like a bunch of birds out there, those boats do."

He cleared his tube and wiped his fingers on the sheets. "It don't mean nothing to me though. Independence Day. It don't mean nothing to anyone anymore."

Mr. Pardal served in the Army from 1965 to 1968, in West Germany. He came home to Staten Island, worked laboring jobs and then was hit by a car. That's when they found the cancer. He has not left the hospital in months. And no one has come to see him.

"Tell you the truth, though, I wish I was out there looking at those long beauties go by, having a cold one and a dog and holding my girl's hand," he said. "Even if I could get out of bed, what could I do? I got a view of an air-conditioning unit."

No one likes to hear about self-deception and disappointment and grief, said Eddie Murach, seventy-two, a retired sergeant major who served in World War II, Korea and Vietnam. But, he says, that is precisely what war is, that is precisely what Ward 8 is. Because whatever war it was, Mr. Murach said, however long it lasted, it changed men from scrawny hometown clerks into men who know the fragility of life.

"I feel sorry for these guys down the hall," he said. "They've got no one."

The sergeant is one of the lucky ones. He has his wife, Mary Ellen. He met her at a root-beer stand in rural Indiana. He sat in his Buick. She sat in the next car over. That was forty-seven years, three children and six grandchildren ago.

She washed him yesterday morning and brought him a pair of binoculars to watch the ships. But the day was hazy and the windows stained with soot. The armada might as well have been in Normandy. Mr. Murach insisted he was no hero. A thirty-year veteran of the Army, he started his career with the Japanese occupation. He was part of the Chosin Reservoir campaign in Korea when the conflict broke out in 1950. He slept in a frozen hole for sixty days. The Army had given its men summer gear for a winter campaign and he watched as men died of exposure. Then the Chinese poured down the ridge, the battalion pulled out, was reoutfitted and pushed back in.

Then came Vietnam. "I was forty, and I had to volunteer because they wouldn't send me," he said, laying bare-chested in bed. The boats below sailed by. "I figured it was a career for me and they were taking guys who didn't want to go. I felt it was my duty."

He has cancer—probably caused by exposure to Agent Orange, he said the doctors told him. He was awarded the Legion of Merit and two Bronze Stars with valor. He spends part of his time in the hospital, part of his time as a high school baseball coach. He loves Buicks and apple pie.

"I've got more blessings than I'm entitled to," Mr. Murach said as he squeezed his wife's hand. "I do wish that all of us could go outside for just a moment and get a gander of those ships."

About twenty-five thousand veterans stayed in the hospitals last year, according to the Veterans Administration statistics, and thirty-five million outpatients visited its clinics. Statistics on visitors are not kept, but Sergeant Clifford Newman of the federal police department, who patrolled the empty lobby yesterday morning, said the respect for people in uniform had declined drastically over the last twenty-five years.

"The price of freedom is not cheap," the sergeant said. "People could invest a little time. Instead of spending the whole day watching the boats go by and lighting off firecrackers, people should have thought to visit a vet."

Carl Passaro sat in a chair in the doorway of his room. "I'm just going to sit here and watch the floors dry," he said. "It's a cruel, cruel thing to have those boats going by and us locked up in here."

Mr. Passaro is eighty-four. He said he saw more action at the race track than in the Second World War as a supply clerk. And now that he is alone and has no visitors, he wishes he had conducted his life better.

"I was a crumb, I admit that," he said. "But even a crumb needs company."

Her Queens Days
Will Become Moscow Nights

Ludmila, a fifty-five-year-old widow, set the supper table. There was bread and butter smeared with red caviar, pickled herring, eggplant, beef, potatoes, chocolate sweets, good teacups and bottles of beer.

She had not seen her son in twelve years, ever since he had gone to America and taken a job moving the furniture of rich people who live in town houses with marble floors and walls painted with real golden flecks. Her son, Vlad, had done well for himself. She could see that. His apartment, in Woodside, Queens, was spare and painted a clean white. It had high ceilings and clear lighting. He was healthy and muscular, and his boy's face had solidified into that of a man. By the look of things, he worked hard, and he could afford to have her come for a two-month vacation.

"Still no wife," she said in Russian, and sighed and petted his cheek. "Always alone—this is bad. When are you going to find yourself a good woman?"

The son rolled his eyes and lit himself a cigarette and sat silently. Then, almost as an afterthought, he leaned over and kissed his mother on the cheek.

"Don't you worry about it," he told her.

Behind them hung a calendar with a print of a Norman Rockwell painting, the one in which a woman and a boy are sitting near a diner window praying over their supper. The dates were marked off with large black Xs that moved inexorably toward the day later in the week when she would board the plane and return to Moscow and her job in the library. It would be the saddest day of the year for the mother and son, half strangers now living half a world apart.

She has a daughter in Moscow and will be a grandmother come December. "Babushka!" she said. "Me!"

Her husband died about ten years ago, and though she does not talk about it, her son worries about her lonesome heart. He could not attend his father's funeral, because he was in New York earning money to pay for the burial. A photograph of his parents on their wedding day stood on the table in a gold frame. Yevgeny was a handsome man in 1968, with a square face and a sharp tie, and, like his son, did not smile for photographs.

They talked about many things at the dinner table: about poetry and architecture and how Moscow is growing so cold now. She was surprised, she said, to learn how the morning light makes New York appear squat and wide and then as the sun moves toward the horizon it grows tall and angular. "Beautiful city!" she exclaimed in English. "Beautiful America."

They did not speak of love at the table; it is not the son's way. He simply called her Mama.

A Jazz Rhapsody
Turned Sour

She lived a long time in Harlem. From its heyday, when the place had swing joints and all-night cocktails, through the sinewy years, the broken glass and rubbled lives, she stayed.

Ruby Jean Johnson told her friends that she preferred to stay uptown, because the rough-and-tumble streets kept her alive. In the end, they killed her.

Mrs. Johnson, eighty-one, was found dead in her apartment on June 26, 1998. The police said she had been strangled with a bicycle chain, raped and beaten so badly that her body would have to be cremated. She was dumped in her bathtub. Detectives surmise that she had let her killer in. The door was locked from the inside, deadbolted three times. He probably escaped through the window.

"It had to be one of them crackheads," said Patricia Tanks, a neighbor. "She let them in her house. Everybody knew what she had in there."

She had furs, boas and mementos from a life well lived, and the word around the neighborhood was that she kept her jewelry in a safe. But after her death, the police said there was no safe, no matter what Mrs. Johnson told friends and neighbors.

No one in her neighborhood knew it, but Mrs. Johnson had been a glittering personality of the Harlem Renaissance, her husband a jazz legend. As Michael McGregor said on the street corner over a bottle of malt liquor the other day: "No one around here knows nothing about jazz. That was another time." They did, however, see the glow of her Tiffany lamps in her apartment, packed with artifacts. "You knew the lady had class," Mr. McGregor said.

A chocolate-skinned woman with silver hair, Ruby Jean Johnson appeared as a young woman in black fashion magazines of the 1930s and early 1940s. Among her friends she counted Duke Ellington, Count Basie and Billie Holiday.

Later in life, she fell in love with Walter Johnson, one of the top jazz drummers of the thirties and forties, a member of Fletcher Henderson's famed orchestra and the man who popularized the use of the high-hat cymbals as jazz's driving beat.

In the good times, he kept his wife in furs and limousines, but when he died in 1977, he left her with little more than yellowing photographs. So when the neighborhood was buried in a blizzard of crack cocaine in the 1980s, she had no place to go. To survive, she created two lives for herself, and kept them separate. "Everybody lives several lives," said her longtime friend Vivian Millinder, seventy-two, the widow of Lucky Millinder, the swing-band leader. "She never told her girlfriends what was going on up there."

On the one hand, she remained the urbane socialite, the elegant woman about town, who friends said carried a silver flask of whisky and went to Lincoln Center for the outdoor music.

The other woman was a recluse, a hostage in her home. Flashy but broke, Ruby Jean was kind to alcoholics and crack addicts, fed them bread from church. She fed them to feel needed, her friends supposed, to buy a little dignity in her troubled neighborhood. She understood what misery was.

Ruby Jean Muckleroy was born on November 5, 1916, in the small dust town of Chattanooga, Oklahoma. In a photo from 1918, the family looks the picture of American rectitude. Framed by a scraggly tree, her father is dressed in a dark suit and high starched collar, her mother in petticoats and a simple linen dress. Soon after the picture was taken, the father ran off, and the mother, single and alone, put the girl in an orphanage, said Brooks Kerr, the pianist and a confidant of Mrs. Johnson in her later years.

She would stay in the institution for eight years, until her grandmother took her out and brought her to New Rochelle. Ruby Jean left her grandmother's house at eighteen and moved down to Greenwich Village with a white woman. To support herself, she racked balls in pool halls, hustled mugs of beer and lived on the kindness of gentlemen.

Her modeling career began on 132nd Street and Seventh Avenue in Harlem. It was there that she first saw Walter Johnson. It was there that she met the German artist. It was somewhere around 1937.

"The way she described it, he was like her Professor Higgins and she was an Eliza Doolittle," Mr. Kerr said. The German's name is lost to time, but Mrs. Johnson told her friends that he taught her how to be beautiful, how to speak, how to be powerful. She modeled for him and for magazines.

Their relationship lasted through the war, then ended. Details have evaporated with time; many of her friends' recollections are uncertain, most others buried in the ground.

It was in 1952 when she really became acquainted with Walter Johnson, a dapper man who spent two hours dressing each morning. He would oil his hair, examine his face for whiskers before cleaning it with a soft sponge. He was so slick even the rain couldn't stick to him, said Harvard Davis, a friend and jazz trumpeter who played with Ella Fitzgerald.

"Neither of them ever had a hair out of place," Mr. Davis said.

She took him in, took his name and they lived for the next quarter century at 660 St. Nicholas Avenue, a marble-walled building in the Sugar Hill section, where many famous black personalities lived.

People say that they were married in 1953, and friends remember the ceremony at a church with a name they no longer recall. They say there were flowers and all the famous people attended.

But at the city's Marriage License Bureau, there is no record of their marriage. It seems that Walter Johnson never divorced his first wife. It did not seem to matter then, friends say, but it would come back to haunt Ruby Jean.

They loved each other, by all accounts. Even when the music turned sour. Jazz fell out of favor, and Walter Johnson got less work. He was never interested in money so, more than once, Ruby Jean had to track down his pay from shady club managers, Mrs. Millinder said, threatening to blow up the nightclub, the manager's wife and his "blue-eyed children." The limousine trips turned into subway rides. By the 1960s, Mr. Johnson was working in a bank, his uniforms custom-tailored. His wife still socialized, and posed nude for struggling painters at the Art Students League on Fifty-seventh Street.

But the neighborhood became depressed, the marble walls in the hallways began to crumble and the couple grew old. Walter Johnson put on his best suit on April 8, 1977, and went to the hospital for stomach surgery. He never came home.

Mr. Johnson's first and official wife staked a claim on everything he owned. Ruby Jean got what was left in her lover's safe-deposit box: two bundles of pictures, wrapped in velvet, of Mr. Johnson's girl-friends. "She cried," Mrs. Millinder recalled, "cursed his name up and down, and then we got drunk."

For the next twenty years, Ruby Jean Johnson scraped along, living on food stamps and a small Social Security check. She pawned her jewelry and lost the rest to drug addicts, who broke into her apartment countless times. Last March, she told Mr. Kerr, the pianist, about a woman who pushed into her apartment and threw her to the ground. Ruby Jean, arthritic and struggling with diabetes, bit half the woman's toe off.

"The fight keeps me young," she told friends. The truth was, the uptown crowd had always been her crowd. Harlem had given her everything. And what little she had left, she was killed for.

"The thing that makes me the most sad," Mrs. Millinder said, "is that of all the beautiful days of her life, the last was her most horrible day on earth."

Saturday Night Fever:
The Life

When Pete Pedone was a top deejay back in the late seventies, when the music was at its peak, he was the main-man-with-the-aqua-green-van, the disco dude who got four hundred phone numbers in the single calendar year of 1979. The world belonged to him and he was unstoppable, sauve, smooth-talking and he had a steady gig mixing wax and eight-tracks for Brooklyn's hottest clubs. He was on fire, he was a supernova and the future was so bright it hurt to stare into it.

Pete Pedone used to see Tony Manero around. They ran the same circles. Manero wasn't much, a scrawny guy who kept mostly to himself in the corners of club Space Odyssey 2001, nothing like the macho dance-floor Casanova played by John Travolta in the movie *Saturday Night Fever*. The real Tony Manero drank tequila sunrises, not seven-and-sevens as the movie character did. Everybody drank tequila sunrises. That was the style in Brooklyn 1977, but the original story, which appeared in *New York* magazine the year before, and then the Hollywood movie got a lot of things wrong. Sure, Manero could dance, but he wasn't all that, certainly not the Godfather of Bay Ridge. There was no Ultimate Face who sauntered in wearing polyester pants as tight as a prophylactic and took the joint over, directing the dancing like a traffic cop. The Brooklyn nightclubs were a neighborhood thing, a place among friends. You came with your tribe but you were only in competition with yourself: how well you could dress, how smooth you could dance, how sweet you could talk. Everybody knew each other. Anything outside the neighborhood wasn't Brooklyn anyhow, not to the Italians. Those areas were wastelands belonging to the blacks and the immigrants.

The Odyssey wasn't a hip club until the picture came out and the movie studio installed the dazzling dance floor with strobe lights embedded in the wood that glowed like giant Jujubes. The Italians rarely went to Manhattan, they didn't need to; they had everything they wanted at home. But to hear the locals like JoJo Gallo, Rob (Sorcerer) Picciotto, Dougie Shemp and Carole Ioia tell it, Manhattanites started coming to Brooklyn when disco topped the charts, looking for a piece of the action. They came like cockroaches, swarming over Bay Ridge with their funky city attitudes. All the pretenders, the lame dancers, the chicken walkers, the Eurotrash sort of killed the scene. Everybody became a stranger. You couldn't tell the girls from the guys.

But for a while, Brooklyn was the epicenter, and Pete Pedone lived on the fault line. The moment was so glorious he didn't need the future; he never thought about it but the future remembered him. It came and went and he found himself, two divorces and two decades later, back in the old club, this time pouring drinks on a Saturday night in Bensonhurst, listening to retreads of the same music he was spinning then.

The Odyssey is a gay club now. A cinder-block building surrounded by auto shops and garment factories with barred windows, Korean delis, Chinese laundromats, few Italians. The neighborhood's changed. No one knows what happened to Tony Manero. "He's probably dead. Murdered," Pete said, he doesn't know for sure, just a hunch. As for Pete Pedone, things haven't gone the way he expected.

Enigma

A group of Mexican boys loiter on an abandoned glass cobbled street, under umbrellas, their voices squealing like faulty brakes. "Yo, dog! Stop stepping on that joint." It's dark, the kids should be home, but they're not because it's Saturday night.

A block over, near the Sixty-second Street subway station, is the club Enigma—formerly L'Amours, a disco club twenty years ago, then a topless bar, a rocker joint and now a discoland again. Like the Odyssey of *Saturday Night Fever* fame, Enigma is the place to be, the flavor of the month, featuring the frenzied, retro sounds of disco, back again; a joke to some, a reunion for others.

Outside, the line ponies up in the rain, wet, bothered and expectant. Inside, the lights dim green; the house is ready to rock. Pete Pedone clips on his teal dickie bow, pats down his blow-dried hair in the mirrored walls as the crowd swaggers in.

It's early. The place is half empty and strained-sober faces glow in the embers of cigarettes. DJ Mad Dog James Kanade spins some familiar oldies until the crowd gets liquored-up and comfortable. He plays the Trammps, Eddie Kendricks, records given to him by Pete and his mother. James is packed into a tight shirt, and his torso looks like ground-beef patties wrapped in cellophane. He is the new young buck, Pete Pedone incarnate, the apostle. He humps and pumps from his booth, imploring the women who straddle the dance floor like nervous lizards to walk his way. They demure and he looks across the club, studying Pete, who is surrounded by a flock of admirers.

Pete Pedone still has the good looks. Almost thirty-six, he has full and black hair, silvering on the sides. A third-generation Sicilian, he's got the Ray Liotta look, dark eyes, olive skin, a hundred-dollar smile, and a thin white scar on his upper lip. It's his beauty mark, the ladies say.

A woman dressed in Lycra pants, silverish unidentifiable material and big hair pulls out a cigarette from her knockoff Fendi bag, snaps it closed and leans over the bar, her breasts slipping out of their moorings. This move happens every week, and Pete Pedone has seen it a hundred thousand times if he's seen it once. He is there with an assiduous flick of the Bic. "You've got the prettiest smile in the joint," he tells her, "why don't you use it?" He lights her cigarette and she melts into a big, fatuous smile.

On the other side of the bar is a heavy woman sipping a red drink from a thin red straw. Nikki says she loves Pete. She comes every week, Friday and Saturday, just for him, silently watching as he bends over, hustles drinks, lights cigarettes. She stands for hours, sipping her red drinks, waiting.

Everybody has a chance at the disco. It's a place of alcohol and dim lights, a fantasy land of sex and make-believe where the clock stands still and responsibilities don't exist. In the disco Pete Pedone is still a heartthrob frozen in time. There are no warts, no pumpkins. Everything is possible.

He notices Nikki, but tries not to let on, not to encourage her. She's fat. When he sees her looking his confidence wavers. He rubs his stomach then smooths his rump, a nervous gesture, trying to let her down gently.

A man meets a lot of women when he's working behind the bar. Especially when he's a handsome Italian bachelor. And Pete Pedone loves women. That's the problem. He loves them too much, and to hear him tell it, they've left his life a delapidated, empty house. His new girlfriend is in the club, a long-legged blond with a taste for good times. As the crowd and smoke grow thicker, his lady disappears. He hasn't seen her in an hour. This makes him nervous. Faces don't like to be stood up, Faces like their women where they can be seen. "She knows where home is," Pete figures. He met her only a month ago while working the bar. He wants to trust her, he tries to trust her.

Roseann

There are only two women Pete Pedone ever really trusted, his mother and Roseann. Roseann Damato grew up on Sixteenth Avenue in a modest brick and aluminum-sided home, attached to the neighbor's house, which looked exactly the same, sharing the shade of a fat elm tree. Roseann went to Lafayette High School in Bensonhurst and hung out with black girls after school, listening to records, practicing dance moves. Roseann was a precocious sixteen-year-old, full-bodied, in 1976. The drinking age then was eighteen and with a fake I.D. she had no problem getting into nightclubs. It was there she became acquainted with the fashions, the moves, the Faces. Her neighbor was Petie Pedone, a nice-looking sixteen-year-old-kid but definitely a boy. She would make him a man.

In her basement after school, they practiced the Hustle, the Rope, the Bus Stop, the Continental Walk. She taught him to dress, turning him on to the wide collar, glow-in-the-fluorescent-lights Huk-A-Poo shirts, and the blue four-inch gum-soled platform shoes. When his friends were listening to Led Zeppelin, he was listening to Kool and the Gang. She took him to his first club.

It was at Orphan Andy's in Midwood. Roseann introduced him to Anthony Apuzo, the house deejay. Anthony wore a gold crucifix, a diamond pinky ring, brown poly bellbottoms, a brown shirt with a floral print and patent leather shoes. He must have been royalty or something, tres chic. He invited Pete into the booth. When Pete saw the racks of turntables and records and the red lights of the control boards, he knew the life of the deejay was the greatest, the ultimate. It gave the kid goose bumps to hear two records put together and the people scream, the crowd freak. It was power. It became Pete Pedone's sense of purpose, his future.

Pete Pedone laid bricks for his uncle during the week, dreaming about the weekends. He thought about the new shirt he would buy with his paycheck, he thought about the new music he would hear. In twenty years, Pete Pedone knew he was going to have his own club.

The kid apprenticed under the music man for a year, carrying the equipment and watching, waiting for his moment. Anthony was a ladies' man, and Pete's break came at a Christmas Eve party at a Wall Street firm when Anthony disappeared with a vice-president's wife up to the executive washroom. Pete worked the crowd for three hours and they loved what he did.

Soon he was spinning in all the big clubs: Gazebo at Sixth Avenue and Sixty-sixth, Revelations at Fourth Avenue and Eighty-eighth, Camelot Inn at East Thirty-fifth and Quentin Road. He finished trade school a year late, majoring in electrical installation, and never thought about college. He bought an aqua-green van to drive his equipment to the gigs. The van had wall-to-wall carpeting, captain's chairs and a bed. He shuttled women in and out the back doors of the clubs, putting more mileage on the inside of the van than on the motor.

Pete Pedone's life was a cocktail party. He had a following. He was written up in *Billboard* in 1981 (as Don Pedone) for being named entertainer of the year by Disconet, a minor record label. He took dancing lessons at Dale Dance Studio in Bay Ridge because "if you wanted to meet chicks you had to know how to dance," he said.

But time marched on. It was 1982 when his father came to him. "You can't do this the rest of your life, son. You got to get a career," he remembered the old man saying. Pete was twenty-two now, the glamour fading, the music changing. His father, a motorman with the Transit Authority, knew people and got his son a job as a conductor. When Pete was a kid, his dad took him on the trains; sometimes he let his boy work the accelerator. So now, when the old man offered, Pete knew he had to take the job, he just couldn't turn it down. Pete didn't want it, never did, never liked getting up at five in the morning to go to the Bronx. It was brain-deadening. The only good thing was, he could still spin records at night. For three years Pete did this, waiting for his dad to retire so he, too, could quit.

It was that year, 1985, when Pet met the future Mrs. Pedone in a diner one night after clubbing. She was a waitress with prerequisite blond hair and the hips. Pete ordered a cup of coffee and her phone number.

Theirs was a big Italian wedding, 330 guests, six black limousines, twenty-six groomsmen. He got married not for love but because it was the thing to do. Eight of his friends had married that year. She made him quit the nightclubs and he found work as an electrician. The marriage went nowhere. They split after ten months. Only two good things came from that marriage, he said: the honeymoon and his daughter, whom he doesn't see often, only every other weekend.

Gun Goes Off

It's Friday, and Pete Pedone has to deliver some electric wiring to a job site out on Staten Island. He has a startup business installing audiovisual equipment in new nightclubs. He also has to get his hair done and his car washed and waxed. All these things have to be done for the weekend, because that's the way things have always been done.

When he emerges from his spare basement apartment with the wire, there is a dull throb, the sound of a firecracker. Police cars and then ambulances. The commotion bubbles out from four houses down. A crowd grows as a group of weeping teenagers carries on in the street. A big, bare-chested kid crumbles to his knees and vomits. A paramedic walks up from the basement.

"Went in one side, out the other," he tells a cop. Suicide.

They bring the kid out from the basement, his skull wrapped in a plastic bag. Pete recognizes Vinnie's tattooed arm hanging off the gurney and he recognizes Vinnie's friends. "He used to come down to the club," he says. The boy's mother arrives home as the ambulance is ready to leave. She screams, "Oh my God!" Collapses.

"He must have been in some serious trouble on the street to take his life that young," Pete says to his neighbor Gino.

"What the hell's wrong with a kid so much to blow his brains out at twenty years old?" Gino says. Pete just shakes his head.

The Worst Year

Pete pulls away in his gray '85 Oldsmobile, which shines like an oiled griddle. He picked it up last year when his other car blew up. He stares straight down Eighty-sixth Street, quiet and preoccupied. "The kid did it at home, probably because he was comfortable there," he says after a long silence. "That's Italian. *La famiglia.* The family."

Stopping for gas, the attendant doesn't understand his English. "Nine, nine dollars! Christ, if you can't speak English, count the money." The attendant fumbles the money.

"Man. Foreigners," Pete says, smoothing his hair in the rearview mirror, adjusting the two-hundred-dollar sunglasses he bought for himself as an early Father's Day present.

"You know, life can kick you, but things get better. Too bad the kid didn't know that. Life doesn't work out like you expect, but you keep on.

"Things are good again for me. I'm moving forward, getting my apartment together. I got a nice woman, I got my business going and I'm working at the club. I'm not going to be there for the rest of my life, but it pays the bills. I'm still going to own that nightclub."

Last year was the worst year of Pete Pedone's life, a year when he was laid off from his electrician's job, the year the car blew up, the year his second wife broke it off with him. Driving across the Verrazano-Narrows Bridge, the traffic is thick, whitecaps break on the water like sparkling lozenges. "Ball of Confusion" plays on the radio. It was less than a year ago that Pete lived on Staten Island, in Oakwood, with his second wife and her four children. They met eight years ago at Pastelles nightclub, and the minute he saw her, Pete Pedone knew he was going to be with her.

The photograph he still carries of her in his wallet is worn and bent. In the picture they have their arms around each other; he with his olive complexion and a shimmering shark-skin suit, she with her long legs and white plume-shoulder dress.

They were happy together, Pete thought; small problems, sure, but nothing serious, a little rivalry with her teenage boy but that would pass with time. Everything was normal, real American, real Italian. He worked and she kept house. He could not see that she was unhappy. She started looking for something else. She went to two-step, country line-dancing classes. Then she wanted to go out to the clubs with her girlfriends to practice the new moves. First she stayed out until eleven, then two, then she asked out of the marriage.

"You know, I still love her, I still want to be married," he says wincing at the memories as though being pelted with a handful of gravel. He fingered the photograph, embarrassed by the sounds of his own admission. He thought he had it, the whole ball of wax, the home, the family and a respectable future. And then it crumbled. "I suppose I should retire this picture," he says.

Regret

It was a cold November day last year when Pete split with his wife. He moved back in with his parents. *La famiglia.*

He saw Roseann next door at her mother's house. She had moved back home, too. She had separated with Sal after nineteen years. She met him at a discotheque in 1977. "When I first laid eyes on him, I knew he was all I ever wanted," Roseann said. Sal. She thought it would be forever.

The two old friends stood out on the porch that cold November day, talking beneath the naked branches of the elm tree, wondering where it went wrong. Everybody they knew went to the clubs, hooked up, got married, had kids, got divorced. Nothing good ever came out of the discos, except a good time. But good times are as permanent as soap bubbles.

Boys' Night Out

Saturday nights are a thing of the past, work nights now for Pete Pedone. Mondays are boys' night out. Manhattan. Grown-up clubs, dinner maybe. Standing in his underwear in front of the bathroom mirror, Pete rubs his freshly shaved chin. "I might not be the best-looking guy anymore, but just give me thirty seconds with any girl." The words hang on the air, and he stops to consider their callowness, his smile drops into the sink. "If I still cared about that anymore."

He walks across his tiled living room floor to the bedroom. The apartment is a sparce, cavernous basement. There is a table, and an enormous leather couch as long as the wall. The only things left from his marriage are the large television and stereo facing the couch.

They are tuned to an oldies disco show. In the refrigerator are cans of cold beer and a leftover bowl of pasta.

Pete wears all black. Tonight it will be Au Bar on Fifty-eighth Street and Madison Avenue, a real players' spot. Along for the evening are Johnnie Sica and Vic Rossi, boyhood friends of Pete, and Freddie Weinstein, an unpopular guy Pete feels sorry for.

The Monday nights started back when Johnnie visited Pete at his parents' house. "He was a mess," Johnnie said. "Crying, feeling sorry for himself. It scared me." This was not the Pete Pedone that Johnnie knew. This Pete would not do. They needed to get him back in the bars.

Au Bar is a place of older gentlemen and young women, cigars, books, overstuffed chairs and Persian rugs. Vic's old girlfriend is there and Freddie's ex-wife. Johnnie, a big-muscled man, dressed in tight black, stands in the corner with a double vodka on the rocks. For a high school dropout who used to work part-time in a beauty supply store, he's done well. Nice jewelry, property and money. One thing is missing, though: a family. He is bad with women. After seeing what happened to Pete's life, he is scared to try.

"It's hard to know how to talk to these women," he said. "When you were a kid, it happened in the van. When you are a man, it has to happen in a place like the Plaza Hotel, or it doesn't happen at all."

It was so much easier back in the day; all you had to be was a good dancer. But when you grow up, you don't dance anymore, you find that life is more than a song and a Hustle, more than a smooth line and a bright smile. The smile fades. People, women, wives get wise to the line. The old songs carry empty memories. Some people realize this later than others. Some never do.

Freddie goes outside to argue with his ex-wife. The police arrive. Vic cuts in on a much bigger man dancing with his old girlfriend. He begs her to come home with him. She blows smoke in his face. Johnnie circles the edges of the dance floor like a chicken hawk.

Pete stands with one hand in his pocket, the other around a drink, circumspect. It's been more than a thousand Saturday nights since he saw those turntables, had those dreams, donated his life to the clubs. "Sure, things didn't work out like I expected, but I'm happy. That's more than most people can say." Right? Things don't work out the way people expect anyway. Do they? The neighbor kid is going to live, not much of a life, but he's going to live. He thought he'd be dead.

Pete downed his drink and ordered another. Life doesn't work out like it does in the movies.

Dot-com Fever Followed
by Bout of Dot-com Chill

He still wears the uniform: leather boots, leather jacket and a dark T-shirt. He is twitchy, he grooms his sideburns and he smokes a lot.

Steve Fine is a dot-com guy without a dot-com and he'll accept a free drink. He is sitting in a bar on the Lower East Side in the middle of the afternoon pulling stolen software from his bag. "This is it," he says to the bartender. "This is my severance package."

"How's your job hunt going, Steve?" she asks. She serves a lot of out-of-work, new-economy types these days.

"Not as good as I thought," he says. "But I've got my unemployment check, three hundred eight dollars a week, and I've got five and a half months left to find one."

He drains his free beer and orders another.

Steve Fine is a thirty-year-old who has become a has-been before he ever became anything, on the unemployment line with 290,000 stock options worth nothing.

He was the art director for pseudo.com, one of the most flamboyant addresses on the Web. The company closed operations in mid-September 2000 after spending millions of dollars without earning a nickel.

Pink slips are blowing through Silicon Alley these days. Pseudo Programs, with 175 layoffs, is by no means the largest of these companies to go under, but its crash has gotten a good amount of press coverage, since its acolytes had crowed so loudly and flown so high.

Building a sort of online television network of video channels, its employees used to boast that they would destroy television as we knew it. The networks are still here, and Pseudo is nothing more than a memory of a brash company gone bad.

It is five o'clock in the afternoon and the bar is filled with unemployed techies who listen as Mr. Fine retraces his rise and fall, from working stiff to master of the new technocratic universe—and back.

He grew up in Scotch Plains, New Jersey, a middle-class community where, he said, Italians lived on one side of the tracks and blacks on the other. Steve Fine called himself Steve D'Fino to anyone who did not know him, because being a Jew meant getting your head kicked in, he said.

His father, an industrial roofer and asbestos remover, went by D'Fino, too. "There was more work that way," Mr. Fine said. It was a solid, middle-of-the-road childhood. There was a Cadillac in the driveway, but it was always aging and Steve Fine wanted out.

"I always thought there had to be more to life than an old car and physical labor," he says.

There was. It wasn't wealth, exactly; Mr. Fine never earned more than seventy thousand dollars a year at Pseudo. But in the new economy, a lot of money wasn't an essential for feeling rich. There were the trappings. In 1995, he began working in a hip ten-thousand-square-foot loft at Broadway and Houston Street, and spent time watching the European women walk by. Those women once would have laughed at him. Now they wanted to party.

Wealth was a state of mind, Mr. Fine said. The dot-com sons and daughters of middle managers—once dropouts and misfits and nerds—were suddenly at the epicenter of a limitless technology. It was a job in which you didn't really have to work. You surfed the Net. In the office, there was the electronic water pipe that five people could smoke at once. The scent was of marijuana, not the must of yellowing books. It was the way out of their fathers' nine-to-five work world. Then there were those options that would be worth millions when some witless investor took the bait.

"We really thought we were going to make it," says David Mulkey, an ex-lighting specialist who earned forty thousand dollars at Pseudo and who now plays music in the subways. "We were making art, we thought. And we were escaping the middle class."

"It was an amazing time," Mr. Fine remembers. "Geeks got girls and people thought we were a club."

For the first few years, Mr. Fine did work hard, more than eighty hours a week, he says. He had, after all, been raised with his father's work ethic. And he believed the work he was doing was important. His job was to design the Web pages for the different channels, design the promotional materials and logos and eventually to manage the mess that went with an out-of-control staff.

Employees smoked grass for lunch and snorted cocaine for supper. They slept under their desks. "It was wild and the Wall Street suits would come to the parties and get high and write us a check in the morning," Mr. Fine says between beers, a hint of pride still lingering in his voice. "We ate from the trough of the venture capitalist pigs."

Pseudo had started as an online radio station in 1994 before expanding to video, featuring boutique channels of hip-hop, punk rock and counterculture programming. It was one of the first Silicon Alley darlings and perhaps better known in the early days for its Warhol-esque parties, which were often held in the loft of Pseudo's founder, Joshua Harris.

"CBS is our competition," Mr. Harris once boasted on television. Now, in the bar, the chalkboard reads *Quit your dot-com!*

"No reason to quit," Mr. Fine says. "Nobody has a job."

Back in his school days, Mr. Fine was a misanthrope who wore a green Mohawk and drank 151-proof rum at the local amusement park. Italian or not, he still got beaten up and the girls made fun of him. He dropped out his junior year but earned his equivalency diploma. He went on to art school and came out thinking he was going to be a famous painter.

But no one was hiring famous painters at the time and he settled for working in a bookstore and then as a receptionist at an audio-visual company. He taught himself computer graphics there and went on to design T-shirts.

"Then, in 'ninety-four, I met a guy at a party," he says. "He told me about this joint called Pseudo."

With three hundred employees, many of whom sat around doing little more than downloading pornography, the company ran through $18 million in 1999; it received $14 million more in May. Investors wanted to see some action. David Bohrman, the former head of CNNfn, a financial news network, was hired to run Pseudo. The suits arrived and things changed.

"It wasn't a freak scene anymore," Mr. Fine said. "The parties faded away and the regular work world took over. In a way it's a relief that I don't work there anymore."

The use of drugs in the office was banned. The content was paired down into a one-channel talk-show format. Pseudo spent a lot of money covering the political conventions in a grandstanding ploy to find new investors. Few tuned in.

"Why would they?" Mr. Fine asked. "Cable does it better."

By the end, Mr. Fine was doing a whole lot of nothing. He was smart enough, however, to put a few thousand dollars in the bank. His savings plus his unemployment checks allow him to make rent, drink in the afternoons and wander the streets of Manhattan with his hands in his pockets mulling over his prospects.

"It's over," he says. "Now I'm crawling back to the corporate dog bowl."

A woman with two-tone hair walks into the bar. She, too, is an old Pseudo hand. She is an Internet consultant now. She "puts people together." Steve Fine hands her his résumé.

He tells her he wants to start his own design firm. Then he digresses into talk about the Web and video-streaming technology. In the next breath he says he is a failure. And then it is dreams about a dog farm in Iceland. Then a farm upstate. He's shell-shocked.

"I'm just down on myself and the whole thing," he tells the woman through cigarette smoke. "I would have been an architect if I was smart."

Runaway Girl

On a moonless night, as the first of the autumn winds sliced through Tompkins Square Park, a group of shivering runaways clutched themselves and dreamed of nothing more than a warm sleeping bag and a half-smoked butt.

Their conversations were the usual ones, about dope and sex for sale and the calamity of their young existences. It is the desperate nights like these that make the dim memories of the homes they fled in Florida and Illinois and California seem brighter. "It's an easy life to get into but a hard life to get out of," said Michael Polo, a twenty-year-old recently up from Florida, who has been beating up and down the highways and railways for nearly five years. "So many middle-class kids are out here looking for freedom 'from' something, not freedom 'for' something. You know what I mean?"

His thoughts turned to Tiffany Giles, a fifteen-year-old runaway from a small town in Louisiana, a chubby, naïve girl he knew as "Sidney" who had escaped his world as improbably as she had landed in it. "Man, that chick was bad news," Mr. Polo remembered. He was one of the first people in New York to greet her and her friend Lisette, two high-school girls on summer vacation who had made their way to

the Big Apple in a stolen car and with three hundred dollars pur-
loined from Tiffany's parents.

Mr. Polo had set them up at a friend's house for a few nights,
remembering his first homeless nights on the streets. By his account
and those of every other broken teenager interviewed in Tompkins
Square and Washington Square parks, the only reason "Sidney"
managed to escape the drug addiction and prostitution of gutter
punk life was because she had parents who loved her enough to
come find her.

"This is the Rotten Apple, cousin," said Ariel, a nineteen-year-old
with fluttering eyelids and a prickly slather of whiskers. "No one goes
by without giving up something. No one."

Tiffany became something of a celebrity and a pariah during her
forty days and forty nights in New York. Her stepfather, who is a firefighter in Jefferson County, Louisiana, was desperate enough to drive
to the city and beg the assistance of his firefighter brethren. Within
two days, every station house in the city was plastered with posters of
the missing girl, and firefighters on their lunch breaks and days off
distributed more than a thousand missing-person fliers.

She was found, wandering in Tompkins Square Park, by her mother.
"It was by the grace of God that we found her," said her mother, Lucy
Smith, who described herself as a fallen Catholic. "I was walking
through the park reciting psalms when I saw this little ragged girl who
looked like a runaway and she needed a bath awfully bad.

"I was scared so I shifted my purse to my right shoulder. Then I
stopped and turned around. I wanted to tell her, 'Please don't do this
to your mother. Please go home.' It turned out to be my baby, with
her hair burned off and twenty pounds lighter. I think Tiffany feels
ashamed."

Mrs. Smith still believes her daughter is a sweet girl, a simple
child who is very easily led. "I know Tiffany wanted to come home
but just didn't know how," she said.

Tiffany expressed no shame and little remorse, saying only, "If I didn't want to be found, she never would have found me." She said her hair had caught on fire when she was frying a piece of meat. She extinguished her head in a sink of dirty water.

Her odyssey began well before she ran away. Tiffany was having a hard time in her hometown, Slidell, where segregation still runs deep and young girls watch MTV and dream of the big city.

Tiffany had been smoking pot and popping pills for more than a year, her mother said. She was failing her high-school classes and running with an abusive thirty-six-year-old man.

"It's boring down here," was Tiffany's reason for running away. "I just had to get away from my parents. I had to go where nobody would question who I was."

She and Lisette said they had stolen Tiffany's sister's Toyota. A day and a half later they found themselves on Broadway, their stomachs full with Big Macs and their eyes full of big lights.

That night, Lisette said, they met three men from Hoboken who got them high on alcohol and marijuana and kept them overnight. They bounced from apartment to apartment, always with men—some prostitutes, some drug dealers. Mr. Polo set them up with some acquaintances who threw them out a week later when they found out the girls were underage runaways. They ran out of money in two weeks.

"I wanted to leave," Lisette said. "I ran away for kicks but everybody turned out to be a creep, and we were broke." She called the police and was sent home on a Greyhound bus. Tiffany sped away in the stolen car.

For the next four weeks, Tiffany recalled, she lived in a hunger- and drug-induced blur. She split time among a Rastafarian marijuana gang from Brooklyn who worked the East Village and sometimes going home with married men. She said she fell in love with a party promoter who plied her with LSD and alcohol and took her to the Tunnel, the nightclub in Chelsea, to pass out fliers. They lived in the projects on Avenue D and she wore his clothes.

Most memorable to Tiffany was a sixteen-year-old male prostitute named Aziz. She bumped into him in Washington Park. "We just sort of stepped into each other and fell in love," she said. "He just seemed so damaged." They went hungry together for three days, sleeping by the chilly West Side waterfront where lunatics howl like dogs.

They drank malt liquor and smoked blunts, spending the lit hours on street corners with upturned cups. People spat at them. "Get a job," they growled.

"I got sort of scared of the whole thing and left Aziz when some men at a peep show wanted to buy me," she remembered. The next evening she got drunk on rum and was taken up to a roof and robbed by a gang of teenagers. A week later her mother found her.

"I'm not too street-smart, not then at least," Tiffany said. "If a guy was cute I would talk to him." Nothing terrible happened, she said blithely. "The city is the best place for a young woman. You can have whatever you want and be whatever you want and no one cares. I'm going back."

The same week Tiffany went home, the parks began to clear out as a generation of lost teenagers took to the road for the warmer climates of New Orleans and San Francisco.

A young woman named Bleu was still in Tompkins Square Park last week, sick from a bad bag of dope. "If I had a wish, I'd wish all the young girls like her would go home," Bleu said in a voice of shattered glass. Bleu, too, first ran away at fifteen. She is twenty-one now and carries a bindle on her shoulder and a monkey on her back.

"They're not accomplishing anything and society is not listening," Bleu said. "No one cares that you feel bad, that your parents don't care. Pretty soon you don't care, and the next thing you know you're wasted away."

Tiffany took a blood test last week. The results were negative.

Sinners and Victims
of Domestic Hell

Family Court is perhaps the saddest place in New York.

It is where society gathers the child abusers, juvenile delinquents, deadbeat dads, bickering parents, wife beaters and the Cains and Abels.

The hallways of Family Court grow more crowded every year as people turn to the system to solve their problems and the government steps to prevent cruelties. Most every type of family feud is dealt with at Family Court except, paradoxically, the dissolution of the family itself. (Divorces are handled in State Supreme Court.)

The crowds at the city's Family Courts are thick, the attitudes are often bad and some stories fall over the cliff of the cockamamie. Recently, one parent told a judge in Manhattan that she slipped in a moment of anger and her hands accidentally wrapped around her daughter's windpipe. The judge could only roll her eyes.

"This is not Family Court, it's a disaster court," said Paul Cooper, a lawyer who is representing a mother at Queens Family Court who is accused of starving her infant with a strict vegetarian diet. "You pull the roof off of this building and you're looking into the bedroom of America. The family is crumbling, the bedroom's on fire and we're asking the judges to be the grandparents here. It gets worse every year."

To say that the system is overburdened is to put it mildly, lawyers, judges and unhappy citizens agree. About two million New Yorkers walk through the metal detectors of Family Court every year as defendants, character witnesses and the like. Sometimes the visit is a good occasion. Three thousand adoptions are consummated here each year. But most of the 750,000 appearances in Family Court mean bad news for someone.

Some Legal Aid lawyers, who among other things represent children against their abusive parents, handle as many as 110 cases at any one time.

The system was devised before the days of crack and the divorce epidemic. Add to that a more litigious society, a greater willingness to report abuse and no compunction about airing arguments in the post–Jerry Springer world, and you have modern Family Court.

"People use Family Court to play out their animosities, and it clogs it up," said Joseph M. Lauria, administrative judge of New York City Family Court. "You get to know some of these families. The good part is we can help with long-term resolutions of family problems."

Family Court is not a tribunal of instant gratification. While you are guaranteed that you will see the judge the day you are called to court, the chances are better than good that you will see the judge again for many more days over the span of many more years.

In civil matters, the courts can attract a surly, frivolous element, since there are no filing fees and the government not only obliges but instructs the do-it-yourself lawyers who gum up the system. These kitchen-table counselors seem to think the definition of *justice* is "give me what I want" and the process of discovery is something like "Yo, the guy in the hallway don't have to pay child support because he don't have a Social Security number, so why should I have to sign over my unemployment check?"

The current family courthouse in Queens is a former public library retrofitted in the early seventies. It is an old run-down building with decaying smells and filthy windows and rows of plastic chairs on each floor. The walls are papered in admonitions: NO SMOKING, NO CAUSTIC CHEMICALS, NO ENTRY, no, no, no.

The referees hear cases in offices no bigger than a broom closet. People—former confidants and lovers—bicker, scream, throw fists. The waiting rooms are snake pits of accusation and recrimination. A woman got stuck between floors in the elevator and when service resumed, her ex-husband was waiting on the third floor to laugh at her.

Take the case of Leon *v.* Gallo, a couple who got along famously until their daughter was four. Then, according to court papers filed by Anthony Gallo, things fell apart between him and Ana Tapia-Leon, the mother of his daughter, and the woman he now refers to as his former paramour.

"For reasons known only to the respondent," his affidavit for visitation rights said about Ms. Tapia-Leon, "and over what appeared to be a very short time, her feelings for me dramatically changed." While the root of their problem lies in this phrase somewhere, neither could explain where the anger began. They have been in court a dozen times over three years bickering about custody.

As if confirmation was needed of his love for his child, Mr. Gallo, thirty-eight, recently showed a tattoo of his daughter's name on his chest. In support of his character, he dressed in new shoes and a tie, and carried letters of reference from his barber and a local deli clerk.

He wept. "I miss my daughter, and that monster won't let me see her."

On the other end of the grubby waiting room, Ms. Tapia-Leon sat alone with her tears. She maintains that Mr. Gallo abused their daughter, although court-mandated investigations have revealed no evidence to its truth.

Ms. Tapia-Leon carried many papers, among them a drawing by their daughter that read "no."

"You see, my daughter doesn't want to see that man," she said, and to that effect she vowed to fight Mr. Gallo to her dying day.

"I'm an educated woman," she said. "I went to university and I keep an immaculate home. I thought these kind of things happened to drug addicts and alcoholics. I never thought I'd be in a place like this, and I blame him for it."

The former lovers eventually got to see a judge near the end of the afternoon. The outcome? Come back in two weeks. Just in time for Father's Day.

THE HUSTLE

THE HARLEM SANDWICH. Three-card monty. The Catsup Bottle. Crab bait. Louisville slugger. Hacksaw. Horse track. Waterfront. Welfare office. Subway train. Preacher. Heathen. He-she. He-man. Never was. Is not. Never will be. Junkie. John. Pimp. Playboy. Princess. Cop. Beggar man. Thief. Shylock. Loan shark. Squeegy man. Milkman. Bagman. Wise guy. Butcher. Baker. Card Reader. Card palmer. Cardsharp. Pool shark. Sharkskin Suit. Sweet-talk. Chicken walk. Cockfight. White collar. Blue collar. No collar. Cat burglar. Coke dealer. House mouse. Snitch. Bowery bum. Precinct boss. Men with soft hands.

You Can't Buy a Thrill

Bobby Platt is some kind of genius. When the sex police came around as part of Mayor Giuliani's crusade to clean up the city, they told him that the topless dancers at his bar would have to cover up. Mr. Platt had his employees wear bikini tops.

When the authorities told him that the ladies could no longer writhe on the mangy carpet, he had them writhe against the mangy wall. When the judge told him the bar could no longer advertise as Billy's Topless, he bought a brush and a can of paint and the marquee now reads BILLY'S STOPLESS.

"I didn't just roll off the cabbage truck," said Mr. Platt, the manager of this no-frills, no-thrills neighborhood go-go joint at Twenty-fourth Street and the Avenue of the Americas. "You can't get around the law. You got to abide by the law."

But the law, which prohibits strip clubs and other sex-oriented business from operating within five hundred feet of residences, schools, churches and graveyards, has brutalized business, Mr. Platt said.

His best employees walked out on him because men were unwilling to tip women in clothes.

"The girls couldn't make a living," he said. "They went back to Iowa. They just disappeared."

He raised the women's wages by five dollars a night. Still, the talent level and the libido at Billy's Stopless have shriveled. About the only thing going up is the prices.

The regulars complain loudly that the humanity has been removed. The margin is so tight that the shots are now measured scrupulously. Exactly one ounce and one ounce only. No more friendly drink. No more shaky hand. A glass of French wine is advertised for $4.50.

"The only thing topless in here are the liquor bottles," said Jesse Disanti, thirty, a music producer and regular patron of the arts. "I guess they've got to make money somehow."

Mr. Platt thinks he knows how. This genius of the G-string has concocted a scheme to exploit a loophole in the law, which allows adult entertainment on the premises so long as 60 percent of the floor space is devoted to nonsexual merchandise.

His plan is to build a wall down the middle of the bar. On the left will be a trough of lasagna and three women clad in bikinis. On the right, near the door, will be two topless go-go girls. "It's as simple as fourth-grade arithmetic," said Mr. Platt, who learned his percentages in South Carolina. "Five women. Three dressed. Two ain't. That's sixty-forty by my calculations."

Built in 1879, Billy's was known then as the Corner, and was one of the most popular nightspots in the city during the Gay Nineties. Both a beer hall and a house of prostitution, the place was closed by the vice squad in 1896.

Mr. Platt vows never to let that happen again.

"We're hoping this wall thing's going to work and we can stay open," he said. "They got us earning it a dollar at a time. It's like selling candy in little bits."

The Exchange Rate
Behind Bars

The buildings that make up the Suffolk County Jail resemble a
Moscow government complex. They are gray, with staggered
green windows and slab walls of cement, all ringed in high hurricane
fencing and razor wire. Visitors are prohibited from bringing gum,
candy or food. No medications. No hats or belts. No sweaters, jack-
ets or coats. No jewelry. No hair curlers. No paper of any kind. No
cigarettes or cigars. No alcohol. And definitely no money. Without
cash of their own, inmates are forced to improvise. Having recently
lived in legitimate society, they are used to a certain standard of living. So the black market flourishes, based on a barter system. Inside
jail, there are six ways to obtain tradable commodities.

1. Charity. Your family or well-wishers may drop money in your
commissary account, which allows you to purchase up to $25 worth
of merchandise twice a week from the jail. (Prisoners fill out order
forms, and the goods are delivered to them on Tuesdays and Fridays.)
Among the more popular items are Devil Dogs snack cakes, going
for 60 cents a pack, and baby lotion to soften the skin, at $1.25 a
bottle. Prepackaged tuna has become a big success since it was introduced to the commissary for $1.50 per bag. (A side of mayonnaise
is $1.) Dictionaries go for $5.50, but few of those are sold, correction

officers report. And at the *Monday Night Football* wine and cheese fêtes, the pate is sliced beef jerky (55 cents a stick) and the cheese is processed cheese spread ($1.60) smeared on the slices of bread provided at mealtimes. The wine is local, made from fermented fruit cups, with yeast coming from scraps of bread.

2. Contrabanditry. An inmate can have dope and tobacco—which was outlawed in the facility during the mid-nineties—smuggled in at the risk of jail time to himself and his confederate.

3. Conniving. An inmate can trade whatever he has been given by the authorities or whatever he has managed to scam from them. This goes for everything from morning coffee to clean socks to prescribed medications from the psychiatric unit that an inmate hides under his tongue.

4. Corporeal. Some inmates trade the only thing they bring in: their bodies.

5. Cards. Everything from commissary goods to promissory notes are gambled in the housing tiers. You can easily tell who's rich by Suffolk County Jail standards: They have soft skin and a shelf full of food. The mopes and card punks walk around in dirty socks or no socks at all.

6. Cribbing. This is out-and-out theft. It stems from the inability or unwillingness to pay your bills, and it is rare. It's not so much the adage "honor among thieves" that holds here, but more like "fear among thieves," says Corrections Officer Lori McKeough of the Suffolk County Sheriff's Department, who works in the commissary unit. It may result in the sharpened end of a toothbrush being jabbed into the neck of the inmate in arrears. Cribbing is usually the work of men scheduled for release in the morning.

When officers believe contraband has permeated their walls, they will shake down and inspect the suspect's cell. Then they check his commissary account. It's a good method for tracking the black market within the jail. Consider the inmate, for instance, who has no money in his account and hasn't had money in his account for a very long time. But when the authorities come to inspect his cell, it is filled with so many items from the commissary that it looks like a cross between a party store and a beauty shop. This means one of three things: (1) He's winning at cards. (2) He's trading away his breakfast. (3) He's dealing dope. "The rule is very simple," says Lieutenant Lloyd Manseau, the forty-nine-year-old commanding officer of security. "Everything is worth something in here. Nothing goes to waste. Except, of course, lives."

One economic postulate of the incarcerated is that if there is a buck to be made, there is a boob to be played. There is no better example of this than the skinny kid who recently visited his friend in lockup. The visiting area contains steel stools, yellow walls and a Plexiglas barrier long enough for forty inmates and visitors to chat at a time. Since the New York State Department of Corrections mandates that all inmates must have the opportunity to touch their loved ones, they are allowed a kiss when their visitors arrive and a kiss when they depart, and for the duration of the forty-five-minute visit they may hold hands above the Plexiglas divider.

This is when the contraband is exchanged. There are only two officers guarding the proceedings, and though each inmate must submit to a strip search following a visit, a full rectal search requires a court order. "A lot gets in—there's no way around it," says Manseau, a silver-haired pragmatist whose youth was lost patrolling the halls of this hole.

The visitors bring the contraband wrapped tightly in rubber balloons, and the savvy inmate will have his pants leg split and his rectum greased. The goods are squirreled away in seconds.

The skinny kid was from Pennsylvania and not so nimble. A guard spotted him, and before the exchange was made, he was snared with three balloons of marijuana, one balloon of pharmaceuticals and two balloons of tobacco. There was laughter among the guards looking through the one-way glass. "He must be new at this," said one of them. "He just earned himself a bed in here."

Three balloons may seem to the law-abiding citizen not worth the risk to one's freedom, but you must consider what the market will bear in the Suffolk County Jail. A balloon may hold ten tablets and enough tobacco or marijuana for ten skinny smokes. Each pill may fetch five dollars, a cigarette as much as fifteen dollars and a reefer twenty-five dollars. The money in these situations is usually exchanged by girlfriends on visiting days.

"Yeah, we had a guy in here who was waiting on twenty-five-dollar bail," said one correction officer. "He was a real pain, if you know what I mean. A real operator. Finally, he got to the point where he was causing so much trouble that the C.O.s [corrections officers] took up a collection to bail him out just to get him out of here. He refused it. You know why? He said he was making more money in here in a week than he could make out on the streets."

Located in the crotch of Long Island where the east end splits into the North and South forks, the Suffolk County Jail is home to twelve hundred people. But when summer ebbs and vacationers go away, there is little to do but crime and the jail population generally balloons to 150 percent of capacity.

An inmate named Peaches says he comes here to convalesce. He is male by gender, but female by occupation, he says. His full name is Charles Wayne Cameron. He is forty-three and has been arrested 145 times and convicted eighty times, mostly for prostitution and petty larceny. He is currently doing time for taking a car, because his trick did not understand that he was simply borrowing it, Peaches explains.

"You can get anything in here that you get in the Hamptons: condoms, heroin, you name it," says the frail, coffee-skinned, blue-eyed hustler, who should know, since he works the Hamptons streets when not in jail. The tony vacation towns are, after all, only ten miles away from the jailhouse.

"A girl like me is a commodity in here, since there are so many guys going to state penitentiary who aren't going to have a loving relationship for a very long while."

Peaches lives in the first-floor-east block—protective custody—home to the rapists, the child molesters and the insane. (Those considered suicidal must wear paper clothes so that they cannot hang themselves.) Anyone may ask to be moved to protective custody if he feels threatened, and when he does, he meets Peaches. The price? Twenty-five dollars in snack cakes and a five-dollar IOU.

"A little bit of weed is always a nice tip," says Peaches, winking. "And if you can't pay, there's always some kind of way to work it off."

There is a card game in fourth-floor-east block. It smells powerfully of urine there. The ceilings are peeling. The floors are wet. There are barnyard noises. Four men gamble for batteries and shampoo and aloe vera gel. Chips are playing cards torn into quarters, and each one represents five cents. Commissary goods are cashed in with the house at face value. At the end of the game, every man is allowed to cash out and take back those products he can still afford. The winner has first pick of whatever is left over.

"Weed, smokes, what have you," says Tito Velez, who is holding two arms full of snack cakes and hair-care products. "Sometimes the game gets so amped up, you got to call your girl to have her drop a hundred bucks in somebody's commissary 'cause you lost so bad," he says. Then he cuddles his cakes like an infant. "But that don't happen to me."

The most popular trade inside is batteries. Used for tape players (twenty-five dollars), the batteries will usually wear down in a matter of hours, because they are not the alkaline type but the paper-jacket type (three for $2.25). The authorities found that when they allowed the inmates to have alkaline batteries, the men peeled the metal jackets off and made shanks to stab one another. Because the paper batteries run down so quickly, inmates will go heavily into debt to be able to listen to some music. The trade is usually something like one pack of batteries on Saturday for three packs on Tuesday, when the commissary reopens.

"It's like a reflection of society as a whole," says Lieutenant Manseau. "It's 'live for today.' Why do people buy SUVs and go into debt to do it? The same reason people trade three packs of batteries to listen to music. Because it's all about 'I want what I want, and I want it now.' That's America. People will go in debt because they don't want to wait. Of course, one person is honest and the other is dishonest, but the premise is the same."

The card game breaks up, and a man goes back to his cell to study a picture of his naked girlfriend. She is bent over, facing away from the camera. The photo has more value than your run-of-the-mill pornography, because she is real in the sense that she is known to somebody on the cell block. "How much for that?" someone asks him.

"A whole balloon," he answers. It is an unreasonable sum and there are no takers.

The Hustling Life

Yoo-hoo!" The falsetto voice rang out over the midtown traffic. The Candyman rolled up in a black Mercedes 550, his hand waving out the sunroof. "Yooooo-hooooo!" he yodeled again. Black Mills knew that call, spun around and saw the custom tires of Candyman's car at his feet.

Black smiled. He and Candyman had been associates back in Boston, well-oiled pimps who'd controlled the streetwalkers along "the Stroll" in Dorchester. Then the Boston police started closing in, so the two hustlers left town. It must have been a year back. They hadn't seen each other since. It was a chance meeting. They stood in front of an after-hours joint on West Thirty-sixth Street. Black was tight with the owner, another old pal from Boston, who gave him free drinks and the house cocaine concession. The Candyman had come to gamble.

The Candyman ducked out of his Mercedes and adjusted his fur-lined coat, one of his women closing the door behind him. Black looked him up and down, impressed. By the look of things, Candyman was on his game. Dressed in an Armani suit and peerlessly shined shoes, he was accompanied by three women in expensive wigs. Four others followed in a white BMW convertible. Framed in the artificial light, Candyman looked the picture of prosperity.

Black was a little ashamed. He didn't like Candy seeing him like this, dressed in his old gray linen outfit and gym shoes, with only one woman. He had come to New York to make his fortune, but the only thing that lined his pockets tonight were a few glassine envelopes of cocaine.

The old friends shook hands. Candyman leaned way back, looking a little disappointed. "What happened to you?" he asked with pity.

Black said, "Hard times, man. Hard times."

Black Mills has a cloudy, tired cocaine nose. It keeps on running and running and no amount of wiping helps soothe it. He has broken the pusher's number-one rule: never get high on your own supply.

There are hundreds of hustles, and thousands of hustlers, in New York. Some, like squeegeemen and panhandlers, are innocuous enough. Their game is about survival, about finding enough to eat and perhaps a bottle to sleep with. Among the more virulent hustles, like drugs and prostitution, competition is fierce, often deadly. Few players at this level make it to retirement. Black, whose mother named him Marc, believes he is the anointed one. "I'll make it because of what I bring to the game," he said, while preparing himself with cologne for the evening. "I bring class and culture. Your nickel-and-dimer don't have that. If you got it going on, you're gonna be the man." The life of a hustle is all image, Black says. It's just like a movie. You must believe in your role and you must never, ever break character.

But when Black Mills came to New York last year, he found it was the wrong time to audition. Whatever else they say about Mayor Giuliani and the police department, pimps and con men know the squeeze is on, especially in Manhattan's visible neighborhoods like Times Square, the East Village and the financial district. Fewer crack and heroin dealers work openly on the streets and in apartment house vestibules. Fewer streetwalkers walk the streets; they have moved into vans or out to New Jersey. Pimps who ran the flesh market with impunity along Eleventh Avenue now work from a few small bars in

Chelsea. The territory has gotten so small that the hustlers are biting chunks out of one another. The game has changed.

In Boston, detectives followed Black Mills's every move the way he followed trouble. He was arrested fifteen times in six years, but never for soliciting. Eventually he was convicted of larceny and assault of a cabbie. He served out the probation and moved away. "He was slippery," said a Boston detective who insisted that his name not be used. "As far as I'm concerned, New York can have him. Out of sight, out of mind."

Black Mills had big plans for himself when he arrived here late last spring. He was going to get away from the hustle; he was going to become legitimate and make his million. That day would come soon, he believed. Maybe a producer would see his handsome face in a club, or maybe he would make his way to a recording studio and lay down some rhymes. Either way, fame would find him. But until it did, he could deal a little cocaine. And if he tired of that, there was always the pimping game.

"I got the knack for slipping in and out of the vernacular," Black said. "I can size up the scene the minute I walk in and take control. I've got skills like no one else. I've been in court so many times, I can speak like a litigator. I've read so many books, I could be considered a scholar. I've had so many women, you could call me Cyrano."

His grace and a certain gentlemanliness speak of good breeding. He sees himself as one of the few hustlers able to float from Wall Street to Washington Heights and never pay for a drink. He has infiltrated a party at John McEnroe's art gallery in SoHo and managed to drink red wine and laugh arm-in-arm with the owner. He chats up a table of blue-haired ladies sipping cappuccino near Lincoln Center and joins their discussion of classical music. But Black Mills has been able to get little else going here, and stories from his glory days don't pay the bills. He sleeps on the floor of a friend's apartment in East Harlem. His buddy Katro N. Storm knew him in his Boston prime. "He had the fliest clothes and was known by all the doormen,"

Mr. Storm recalled. "He wore fifteen-hundred-dollar silk shirts and went to clubs where people appreciated the threads."

By the age of twenty-five, Black Mills controlled a sizable piece of the prostitution business in Boston, the police and associates say. A dropout from Morgan State College in Baltimore, he had a sharp business mind and managed to build an empire of eight girls who worked from a handful of apartments he rented. He kept a loft in the blue-collar section of Dorchester, complete with skylight windows, modern furniture and naked hostesses, who would refill his guests' Champagne glasses at the snap of his fingers.

"He ran a tight operation," remembered a pimp called King Beef, who was introduced to the Boston scene by Black. "The cops wanted him bad, but they could never stick anything on him. The only problem was, you could never bring your girl around 'cause he would steal her."

Like a magnet, Black could attract people, but like a magnet, he could repel them. He admits wrapping women in boutique clothes, then beating them into submission if they refused to turn tricks. "Never let a woman think she's too good to work the streets," he said. By the time he left Boston, police records show, he had been charged with assaulting women and once with violating a restraining order. In each case, the woman decided to drop her complaint.

The Eyes Still Shine, but the Skin Sags

When Black Mills had a clear head, friends say, he steered clear of drugs and could give freely of himself. The only payment he expected was an acknowledgment of his kindness. His roommate, Mr. Storm, remembers one particular evening: In a blizzard, a coatless addict was sitting on the sidewalk begging change. Black stopped and said, "Brother, I can't give you no change. You'll just smoke it away. Them drugs ain't going to do you no good. Hear me, they'll lead you to ruin." He gave the man his thousand-dollar coat and walked away, leaving the addict in disbelief, his nose running on to infinity.

"It kind of makes you sad to see him now," Mr. Storm said. "He was as sharp as a sword in Boston. Now he's as dull as a butter knife. It's like there's two people in that body. He's starting to believe the lies he's telling. You know, you're only young and good-looking for so long. . . . He's got to get out of New York. It's eating him alive."

It is a dank, cold morning. The rain casts a monochromatic pall of gray. Black, a tall man, walks across Second Avenue. A solitary figure, he wears a black leather suit, his eyes have a patent-leather shine. He still looks good, possessing the last bit of youth, a nut-brown complexion, strong jaw and reedy mustache. His skin, however, sags under the burden of alcohol and cocaine. The suit hangs loose, twenty pounds too big, and his nose is running.

He approaches a beat-up bottle blonde, chubby white legs and a crooked smile. It is too cold for her saucy skirt: "Hey, baby, you looking real good. You got a boyfriend?"

"Hey, sugar, what you need?" she asks in a coy Southern drawl.

"Your name, baby, your name."

Diamond, she tells him.

"Diamond, I asked you a question. You got a boyfriend?"

"No. Well, I did but . . . ? I don't . . . No, I don't got one no more."

She pulls a menthol cigarette from her purse. Black strikes a match. "You look like you could use one," he says, smiling.

"Yeah, maybe I could," she says, putting her cigarette to the flame.

They walk to the Playhouse sex club in Times Square. The neon sign reads GIRLS. GIRLS. GIRLS. XXX PEEP SHOW 25¢. Inside, Black and Diamond sit together, soft and familiar now. The peep show window flickers open and closed. She sits on his lap as he snorts powder off a key. She smokes from a crack pipe. They are falling in love, he says. Maybe, she says.

"Look, baby. You a ho and I'm a pimp. You want to work for me, or do I got to beat you outta this booth?"

Diamond doesn't say anything, her head immobile as he squeezes her jaw. She sees violence in his eyes, and the pain brings mascara-muddy tears to hers, distorting the blue raindrop tattoo in the corner of her right eye. She was once a hooker for the Crips gang in San Diego and is used to this sort of thing now, she says.

They walk back through the rain to Grand Central Terminal. He is almost dragging her on her tattered heels. She doesn't know where she's going. Uptown. East Harlem.

Looking over His Shoulder Wondering Who's the Cop

They spend three days in Black's small room, on a pallet of foam rubber. He packs powder into his nose with a plastic card, but the crack she smokes irritates him.

Still, he goes out to score two dime rocks on credit for her. When he comes back, he studies her ragged, sleeping body. Diamond, he says, disgusts him, but he thinks she can be manipulated. The coke hustle is wearing him down. Running uptown and down, always looking over his shoulder, wondering who's the cop. When Diamond awakens, she finds a pastrami sandwich and a carton of orange juice. It looks as though he cares.

They talk. She tells him she's tired of her old man, a tyrant with a Cadillac and a solid fist. He controls a stable of women on Tonnele Avenue in Jersey City and is a tough boss. He slapped Diamond all the way to Manhattan. Black nods sympathetically. Maybe he and Diamond can do business.

A few days before meeting Diamond, Black suffered an asthma attack. But that wouldn't stop him from making his evening rounds. He stood in front of the bathroom mirror twisting his braids, getting ready for a night in the clubs. He looked haggard, dark rings under his eyes. He hacked phlegm into the sink and wiped his nose.

The apartment was littered with empty packs of cigarettes and malt liquor bottles. A calendar from last year hung on the wall and a crazy orange oil portrait of Khalid Muhammad leaned against it. *Sankofa,* a film about a black woman who falls back into the time of slavery, played in black and white on the television. Black emerged in a corduroy outfit, the shirt open to his navel. He and Mr. Storm stared at the screen.

Black said, "'Member, in all-white class, you'd see a movie like this and it'd be presented not beautifully but like some jungle-bunny thing?"

"Yeah, I used to get embarrassed."

"Yeah."

"Or when you did plays, you always got the slave part," Katro said.

"Yeah. Seems like I was always Leroy. That's the slavemaster's mentality. Society don't want to see a black man rise." Black shoveled a key full of coke up his nose. Then another. His sluggish eyes came back to life. After a few minutes the picture turned to static.

"The machine's tore up," Katro said. Black stumbled over to fix it. "It's tore up like you, and you gonna tear it up worse."

"Who's tore up? Did I say I was gonna tear it up?"

"Don't come across like that. You tearing it up."

"I'm not gonna tear it up, mother."

"You put another tape in that machine and it's gonna be tore up," Katro said, snatching the remote control from Black. Black started to shake. "You know what you are? A punk! A certified little punk."

"Well, you know what you got to do. Git. I'm leaving and locking the place down, so you got to go."

"When you gonna be back?" Black asked, his voice instantly contrite.

"Don't know. All I know is you got to go."

It was past midnight, and Black took his coat and hat and descended the stairs onto the short block. In the daytime it is alive with respectable people, storefronts, a restaurant and a candy shop. At night, it becomes a netherworld of iron gates, gangsters and crack-heads. In the few short months that Black has lived uptown, people have noticed him and his aggressive attitude. The hustlers have grown wary. They say few cops come up here, not yet.

Frank was sweeping snow from the stoop. Frank is an old-looking hustler whose game is to clean the steps while keeping an eye on the door of Black's building. This might earn him a couple of bucks. At forty-five, Frank has been through the system, married four times, and is satisfied that he has lived a clean enough life to not have to look over his shoulder.

"What up, player?" Black mumbled on his way by.

"Not much, little brother," Frank said. "Watch out for yourself tonight." Leaning on his broomstick, Frank watched Black turn the corner, then swept his footprints away. "If you living like you can't lose, your day will come," he muttered.

Black made his way to the upper reaches of Amsterdam Avenue to a rubbled tenement with no doors. Inside the foyer, underneath a flickering light, stood a skinny white boy with a knit cap pulled down to his eyes. "Poppy's not here," he said in a whining, nasal tone. "Poppy said he'd have the dope soon, but Poppy's not here." Black gave him a menacing look and the white boy put a hand over his cleft lip and slunk back into the corner.

Poppy, a young Dominican, was on the third floor, behind his desk with an electronic scale. Upon entering the filthy apartment, Black was patted down. "*Que pasa*, Poppy? Can I get a deal? I come here all the time." Poppy looked at him as though he'd never seen Black before.

Poppy said seventy-five dollars for two and a half grams and watched as Black laid out fifty-eight dollars, the last eight in singles. "Come on, Poppy, gimme a break." Black was working him. The longer the deal took, the better his price. An urgent pounding came to the door. Poppy fumbled through the money and gave the foil to

Black who passed through the door, past the agitated customers and an armed goon, down the stairs and out the building. He kept his head low. He knew the police could be photographing him from this window or that. The white boy was long gone.

Downtown, the action around the Chelsea club was slow. The cold had kept all but the most die-hard partyers home. The bartender, a woman, set a drink in front of Black, who admired himself in the mirror. Not everyone can take a Dominican for seventeen dollars.

Growing up, Black was going to be a businessman or a doctor. He watched his mother work hard as a social worker and get less than she deserved. She wanted more for her son and made sure he was exposed to books. When she could, she took him to museums. His mother couldn't afford to keep him full-time and he bounced among relatives. "I learned to be charming. I learned to make people like me," he said. "It was a survival thing."

The kids in Dorchester liked Black. They thought he was a doctor or a lawyer, the nice man who handed out fifty-dollar bills for good grades. He was their hero, someone to emulate. They didn't know Black was a pimp.

The yuppies at the club liked Black. He was exotic, their connection to drugs and a taboo world. Black hustled them, sold them coke at a substantial markup they were eager to pay. He sold more than enough to break even. The rest he snorted and floated high above himself. He was where he knew he belonged: in the center, on top. The keys to Mr. Storm's apartment became irrelevant. He went home with the bartender.

Driving to New Jersey Low on Money

Black and Diamond head through the Lincoln Tunnel in a borrowed car. The night is wet, and the wipers sweep to the rhythm of Curtis

Mayfield. Diamond is going to turn tricks, and Black has agreed to be her new man. It will cost her a down payment of fifty dollars. He is a little nervous, not so much about his safety, but because he is dead broke. He's going to get some money somehow, even if he has to stick someone up. They've decided to work New Jersey because Diamond knows the scene. Manhattan makes Black nervous. The police are crawling all over the West Side and the pimps are trigger-happy.

Black has forgotten his stiletto. "Don't worry about it, baby," Diamond reassures him. "I got my own." Boston Black would never have made that mistake. He has lost some face with the hooker. Annoyed with himself, he tells her to shut up.

Diamond is dressed in Black's white Naugahyde jacket and the short skirt. He rubs her thigh and asks if her "old man" will be around and what sort of car he drives. "Cadillac, right? If you see him, run," Black says. Diamond giggles, reassures him again and takes a cigarette.

Tonnele Avenue is a strip of fast-food shacks and motels with eighteen-wheelers parked in the lots. Turning into the Spinning Wheel Motel, Black sees two Asian women in vinyl working as a duet. Diamond knows them. She knows everybody here. Black gets out of the car and tells her: "Now get out there, baby, and do us some money."

Diamond stands on the shoulder of the road and waves to passersby. Black looks for a spot to lie low. He doesn't notice her running across the street to where a burly woman is waiting. They hug and run down the road to a crack motel. Diamond is the burly woman's hooker and part-time lover.

Black runs after them. But by the time he reaches the motel, they have already locked themselves in their second-floor room. "She don't want no trouble," the woman yells. Black's Naugahyde jacket comes twirling over the balustrade.

He stands in the rain, his nose dripping, the player realizing he just got played.

What's a Few Bloodstains?
It's an Apartment!

It has long been a not-so-well-kept secret that there is, among New Yorkers, a certain ghoulish, opportunistic element who, seeking better habitat, has been known to peruse the obituary pages in search of a freshly vacated living space.

Landlords tell of these people standing, hats in hand, waiting for the relatives of the newly departed to return from the funeral so that they might make an offer before the FOR RENT sign goes up. But the real estate market has gotten so taut in the last few years, and a decent apartment at a reasonable rent is so rare, that a new, more gruesome stratagem is being employed.

Instead of the death notices, apartment seekers are now turning to the police blotter. And they are not showing any signs of squeamishness about campaigning for the former dwellings of homicide and suicide victims, no matter how heinous the crime or how many pints of blood have stained the finished-oak parquet floors.

"You just would not believe what's going on out there," said a building superintendent in the East Village, Zbignew R., who is loath to use his full name when railing against prospective tenants, because, after all, they are how he makes his living.

"Some people don't have a problem with natural death—you know that happens all the time, and it's a natural thing," he says. "But when a guy puts a pistol to his head, and the word gets around the neighborhood, and the next day you got a guy banging on your door looking for an apartment for his brother, well, that's a bit beyond the reasonable."

Landlords, supers and property managers throughout the city marvel at the macabre ingenuity of today's apartment hunter.

"It's like the predator and the prey, the hunter and the hunted," said Joe Pistilli of the Pistilli Realty Group in Astoria, Queens, who has holdings from Flushing, Queens, to Morningside Heights in Manhattan. "I've got tenants banging on old people's doors in my buildings trying to figure out if they've died yet."

Usually a scavenger will wait until the carrion is cold, but the Gotham buzzard is a different breed. At one of the city's empty—and somewhat infamous—nests, potential renters did not even wait to learn the fate of the tenants.

Those tenants are Camden Sylvia, thirty-seven, and her longtime companion, Michael Sullivan, fifty-four, who disappeared on November 7, 1997, from their three-hundred-dollars-a-month loft apartment on the fifth floor of 76 Pearl Street, in lower Manhattan, after having an argument with their landlord, Robert Rodriguez, over a lack of heat.

A week later, Mr. Rodriguez vanished from his upstate home, telling his family that he was going to Manhattan to answer questions from detectives. He did not resurface until two weeks later but has remained mum when it comes to the police.

When the authorities found a sneaker-clad foot underneath a pier near the World Trade Center on February 1, 1998, they thought it might belong to Ms. Sylvia, because she was reportedly wearing running shoes when she vanished. At this point, things took a bizarre turn. A man who works for Mr. Rodriguez said that within a week after the foot was found, more than a half-dozen bargain-hunters called to ask if the apartment, despite its lack of heat, had become available.

"I want to reiterate that there is no apartment for rent and it is not on the market," Mr. Rodriguez's lawyer, Joseph Marro, said last week.

The episode brings to mind an East Village studio apartment I once inhabited. The guy above me was a mellow type, who listened to the not-so-soothing sounds of a wave machine. It may have been that wave machine that drove him to kill himself with a bullet to the head. There were inquiries about his apartment before the fresh paint had dried.

The new tenants in my old neighbor's apartment had nothing to say, but others in the building were understanding. "You do what you gotta do," said one man still dressed in his pajamas in the middle of the afternoon.

And Manhattan, as crowded and expensive as it is, is not the only borough where good taste gives way to a good opportunity. Take the case of Lourdes Ochoa, who was stabbed in the heart in her apartment in Bushwick, Brooklyn, by her husband. The police said it was a family dispute. Mrs. Ochoa's husband was arrested and charged.

Some Ecuadoreans who live in the building, which is in a neighborhood heavily populated by Ecuadoreans, told the landlord that they would never rent the apartment, because, as a rule, they are a superstitious lot. The landlord reports, happily, that a man in the building had an aunt who needed an apartment. Not even a week's rent was missed.

The Shantytown of
the He-Shes

It's four-thirty P.M., the sky is litmus blue and the girls are still in
bed. There are six in a single room, three to a bed, their wigs hanging on sixteen-penny nails. By gender they are male, but by profession they are ladies of the evening.

Work is just outside the chain-link fence that cloisters their river-
front neighborhood from West Street, where the business day begins
at evening rush hour. The neighborhood is a shantytown sorority of
crack-addicted prostitutes, buried in filth and refuse on an abandoned Hudson River pier between West Twelfth and Fourteenth
Streets. It is a gray mix of makeup and dollhouses, shadows and sex.

In the middle of the pier is a small, tattered shack surrounded by a
garden of rotting clothing, decapitated dolls and worm-infested
chicken carcasses. It is the sometime brothel of J'avon English.
"Jesus don't come around here 'cause he ain't got no money," J'avon
purrs, "and the devil's just too plain scared."

For J'avon (pronounced Zha-VAWN), Noonie, Venus and the other
transvestite prostitutes who occupy the shantytown and refer to themselves with feminine pronouns, the pier is a communal sanctuary of
sorts, a place to escape mainstream societal mores. But the lack of
those mores has also made it a forbidding place of drugs and violence.

When he works, J'avon wears a tight red miniskirt, a black brassiere, a brown frosted wig, bright red nails and red six-inch spike heels—size twelve. He wears too much base, giving his face a cheese-cakelike quality, and worries about the ravages of age; he will be thirty-three in three months. A languorous five feet ten inches and 140 pounds, he has a big, masculine back that betrays his biological gender, as does his deep, if demure, voice.

J'avon usually charges fifty dollars for sex, but on this occasion he's looking for only five bucks so he can get a hit of freebase cocaine. "It's the weekend," he says, nibbling on yesterday's bagel. "It's supposed to be your vacation. Since I can't make it to the Hamptons this weekend, I'm just going to need five to start mine."

On any evening, especially Friday and Saturday, J'avon and other prostitutes line up on and near the transition between Eleventh Avenue and West Street, negotiating prices and jumping into cars. They have been there ever since the police started a drive to clear the meatpacking district—south of West Fourteenth Street and west of Greenwich Street—of prostitutes, said Ben Green, chairman of Community Board 2. The Hudson River Park Conservancy plans to build a bike path along the waterfront, and the community board is seeking a place to relocate the occupants of the pier. "We want to do it in a humane way," Mr. Green said. "We don't want to displace people, we want to get them services."

The community, for the most part, is tolerant. A nearby taxi garage gives the shantytown dwellers all the water they need. A local baker gives them fresh bread or bagels when they want it. "We have no problems," said Carlos Correa, a neighborhood florist. "The drag queens and the homeless go about their business and keep to themselves. It's tranquil."

A communal bucket serves as toilet, bowls serve as showers and the transvestites are always looking over their shoulders. Violence lives next door; his name is Everyman. He is a client, a neighbor or a "husband du jour," such as the one Venus said beat him until his eyes "swelled up like a bullfrog's." And even in this world of outcasts, there is social stratification. Along a pier just south of the one occupied by the transvestites is a homeless community of comparative luxury. The occupants have built a riverside patio with lawn furniture, an oven, toilet facilities and a canopy to shield them from the sun—and the eyes of idling motorists. American and rainbow Gay Pride flags slap the wind.

It is all off-limits to the transvestites.

"Those walking scarecrows over there, we don't mess with them," said Vinny, a homeless man in black spandex shorts. "Look at them. They're pigs, leaving their mess everywhere, doing dope. We just leave them alone."

Indeed, the north pier occupants admit that life there is getting progressively worse. The cocaine problem is getting out of hand, J'avon admits, and people are stealing too much, says Dean Blair, a fifty-two-year-old drifter, who is the unofficial superintendant and mayor of the shantytown.

But the prostitutes say they have few other places to go. Mr. Blair, who built and maintains many of the thirty or so shanties on both piers, charges no rent and at least makes a cursory effort at establishing some order. His rules are: Don't steal, keep the place clean, mind your own business and try not to draw the attention of the police.

Indeed, the entire atmosphere of the pier is designed to deflect attention, whether from the police or anyone else. It is cordoned off by a chain-link fence, perhaps ten feet high, beneath a decaying arch. It marks a passageway between the harsh reality of the street and the closed society of the transvestites.

Two hours after setting out to make five dollars for drugs, J'avon emerged from that passage with sixty dollars and a meal of fried chicken gizzards. He tossed off his heels, lit a cigarette, cuddled up with his shack-mates, Venus and Noonie, and spoke of the events that led him to the pier.

J'avon says he grew up in a middle-class Long Island home, the son of a Nassau County health worker and a nurse. He says he always knew he was a woman.

He led a "normal" childhood, he says, graduated high school and at age eighteen came to Manhattan, where he attended cosmetology classes by day and turned tricks by night. He lived the life of a party girl, wearing fine women's clothes and drinking gin in the best hotels. For his overnight company, he charged three hundred dollars.

Then J'avon fell victim to crack. He split time between his parents' home and prostituting himself on the street. He started taking female hormones, which enlarged his breasts and softened his voice.

His first trick, he says, was a spur-of-the moment decision. J'avon and a friend went to the Crisco Disco, a now defunct gay club just across from the pier. They had no money, and their smooth talk wasn't working with the doorman. They needed cash, so J'avon and his friend walked a few blocks south to "the Track," a notorious stretch of West Street frequented by young male prostitutes. His friend got in a car and came back ten minutes later with forty dollars.

" 'Where'd you get that?' " J'avon remembers asking. "But I knew where she got it."

A big black Cadillac rolled up to them. The man inside wanted J'avon, and his friend pushed him in. J'avon performed a sex act, then cried. The man gave him a hundred dollars.

"I couldn't believe what I had done," J'avon said. "It wasn't the gay sex—I'd done that. It was the prostitution. I just couldn't believe it. I felt so low." J'avon and his friend went back to the disco to wash away their debauchery in alcohol.

Noonie, twenty-four, was also "always a girl." He was a prostitute by age thirteen, had an apartment by fourteen and a car by sixteen. Somehow, he managed to finish high school.

Noonie said his mother died recently of an aneurysm. They were very close, he said, because they had a common enemy—an abusive father, who, Noonie says, once belted him unconscious and locked him in a closet. An intravenous drug user, he died eight years ago of AIDS, Noonie said.

He winces at the mention of AIDS. They are crack addicts, Noonie and the others say, but they don't touch needles, and they use condoms.

J'avon and Noonie both say they don't have to live on the pier. Noonie could go to the Lower East Side apartment in which he grew up but says the memories are too painful. J'avon says he can always go home to Long Island, where he says his parents don't know what he is or what he does on the streets.

"I'd like to get out," J'avon insists, "but this life's like moths to the flame."

Raffle to Benefit a Charity
Close to His Heart

Roy Dean is as well polished as a mahogany rail, a sharp man in a stiletto suit. He wears a clean chin, a wide-brimmed hat and wingtip shoes. In his pockets he carries a cigarette holder, a kerchief and a stack of small pink raffle tickets:

A Pre–Mother's Day Cocktail Sip Saturday May 13
John's Recovery Room 535 Lenox Avenue
1st Prize: Woman's Diamond Ring, 2nd Prize: $200,
3rd Prize: $100
Donation: $2 per ticket, Donation: $9 per book
(Winner Need Not Be Present)

Roy Dean was the sponsor of the raffle and the event was held for the benefit of himself.

To the charitable-minded this may smack of rank self-centeredness, but Mr. Dean sees it differently. "Can't think of no one more needy than me," he says," and it's a whole lot better than working."

It is known around the Harlem gin mills that Mr. Dean is a refugee from the shoulder-to-the-grindstone workaday world. It is also known that around the major holidays there is money to be made. So this rakish man will slip into his suit, button down his solicitude and go from bar stool to bar stool peddling tickets with all the importance of a life insurance salesman.

"You need something for the future, and I'm trying to offer you that future right here for a mere two dollars," he tells an elderly patron of the Princess Lounge at West 116th Street and St. Nicholas Avenue. Many don't buy. They suspect the diamond is a dupe and the cash prizes predestined for the pockets of Mr. Dean's distant relatives. But many do. These sales can be laid to the dreams of retirees or the jumbled judgment of the intoxicated.

Then there is another type of buyer. Mr. Dean is thin, excitable and hungry-looking, and some white people drinking uptown are flustered by his staccato hard sell. Mr. Dean can often sell them a book of tickets, secure in the knowledge they will not show up on raffle day.

It is a clean bit of alchemy as Mr. Dean transforms five pink slips of paper into two whiskey-and-sodas and a five-dollar bill. The pre–Mother's Day Cocktail Sip does in fact take place, at John's Recovery Room, a run-down bar on 137th Street, just up the block from Harlem Hospital. Men sell seafood on the corner and customers must show their faces in the plate glass before being buzzed in. The place is decorated with foil and balloons, and a tub of fried chicken cools on the back table. It is a friendly crowd: cocktail hour for the elderly and retired runs from two to nine P.M.

First draw is called for five-thirty, but five-thirty comes and goes. Mr. Dean, distracted, darts in and out, and the evening falls behind schedule. The draw is pushed to seven, then nine. The chicken grows cold and the old people sleepy; ten o'clock and still waiting.

A man named Franklin can take it no more. After drinking for hours, he makes his way to the door. "The chicken's turned to rubber and so's my legs," he said. "Hope my old bird ain't waiting up for that ring."

The prizes were raffled off in the early morning hours, the bartender says. The winner of the diamond was a big woman and the ring did not fit.

The Way to Live?
With Your Feet on the Table.

A man named Mikey was drinking at Pete's Tavern, the dark old saloon down in Gramercy Park. It was one of those dog-day afternoons, a Sunday, and the city was empty except for the half-million people who were left to pay the bills.

When possible, Mikey pays no bills. And for a man of wit this is usually possible, he said. Heavy lifting is for suckers. And honest men are suckers. A man should live with his feet on the table, Mikey explained, in a nasally, arrested tone. "That way your woman can easily reach your feet to wash them."

He introduced himself as Mikey, nothing more. He assured the man who bought him an orange martini that he was misunderstood when he was overheard on the saloon's pay telephone threatening to rearrange a woman's anatomy.

"You know I love the little girl," Mikey said, and here he smoothed his chest hair. "I love all my girls. But in all honesty, when I tell a woman that I'm going to be around, I expect her to be around." It was easy to figure that Mikey had no cell phone since he was beating his fist into the pay phone. How did he expect a woman to find him if he carried no phone?

"I just expect it of my girls," he said. "I expect them to feel me at all times."

Mikey is a man in his late forties. He resembles Walter Matthau, and speaks in an Arthur Avenue accent. He wore a pressed white track suit, leather sneakers, a gold bracelet, gold necklace, gold ring, gold watch. He lives alone in Forest Hills, Queens, and has an opinion on everything but himself. "My life is five minutes old," he said, and ordered himself another martini. His life consisted of some jail time, some ponies, some acting. The usual. "You can cover my life in half an hour," Mikey said.

The martini arrived, and he lifted it as if to say, "Thanks, sucker," to the man who would eventually pay for it. Mikey's "little girl" strolled into the bar a few minutes later. She was done up in leather: leather skirt, leather blouse, leather pumps, leather face. Her face was as dry and creased as a lizard's.

"She's one of my girls," Mikey said from the side of his mouth. "She works for me." What he meant by that, exactly, he would not say. But he bought his own drinks from then on.

"Say, pal," he said. "How would you like to earn some easy money?"

"I like easy money," the man said. "What do I got to do?"

"Real easy," Mikey said. "Just pick something up for me."

It was arranged.

Fame Stinks[*]

Jayson Blair, an enthusiastic, eccentric reporter for *The New York Times* and fixture at Robert Emmett's pub in midtown Manhattan wandered into the bar the other evening around a quarter past eight.

Though Mr. Blair somewhat resembles Gary Coleman (the elfin, erstwhile child actor), no one seemed to mistake him for Mr. Coleman until a few hours later, when Mr. Coleman himself entered the bar.

The meeting was prearranged by a mutual friend of the men, the reasons being too salacious and convoluted for this space.

Nevertheless, confusion reigned. Ollie the barman brought out two phone books for the men to sit on. Things large and small were compared to the size of Mr. Coleman's skull. Mr. Blair, currently traveling on the wagon of sobriety, ordered coffee. Mr. Coleman, who has no kidneys, ordered Coca-Cola.

---

*This story was submitted to the *Times* on February 1, 2002, but never ran. The editors felt it struck too close to home. Mr. Blair later achieved some measure of notoriety when it was discovered that his dispatches from the heartland had actually been written from his Brooklyn apartment. Gary Coleman went on to run as an independent for the governor of California. And lost.

Though Mr. Blair wears a beard and towers a full six inches over the four-foot-eight Mr. Coleman, the similarities between the two men are striking. Consider:

Both are insomniacs, prisoners to manic periods of highs and lows. Neither dreams regularly. Mr. Blair, twenty-five, has a younger brother named Todd. Mr. Coleman, thirty-two, has an older television brother named Todd. Mr. Coleman is famous for the line, "What you talkin' 'bout, Willis?" Mr. Blair, a gossip, is known for the line, "Hey, what are you guys talking about?"

Both are excitable black men given to wild hand gestures and possess loud cackling laughs. Neither has that special woman (Mr. Coleman insists he is still a virgin) and, most important, both are trying to extricate their working lives from their private ones.

"Fame," snorted Mr. Coleman, star of the eighties hit *Different Strokes* who lost a $20 million fortune through bad investments and good friends. The money dissipated, the cherubic little boy grew into a bitter little man and the producers stopped calling. All he has left is his threadbare celebrity and a job as an on-line love columnist at www.ugo.com.

"If I could give fame to you, I'd have to hate you," shouted Mr. Coleman, causing the late-evening diners to periodically look up from their plates and see double.

"Fame is more a punishment than a blessing. Every mistake you make is there for everybody to judge. You're laughed at and ridiculed."

He went on: "Fame stinks without money."

Mr. Blair, who recently took a few weeks away from his job as a business writer to tend to his inner being, said, "My situation is the opposite. I enjoy my professional life. It's just that I've had no personal life for two years. It's all wrapped into work."

"What do you have to complain about?" Mr. Coleman asked. "What are you? Five-foot-two? You've got nothing to complain about. If I had your height, I'd be on *NYPD Blue*."

The Gambler

The old man was born under a bad sign. His mother's innards ruptured while trying to birth him into this world. He made it, she didn't and that's about where his luck ended.

"I don't care about nothing," the old man keeps telling himself, " 'cause I don't got nothing. My luck dried up, and I'm ready to die, so forget about it." But that doesn't stop him. That doesn't stop any of them. Four or five times a week they're there at the horse track. They bring a little money and a hunch they usually mistake for wisdom. They usually lose, and when they lose big they feel sick, like they're dying.

These kinds of players you see at the track go home to their cold rooms, take off their oily caps, take out their ruined teeth. They think about the emptiness, the nothing, wondering why they did it, wondering where it all fell off, wondering why they bet forty bills on a twenty-two-to-one long shot and then died just a little quicker as they watched the nag never get out of the gate, never challenge and run last the whole way. Once again they've come home with nothing, having known it would turn out this way.

"It's a sickness," the old man, Pete Hionis, said. He is a man who once had it all. The family, the uptown apartment, the luck. Now, at eighty-four, all he has is a pension and a roommate he's had to take on to make the rent in Astoria. He never saw it coming. "There used to be so much opportunity, so much money coming in, that even a guy without an education could afford to blow a few hundred a week at the track with strictly fifty-dollar bets, when fifty dollars was worth something," Pete says.

To really make it at gambling, to avoid labor, you had to have a bankroll and you had to have a hustle. You had to know how to cheat, palm a card or groom an inside tip. Otherwise, the odds would eat you up. But that's all over. These days you can't touch the cards at a casino, and you can't rig the Lotto and you can't swindle the bookie, because the race results come by satellite instead of the evening papers.

So the era for punters like Pete faded away. The opportunities became fewer, the fun became habit and the fifty dollars snowballed into thousands. He married the horses, and the family took its leave. Pete is an old, sick man now, gambling his pension away, waiting to die. He doesn't even bother with a burial plot. Better to leave the mess for someone else.

"Sometimes there are some winners," Pete says, but the winners are rare. The survivors are most often quitters. They played a few hands, a few horses, maybe even for a few years, but soon enough they realized the game was stacked, the bettor was supposed to lose, and they just up and quit like an old car battery. Then there are the losers, the people who could never stop. These are the ones whose only company on Christmas night is a can of cold pineapple chunks and dirty fingernails.

On the ground outside the door of the aluminum-sided house in Astoria was a small pile of dust and ashes and a used nose rag. The mailbox was smeared with sprawling fingerprints, and it looked as though someone had staggered up and grabbed onto it to right himself. Beyond that, no one really knows much about Pete the Greek's home life. He meets his few friends at the local Burger King.

"A man should treat his home like half a ham sandwich," old man

Pete says. "See, the half a ham sandwich is yours, just yours; there ain't enough to share with someone else, so forget about it. You can get your own anyway, you bum, so don't ask for it. Don't ask for none of it, not a bite, not a crumb."

No, you have to mind your own business, and Pete will meet you down at the Burger King for a cup of tea, because he can't eat anything anyhow. The guts are gone. The cancer ate them up. All the intestine-turned-stomach can take is tea and Jell-O. Or on a good day maybe a poached egg. "What's the use, anyway?" Pete says. Food just gets in the way of death. Just slows it down. Screws it up.

"I'm an old sack," Pete usually says after an afternoon of losing. He says it like gravel, like Don Corleone, if Don Corleone was Greek. Like the Don, Pete isn't afraid of death. He's just afraid of dying without grace. Besides no stomach, he's got bad eyesight and can't see a decent set of cards. He's had so much chemotherapy his hair's about gone and the eyeballs have gone saffron yellow. He lost his stomach to nerves. Too much gambling gave him ulcers and gastritis and cancer, he figures.

He's had ten surgeries on his guts and has been exposed to enough radiation to light Akron, he said one morning at the Burger King while demonstrating how to cheat at knock rummy and bridge. To prove this, he undid his black wool coat, unzipped his pants, lifted his sweater, a flannel, a T-shirt, peeled back his thermal undershirt, pulled down his thermal trousers and revealed a gnarled torso, a road wreck.

"I gotta go check into the veterans' hospital again," Pete says over and over. His kidneys are killing him, and he's cold. "I'm going to go there and die," he said.

But there is no way, even in his fever of self-pity, that he could ever do that, wait to die alongside men in open robes with sores on their hind ends. The blubbering gums, the D.T.s, the howls of lunacy well past midnight. The taste of cheap cigarettes near the foyer.

"Only thing is, they don't got no action in there," he says. To Pete, gambling has always been work. Most people don't know work, he says. Work is having it and having lost it and having to live with that. Gambling for a lifetime takes guts and a little luck, Pete says, but since he lost his guts to cancer and his luck ran out a long time ago, Pete's appetite for chance is at least in part fueled by dementia.

In truth, the hospital will never do, so Pete is going to kill himself at twenty bucks a shot. Down at the Aqueduct Race Track in Queens. Pete has been going to tracks nearly every day for fifty years. He's spent more time with the ponies than with his daughters.

"They don't even know me," Pete said through a nose rag that he dropped to the ground after clearing his cavities. "I don't know them, either. I know the ponies, that's all. The ponies. I'm a spent-up old stupid man who lost a million dollars at this track and the card tables. I'm ashamed to even have my family see me like this."

If a man could get rich on slow horses, then Pete would be a millionaire, but it doesn't work that way. It's not supposed to work like that, and Pete knows this. Still, every day the car service comes, and the driver has never seen the inside of Pete's place. He just waits on Thirty-third Street in Astoria, idling.

A Greek's Odyssey

Panagiotis Hionis was born on the day after Christmas 1913 and has gambled ever since, when his mind served him right. While growing up in Cephalonia, an island in the Ionian Sea, he won money against the local boys by shooting rabbits. His father was a wine and oil maker. Pete decided to leave Greece when he read about Hitler in the newspaper. He got a job as a purser on an ocean liner and jumped ship at the Fifty-eighth Street Pier when he came to New York in 1939. In his military I.D., he looked young and full of hope, with a thick neck in a wide open collar, a smile as if he were invincible and knew it all.

President Franklin D. Roosevelt told illegal aliens like him that either they fought in the war or they went home, which would have been suicide with the Germans goose-stepping all over the place. Pete served in North Africa in the Fifth Army and was with General Mark Clark when he invaded Salerno, Italy. Pete got rich playing cards and running bootleg lye (for soap) and wine through Italy near the end of the war. He came back to America in 1946, lost his money in a stock-market downturn, blew the rest at the track and joined the merchant marine for thirteen years.

When he got back, in 1959, he opened the Neptune Diner in Coney Island. He gambled, sold the diner, opened another, the Olympic, at Forty-ninth Street and Eighth Avenue, near the old Madison Square Garden. That went for a couple of years, until, he said, he realized his partner was skimming the till. He quit and opened another one at Fifty-sixth and Second. He said he was never interested in the diners even though they made money.

Instead, Pete went to the Italian and Greek parlors to play cards. He worked for the bookies and ripped them off. His scam was to slip bogus bettors' receipts into receipts he held for bookies after associates would call him from, say, California with the race results before they were announced in the evening papers. A confederate cashed in the phony receipts. He left the shops up to his wife—his ex-wife, he said. He divorced her after thirteen years and two daughters, he said. The marriage was a trick, he said, a bad bet. After the war, he promised an old friend he'd marry a cousin who was stranded in Greece. Strictly a green-card arrangement. Go to Greece. Pick her up. Marry her and bring her back. It was supposed to be a short-term obligation.

"What the hell, I stuck with her. She was terrible. Couldn't keep a house. Couldn't do nothing. I got two daughters, but she was bad luck."

Pete says he cheated on her a hundred times. He likes to say she's no longer alive and so unable to vouch for his character. But his wife is alive. It's just that Pete traded it all in: the daughters and the granddaughter and the photo albums. All he got in return was sickness and isolation. Better to put it all behind him. His wife, Annie, holds no bad feelings against the man. "He never was responsible for anything, except the horses," said Annie, who lives with her two daughters and son-in-law in Rockaway Park. They never did get a divorce, and when Pete almost died during one of his operations in the eighties, he came to live with her, and she nursed him. Pete likes to say it was a thirty-year-old bombshell with a cocaine problem who nursed him. It's a fantasy. Lonely old men get that way, his wife said.

"He doesn't want anybody anymore," Annie said. "He never did. He stayed with me and my daughters for a few months, but all he did was go to the track."

Pete used to go to Stevie's card crib over the pizzeria at Seventy-first Street and Second Avenue. He also played in the famous nine-day, no-limit marathon held at the Knossos Heritage Society in Astoria. Pete and his buddy Michael Diamantis kept a four-bedroom apartment at York Avenue and Seventy-second Street and three girls when things were good.

"In those days, it was the best," the white-haired Mike said, sitting down for a cup of coffee when his old pal Pete stopped into his diner the other week in Maspeth. It was good to see old Petie. He's been sick, and Mike was happy to see him eat a plate of eggs. Mike quit all the bad habits a few years ago after he lost his house to the ponies and poker. He still has a restaurant, and his wife stuck by him, so he's able look back and laugh.

"Rent was cheap then, the shylocks would give you a grand for a hundred and thirty dollars a month and there was no problems," he said. "The only problem was we lost just about everything gambling. But I wouldn't do nothing over. Well, maybe a few hands of poker, but that's it."

Kostas Lambrakis was the host for the poker parties. After 150 years of struggle and turmoil and civil war, the Greeks who made it to America prospered in the sixties and seventies, he said.

"For a long time, we had nothing and then suddenly we had everything," Mr. Lambrakis said. He said that gambling has been in the Greeks' blood since the time the gods destroyed the Titans and rolled the dice to divide the universe.

"The horses, the cards, dice and cockroaches—you name it, we bet on it," he said. "But in the long run, you are a loser, not a winner. If you forget this, you end up broke and empty and sick."

The Action at Aqueduct

Post time at Aqueduct is half-past noon. The whole track is full of crazy people. They line up at ten A.M. waiting for the gates to open. Some come and drink and sleep the entire day and never see a race. Others buy coffee after coffee and just mumble to themselves as the counter girls repeatedly wish them good luck. Occasionally, someone stands out in the cold, his elbows on the rails, whimpering to horses, telling the beasts that nobody loves a loser.

There used to be a lot of Greeks, Pete says, but now the colors and ethnicity are mixed, most people are old and there is no tension, because the only color that matters is green. It's not as if there is no fun. A younger man throws his racing form, rips his tickets and cusses and kicks, which makes for better entertainment than the horses. The old-timers laugh and cover their mouths so this Rumpelstiltskin cannot see their laughter.

The Rumpelstiltskin knows Pete—everybody knows Pete, although few bother Pete when he's gambling—and gives Pete a courtly, "Hello, old-timer."

"You shouldn't be here," Pete tells him. "You don't belong here. Don't start playing the horses, I told you. You're gonna lose everything."

"I got a hunch, though, Pete," Rumpelstiltskin tells him.

"Oh, you gotta hunch? Well then, go ahead," Pete says.

The race track is dying. There are too many ways to bet now. The lottery, the casinos, the off-track betting parlors. And who wants to watch burned-out people gamble away their pensions or their children's Christmas gifts? Who wants to hear men run through the lies they're preparing for their wives?

Pete was there the last weekend of racing before the Christmas break. He bet loser after loser, trying to pick the win and place horses—which is called an exacta—at fifteen dollars a race, or 1.2 percent of his monthly pension.

His system goes like this, and pay attention—it's good free advice, he says:

1. Watch the odds. If a horse is listed in the morning as a ten-to-one shot and drifts down to, say, five to one, it may be a good bet. Something must be up because people are not dumb with their money. Never bet a horse that creeps up in odds. A horse listed at ten to one in the morning and closes at twenty-five to one is a bad bet. If the money drifts away, it's usually for a reason. Stay away from long shots, and if you have to pick a long shot, twenty to one is the longest shot you want to take.

2. A horse that runs is better than a horse that closes. Grandma loves a closer, a horse that moves up in the course of a race but rarely wins. What Grandma doesn't understand is that the horse is lazy and is in reality only passing tired horses. A pony that consistently runs at the front of the pack at least has a chance. Remember, appearance doesn't count for much. Shiny coats, big chests, bright colors don't mean anything. The experience of the jockey and the trainer count for more than superstition.

3. Never bet the rent.

On the last race of the day, Pete was down $140, and put two dollars on Quiet Trail, going off at five to one, and Sovereign Gem, at nine to one. Sovereign Gem's odds shrank from a morning high of fifteen to one, and Pete liked the trainer. In the race, Quiet Trail led wire to wire and Sovereign Gem placed second, and Pete's exacta paid a neat $130, putting him down just ten dollars for the day. All things considered, a win. Pete went home that afternoon feeling not so sick, feeling like it was going to be a good Christmas.

On Christmas Day, Pete sat around his apartment waiting for a call from his family. By two o'clock in the afternoon, he knew the call wasn't coming. He packed up his nine hundred dollars cash, went to the Port Authority and caught a bus to Atlantic City.

He arrived at five-thirty P.M. and looked for a blackjack table with a ten-dollar minimum so he wouldn't blow the whole wad. The lowest table at Trump's was twenty-five dollars. The same at Bally's. The same at all the casinos. So Pete bought some chicken he could not eat, waited for the seven o'clock bus to New York and made it back to Astoria by eleven P.M. He took off his coat, opened a can of pineapple chunks and blew his nose.

SQUAD 1

IT DID NOT SEEM to me that those thousands of people, men and women, who rushed to Ground Zero on the morning of September 11, 2001, were heroes. They were just good people raised by good people and they answered the call. That is how it is supposed to be.

We didn't believe our society had people like that anymore. We didn't know what to call them. So we called them heroes. Like my mom said of the rescuers that day and the many days after: "It's good to know we still have substantial men in this country. Tell them thank you."

Indeed.

These stories are dedicated to the unborn grandchildren and great-grandchildren of the men of the Squad 1 firehouse. This is how it was. This is how we lived. Your grandfathers were substantial men.

Dave Fontana's Legacy

Mommy, is Daddy dead?"

The little boy said it right there at the Burger King. "Yes, Aidan, Daddy is dead," said his mother, Marian Fontana. She decided that the raw truth about her husband, Dave, was best.

Daddy was buried in the rubble of the World Trade Center trying to save people's lives, and he died doing something good.

The boy thought for a moment.

"You're a liar," he decided. "Daddy's not dead."

So the little boy planned a welcome-home party, and his mother planned a funeral.

The struggle between denial and acceptance occupies the lives of those left behind by Dave Fontana, one of twelve firefighters from Squad 1 in Park Slope, Brooklyn, who were lost in the attack on the twin towers. It resounds in a wistful five-year-old son and a heartbreakingly practical widow. And it extends beyond family, to close friends like Sean Cummins, a fellow firefighter at Squad 1 who survived, but—like the others who lived—battles the guilt.

The story of death has been well documented in these, the first few weeks following September 11. But there is also the matter of living. The people of Dave Fontana, a ten-year fire department veteran, are dealing with living in their own ways. His son, Aidan, talks about a party that will never be. His wife, Marian, prepares for a funeral without a body. His friend Sean mops the firehouse floors, unable to deal with idle time.

When the people of Squad 1, an elite fire and rescue unit, speak of that day, their eyes settle on some point far away. They are the same eyes as the widow's. Guilt is part of it. Many of the firemen had asked others to work for them that day. Marian asked her husband to work the night shift so they could be together for their anniversary.

Then there is a boy who just wants his father.

Mr. Cummins prefers to work in the rubble rather than face Mrs. Fontana. With luck, he said, he would bring her Dave's body or a helmet or a scrap of his uniform, anything so that she might have something to visit on Sunday afternoons.

Mr. Cummins, thirty-eight and Irish born, is physically robust and emotionally reserved. He is no more than five-foot-eight, and like the others at Squad 1, he has a muscular neck and forearms, and his hair is cut close. He is a husband and father, but there is a part of him that does not belong to his family. There is his life in the fire department. When he sat to talk about his friend, he could not sit at all. He poured coffee, he wrung the neck of his mug.

It was nearly two years ago that the men worked together on Mr. Cummins's first shift in the firehouse. They had the same kind of one-line humor.

"Ah, we had good times together," he said in an Irish brogue. "We had good times together."

The families overlapped at the firehouse, as all the families do. There were the Christmas parties and the summer picnics. But the couples never got together outside the firehouse. They were young, and there was always time.

"We always said, 'Let's do it, let's get together,'" Mr. Cummins remembered. "It never happened, and now unfortunately it never will."

Mrs. Fontana, her head full of scattered details, worries about Sean. "He usually laughs so much, he's such a happy man," she said the other afternoon as she got her hair colored at a salon. "I hope he's going to be okay."

A thirty-five-year-old artist, Mrs. Fontana canceled her one-woman comedy show scheduled for January 2002. "I know Dave would tell me to go ahead and do it," she said. "I just don't think I could laugh, though."

These days, she spends her time going to funerals and working on the details of her husband's pension. The boy, at least, has school, but they all talk about his dad there.

And, quietly, Marian Fontana allows herself to remember her husband.

He died at the age of thirty-seven on September 11—their eighth wedding anniversary. He was one of those rugged men that women go for. He was big and muscular, with dimples, a square jaw with a cleft. He wore a crew cut and had serious eyes set back in his skull. He was a college graduate who majored in sculpture. He took yoga classes, and the women at Public School 321 called him Mr. Mom. He read to the children there. He was the only fireman from the station house who lived in the neighborhood, and he was popular.

Mr. Fontana was known as the type of man that other men wish they could be. He was a doer, a good husband and a better father. He was a fireman not because he needed the benefits but because he could be of some benefit to someone else.

It was a beautiful morning when he came off the night shift on September 11. He called his wife and told her to meet him at nine o'clock. They planned to bounce around Manhattan, take in a museum and celebrate. Then the call came. Five alarms.

The time of day would prove especially deadly—a shift change when the crews overlapped. Eleven men piled on the two trucks and raced to Manhattan.

"A lot of guys around here think, 'It should have been me,'" said

Mr. Cummins, who was supposed to be on duty but switched because his mother was flying back to Dublin. "But you can't think that way." His voice drifted off and he thought about the man who drew his straw, a name he will not mention.

Just after the collapse, Mr. Cummins arrived on Church Street. A firefighter from Engine 211 was the only soul, a hulk in a mask, the sole survivor from his truck. "Come on, guys," the hulk said to Mr. Cummins. "We can put it out."

Mr. Cummins spent three straight weeks on the pile, crawling through holes, rapping on steel girders.

Last Tuesday, October 2, was his first shift at the station house since the collapse. He has talked to Marian only once. He has seen her at funerals, but other than that, he cannot face her. He has three children himself: Sean, seven, and four-year-old twins, Hannah and Tara. His wife, Maureen, said that when her husband comes home to Rockaway Park in the Rockaways these days, he clings to them.

"Why me?" he asks his wife. And naturally she has no answer, because there is no answer.

And Marian Fontana asks herself the same thing. The smell of her husband on his clothes makes her sad. Wine salves the sadness, but then the morning comes and the right side of the bed is still empty.

It is hard doing normal things, Mrs. Fontana said. At the beauty shop, they talked about snorkeling in the Caribbean and bottled water and such. The street was filled with the screams of happy children on the playground. The tide of time rolls on, irreversible and unfair.

In the neighborhood, the fliers for the missing and dead are already papered over with ads for luxury apartments. The leaves are changing color and falling from the trees, Sean Cummins digs through the rubble, and Marian Fontana plans a funeral.

The Empty Coffin

The funeral could not have been more beautiful had there actually been a body.

The priest still wore his white vestments. The pipers still played. A thousand heavy hearts wiped their noses and stared at their shoes. The veneer was there, but the coffin of firefighter Dave Fontana was empty. It was a prop on loan from the local funeral director.

When the mass let out, the limousine followed the pallbearers who in turn followed the caisson. Aidan sat inside the black car wearing his father's helmet.

"Mommy," the boy said to his mother as he stared out the window at the spectacle of a thousand firefighters saluting him. "I'll remember this day for the rest of my life."

"Good," Marian said. "That's why we did it—for you."

It was the first time Aidan acknowledged that there would be a life without Lieutenant Dave Fontana. Daddy was dead. He finally believed it, and he returned the salutes of the firefighters.

The widow cried and wiped her eyes and tried to appear as though she was happy. But there was no happiness anywhere inside her. Grief is not a neat little package, she said. An empty box does not change what happened. She would happily move forward if she could figure which direction that was.

The borrowed box was supposed to be the first step in a new and normal life for the family and friends of Dave Fontana. It brought that, but it also brought strange, unexpected effects.

The little boy has grown sullen now that he understands the meaning of September 11. He throws tantrums when it's time for bed, something he never used to do. The widow is less content than before. Her days are still consumed with bills and paperwork for the fire department.

Mr. Fontana's fellow firefighter and friend Sean Cummins sits and waits with other members of Squad 1 for a good fire—a fire in which nobody gets hurt but there's some action to take their minds away from the wilted flowers sitting in pitchers of black water. They have carried coffins at a half-dozen funerals and they'll attend a half-dozen more.

Mr. Cummins has trouble with the mock funerals. "Carrying empty caskets, it doesn't feel right," he said at the wake as he stood away from a group of firefighters who were dusty and carried the unmistakable stench of Ground Zero.

It is mostly firefighters they are finding, he said, because bunker gear is not easily destroyed and has the preservative qualities of a rubber bag.

"With a little more time," Mr. Cummins said, "I'm sure we could find Dave. With just a little more time."

The combination of the funeral dress blues and his small frame gave Mr. Cummins the appearance of a steeplechase jockey. He looked into the warm sun and commented on the incongruity of the day. The shadows of the branches danced in the stained glass. The dead leaves blew down the sidewalk, making a scraping sound.

"Ah, good Lord," Mr. Cummins said as he put on his white gloves and prepared to stand over an empty coffin. "I hope it's like this when I die and not a miserable day. Rain, now that would be awfully Irish."

Rockaway Park, Queens, where he lives, is in an Irish enclave on the west end of the Rockaway Peninsula. His house is of the Queen Anne style, large with white siding. There is a flag in his and every other yard, and one morning last week a fire truck was on the block checking hydrants. The place has a seaside New England feel, except that it is twelve miles east of Manhattan, and about ninety people from the neighborhood died on September 11.

One of those missing is Gerard Dewan, a firefighter who lived in the Cumminses' basement. He was assigned to 3 Truck in Manhattan and his room is exactly how he left it, his bed made, the newspaper from September 9 on the table.

There is to be a funeral for him in Boston. And again there will be no body. Sean and Maureen Cummins will attend. Then they will return home and pack the remnants of his life.

"He didn't have anybody in New York," Mr. Cummins said as he stood in his bathtub repairing some leaking pipes, a job he had put off for six weeks. "Gerry really found a family here with us."

The small details of domestic life are monumental tasks these days, Mrs. Cummins said. The pipes still drip, the garden needs tending, the children still need to be put off to school. Then again, she said, married men are more fortunate. At least there is a routine for them.

"I know there is a part of him who wishes he were in the towers that day," she said as she put on the kettle. "He is tough in public, but he's weak with us."

Mr. Cummins has installed a fake fireplace in his living room so that he can sit with his children and stare at the electric flames. It reminds him of simpler times in Ireland, where he grew up. He can sit for hours and say nothing.

Mr. Cummins and Lieutenant Dennis Farrell, the leader of Squad 1, were supposed to speak at Mr. Fontana's funeral, but neither did. Mr. Cummins could not bring himself to regale strangers with stories of their firehouse antics. And Lieutenant Farrell felt he had spoken at too many funerals already.

He, too, was close with Mr. Fontana. As leader of the squad, he has taken on many of the burdens of putting the station house back together. The widows of his men turn to him. He's a strong man. They will have to put their own homes back together, but it's nice to know the lieutenant is there.

Aidan Fontana is starting to cope better at school. When Mrs. Fontana drops him there, he doesn't cling so much. That's progress, she said. The kids made him a book to make him feel happy. It told stories about him and his father. He said he liked it. He likes the letters and presents people send him, too.

He points out pictures of his father that are scattered around the living room and speaks of their time together in the past tense. He's got good memories of the beach, of being kissed by him.

It's worse for his mother. She has wept publicly only once, at the funeral as she delivered her husband's eulogy. She spoke of how they fell in love many times, how he proposed in the park in the thunder and lightning, how he would whisper "I love you" in the sleeping boy's ear so he would know it deep in his subconscious.

Mrs. Fontana threw a large party after the funeral, and many of Dave's admirers drank and ate and laughed late into the evening.

The coffin was returned and she packed her bags to run away for the weekend. The apartment was littered with details of the funeral.

"It wasn't a funeral for me," she said. "I didn't have a body. I don't feel closure and maybe I never will."

The First Holiday

The first call of the Thanksgiving Day 2001 shift came in at nine-eighteen A.M.

"Ten twenty-six!" the call box bleated. The driver started the fire engine and the men jumped into their boots, pants and suspenders, which stood next to their lockers like mannequins. "Ten twenty-six!" the call box bleated again. A stove fire.

"They burned the turkey already," Firefighter Bob West said. "You shouldn't stuff the turkey until after you cook it." That's what his mother told him, anyway.

It was shaping up to be another normal holiday for the men of Squad 1. But normal is a relative concept nowadays.

Thanksgiving, it seemed, had come around to its original meaning, less about football and overeating and Christmas commercials than about an appreciation for life. In the aftermath of the ambushes on the World Trade Center and the Pentagon, people across the nation stopped to consider and appreciate what they had and what they had lost.

There is a mother in Mississippi with a son in Afghanistan. He is alive, and she is grateful for that. A war refugee from Guatemala has made a life for her children by shining expensive shoes on Wall Street, and she is grateful for that.

Then there were the six men working at the small brick firehouse, surrounded by grandparents and wives and children, and they, too, were grateful for a few hours of the regular life. Their evening would be spent combing the smoldering pile of the twin towers for bodies.

The firehouse is still decorated in purple bunting and wilting flowers from the funeral of Lieutenant Michael Esposito. Then there are the other eleven men Squad 1 lost that dark Tuesday morning: Amato, D'Atri, Russo, Cordice, Bilcher, Siller, Carroll, Fontana, Box, Garvey and Butler.

Firefighter Robert Maddalone is one of the new men assigned to the house, and while basting the turkey, he perhaps said it best.

"I'm thankful I'm alive, but I feel guilty I'm alive," he said. "I'm trying to remember the guys who aren't here. Their wives and children. It's a hollow feeling. You try to laugh sometimes to keep your sanity, but you feel bad about laughing."

The turkey came out well—moist, with crispy skin, despite the men's playing with the stove's thermostat as if it were a radio dial.

A typical phone conversation went something like: "Happy Thanksgiving, Dad. Is Mom there? . . . Hi, Mom. How long do I cook this bird? . . . Sixteen pounds."

In the corner, Sean Cummins was playing with some walnuts, making some anatomical references to them in the style of the barracks.

The past ten weeks have been the worst in his life. There was the Trade Center collapse and the death of thousands. There were the weeks on end searching the wreckage. There were the funerals of his company comrades and a dozen more of other firefighters. There was a scaffolding collapse that killed five. A fire that took the lives of three children. And the airplane crash that hit his neighborhood, leaving 265 dead.

Even so, Mr. Cummins has things to be thankful for. There is his wife, Maureen, and his three children. There is also the work he does.

"Tuesday morning we found a man in the pile," he said. "We dug him out, and he had his wallet in his pocket. I was hoping they would notify his family by Thanksgiving. That would make me feel good."

Around noon, Daniel A. Nigro, the chief of department, the top-ranking uniformed fire official, stopped by on his own time. He came to check the men's morale. He came to say hello to their families. He came with a lump in his throat. "The department is going to get through this, men," he told them. "I don't know what the future holds, but we'll all get through this."

The room fell silent, and the turkey made the hissing sound of falling rain.

The turkey was pulled from the oven just after one P.M. The neighbors came by with fixings. A call came over the box about a drug overdose. A tattered woman on the graffiti-scarred corner of Degraw Street and Fourth Avenue in Brooklyn was slumped in a doorway with her forehead to her knees. She had just come from the soup kitchen.

"What'd you eat?" the men asked her as a priest looked on. "Nothin'," she slurred. "Jus' turkey."

"Uh-huh," one man said. "That's an awful lot of turkey."

Off she went in the ambulance, and life in New York went on, just like the old days. Back at the firehouse, the turkey was still warm.

Bart Codd, the new captain at Squad 1, said grace. "Personally we have things to be thankful for," he said, scratching his bowed head. "But others don't. Let's keep that in perspective. Amen."

The men ate, watched the Detroit Lions lose, piled into their engine around five o'clock and drove down to Ground Zero, full of roast turkey, sauce and yams.

Theresa Russo called as the men were on their way out. She has lost her husband, Michael, a lieutenant at Squad 1. He and eight others have yet to be found. She just called to wish the men a happy Thanksgiving and to thank them for the job they do.

The six firemen arrived at Ground Zero around five-thirty P.M. and to their disappointment were assigned a backup role. No action.

They watched with their hands in their overalls as other men picked and raked through the scrap and the black dirt that is not dirt at all but pulverized building.

A police dog sniffed, and tourists peeked over the barricades and took photographs with their cameras over their heads. "Surreal," Mr. West said.

Floodlights and smoke and the unmistakable stench. In the sky stood the green splendor of the Woolworth Building, a beautiful testament to humankind, and the firemen stood to consider it for a time. Below, was the wreckage and horror. "The very worst of mankind," Firefighter Billy Reddan said.

Cigarette embers glowed in the dark recesses, and more than 150 men and women spent Thanksgiving evening here, working.

The scene brought to mind an image that firefighter Tom DeAngelis painted that morning at the firehouse as he was coming off the night shift and the turkey was put in the oven.

"There was a dark alley around Ground Zero, near Washington Street, I think," he said. "It was four o'clock in the morning, and a man was there with a bucket and brush scrubbing the rescuers' boots. A regular guy stooped over in an alley doing that, just wanting to help in some way. Where's the glory? To me, he's a hero. I'm thankful to that guy."

Bill Noesges, a night foreman of the operating engineers, was among the workers at the Trade Center site, talking about his wife and children and Thanksgiving.

"To a person, we are proud to do this job," he said. "You couldn't tear me away from here, not even for the holiday. When it's all over, though, someone is going to have to reintroduce me to my wife."

However it may have sounded, firefighter Eddie Cowan said he would give his two legs to make everything back to the way it was on September 10.

An impossible wish, but at least it wasn't raining.

A Jacket, an I.D.

The remains of Lieutenant Dave Fontana were found last Thursday, December 6, in the wreckage of the south tower of the World Trade Center. In an emotional bit of synchronicity, the remains of firefighter Gerard P. Dewan were also recovered. Firefighter Dewan was the tenant and friend of firefighter Sean Cummins, who in turn was a friend of Lieutenant Fontana's at Squad 1.

Since Lieutenant Fontana's coffinless memorial in late October, Marian has become politically active, emerging as the spokeswoman for a group representing family members whose relatives and spouses have not been found since September 11.

"I'm not sure how I feel," Mrs. Fontana said. "Mixed, I guess. I was happy that they found Dave, but I'm not feeling the closure I expected to get."

The lieutenant's remains were found by rescue workers, while Mrs. Fontana and her son were visiting Hawaii. That same day, Aidan learned to surf. It was an important moment for the family, Mrs. Fontana said, since her husband was a surfer and a lifeguard on Long Island in his younger years.

Mrs. Fontana is planning a small funeral service for her husband at the GreenWood Cemetery in Brooklyn, noted for its natural beauty and Victorian monuments. Lieutenant Fontana will be laid to rest in the shade of a beech tree, she said.

A firefighter from Squad 1 who was among the workers last Thursday said he knew they had found a fireman by his jacket.

"We didn't know it was Dave right away," the firefighter said, asking that his name not be published because, like many firefighters, he was working on his own time and thus unauthorized to be at Ground Zero. "It was dark, late at night, and you are never sure of the time. But it was like we got something and then we got something else."

The firefighter paused for a moment to compose himself and continued: "In a way, it makes me happy. We accomplished something for his family."

Lieutenant Fontana was not just a firefighter, the people who knew him say. He was a Renaissance man: a sculptor, a fire department historian, a prankster. He was well known for his devotion to his son.

After the body was recovered, it was draped in an American flag and driven to the Bellevue Hospital Center morgue for official identification.

The remains of Firefighter Dewan, thirty-five, were also found last week, and his and Lieutenant Fontana's names appeared side by side on the list of the confirmed deceased.

Firefighter Dewan was among the first firefighters to enter the twin towers. Along with eleven others from Ladder Company 3 / Battalion 6 in lower Manhattan, he never made it out. It was his first day working at the firehouse. A small family ceremony in Boston, where he was born, is planned for today.

Firefighter Dewan had family ties to the Boston fire department, but because of a lack of job opportunities there, he began in the New

York fire department. He is the first member of his family to die in the line of duty.

"At least there is closure and he can be buried," said Maureen Cummins.

As of yesterday, there were 117 confirmed deaths of the 343 fire-fighters who were presumed lost, fire department officials said.

Star Without a Script

Marian Fontana, struggling writer and actress, has found fame. Or rather, fame has found her.

It is in the role of the Fireman's Widow, a woman both drawn to celebrity and repulsed by it. CNN routinely sends the limousine. She met with the president of the United States last month. She was the guest of Senator Hillary Rodham Clinton at the State of the Union address last week. She has been quoted in scores of newspapers, and they know her name from Britain to Hong Kong.

She even turned down *Oprah* twice.

It is an excitement mixed with guilt that consumes Mrs. Fontana, especially at night when she rolls over and sees her husband's shoes still tucked halfway under the bed. She wonders whether she can ever be seen as anything more than the widow of Lieutenant Dave Fontana. And if she tries to step out with her own work, will people think she is exploiting his death?

When she feels alone like that, she asks, just as her son does, "Where's Daddy?"

"Sometimes, I have to stop and ask myself, Am I being authentic? Is life out of control?" Mrs. Fontana said after she walked into her basement apartment in Park Slope, Brooklyn, late again, stuck at another meeting at fire department headquarters talking over money and pensions. Her son, Aidan, and his playmate were already home, having been picked up from school in a fire truck.

"Sometimes I wish I could walk away from all this, delete all the messages, raise my son and write my comedy in peace," she said.

Thousands were changed by the blazing, beguiling cameras: victims and survivors, fathers and children, firefighters and working people held up by the world as heroes, their emotions and opinions shuttled into living rooms across the globe. And the cameras eventually left them, as they left the survivors of previous American tragedies, sending them back to obscurity.

There are a few characters left in the hot lights. One of them is Marian Fontana, thirty-five, the fireman's widow.

"I took this on to distract myself," she said wearily. "And now there's almost nothing left of my own life. I'm struggling to find it."

At some point, she would like to return to life on the stage, to crawl back into the skin of her characters, like Dizzy Kane, the bassoon-playing kook with buck teeth and a pet dog, that have been regulars Off Broadway. She has not written a sketch since August.

But circumstances push her toward the corridors of power.

It began some months ago, when City Hall decided to scale back the presence of firefighters at Ground Zero. Mrs. Fontana threatened a protest by the firefighters' widows. She knew, and the firefighters' unions that backed her knew, that three hundred angry wives would make for more sympathetic pictures than a mob of angry firefighters punching out police officers. Eventually, Mayor Rudolph W. Giuliani retreated, and the recovery continues.

So, this single mother living on a firefighter's pension—and the unpaid president of the 9-11 Widows' and Victims' Families Association—finds herself one of the most important nonelected, non-moneyed people in New York. So important that politicians and developers agree that she will have to be appeased before any construction begins on a memorial or office complex at Ground Zero.

"Mr. Silverstein definitely wants to talk to her and representatives from all the concerned groups," said Howard J. Rubenstein, a spokesman for Larry A. Silverstein, the holder of the World Trade Center lease. "It's terribly important to him to be as helpful as possible, including a suitable memorial."

When her husband was alive, they were a relatively quiet couple. Unlike most firefighters, he did not take a second job; he wanted to spend time with his boy. She cleaned. He cooked. She wrote. He made art. The family camped and spent time on the beach.

Politicians seek her out for the photo opportunity. Strangers eavesdrop on her luncheon conversations. Oprah Winfrey's producers wanted her to talk about the scrum that has erupted over the federal compensation fund for the victims' families. Mrs. Fontana declined.

"I'm not even interested in the money," she said, pouring a glass of wine, the small apartment cluttered with scraps of paper, plastic bags and a broken blender. "I'm used to not having money. I'm an actress, and my husband was a firefighter. I'm more interested in people not forgetting what happened. It seems people have begun to lose interest."

It is common now to hear people around town say that the catastrophe of almost five months ago seems as if it happened five years ago. Work moves along and there are layoffs at Ground Zero. Some Muslims feel safe enough to chant verses of the Koran on the subway trains again. Politics and business scandals have taken over the front pages. And opinion has begun to turn against the widows, at least among some people.

A few weeks ago, Mrs. Fontana appeared on a radio program on WNYC-AM for a discussion of her life, the benefits fund, Ground Zero and a possible memorial when a young woman was put through.

"I get the feeling they want to be set up for life," the woman said. "I mean, if their husbands had died in another manner or weren't firefighters, you would have to make do with what you got. There's just a feeling that no matter what you get, it's not enough."

She went on: "It's making me very angry. I gave to charities. And you're getting this tax free and you, like, just want more and just it's never enough."

One would expect Mrs. Fontana, like so many other survivors, to lose her composure, to raise her voice, to at least hiss: "How dare you."

Yet she held her composure and went on to explain for perhaps the fiftieth time that week her position.

"We're very grateful for everything we got," she told the caller. "We're not asking for millions. All I'm asking is that what we get is fair from the fund. We shouldn't get any more or any less than what everyone gets. I could care less about the money. It's more of a moral issue."

In truth, the money part bores her, she said. Actuaries and professors and lawyers. But that is part of the role that is at once the lightning rod and the rock. A theater graduate from Sarah Lawrence College who was raised in Staten Island in a family where there is no memory of anyone ever having voted for a Republican, Mrs. Fontana is not what many consider to be the typical New York City firefighter's wife. She is disobedient, headstrong and practiced in the art of street theater.

She is unpracticed in politics, and she speaks her mind. Yet she is capable of amending her outlook. She finds Mr. Giuliani to be "caring" and believes that Governor George E. Pataki is "genuine."

Mrs. Fontana, along with other survivors, arranged a rally a few weeks ago at the Park Avenue Armory to protest the rules for the distribution of the federal money. It looked like a political convention, with the large American flag behind the dais and the television cameras and the journalists from across the world feeding on cheese and crackers at the buffet table. About a thousand family members attended, along with the governor and the mayor.

It went smoothly until Mayor Michael R. Bloomberg spoke of "an appropriate, lasting, eternal memorial." Some in the audience hissed at the mayor's innocuous trial balloon, and Mrs. Fontana's face went hard. It all seemed to presage the rumble when talk of development of the sixteen sacred acres begins in earnest.

Hours later, after the camera crews had left, Mrs. Fontana was still there shaking hands in her blue power suit, her husband's family waiting patiently in the foyer.

"Your husband is buried next to mine, and I guess that makes us soul mates," a widow said. "Thanks for the work you're doing," she added. "It's important to all of us."

The gratitude of the family members and her jumbled feelings of anger and devastation keep her going, even though on many nights she arrives home past midnight and the baby-sitter has already put her son in bed. Underneath it all, she is still a woman who lost her man, a mother of a confused little boy.

The boy sang to himself one morning in the bathroom mirror, "Mommy is going to die. Mommy is going to die." And Mommy sang back, "No she's not. No she's not."

This is her life away from the cameras and the microphones, a woman playing both mother and father. When she tried to put the boy on her shoulders the way Daddy used to do, she threw her back out. She has put a will together, but has few assets beyond some bank accounts and has not found the time to sign it.

At quiet moments, she wonders if this hectic life is what her husband would have wanted for them. And, being human, she wonders if there will ever be another man in her life. For now, there are just memories of the man who proposed to her in a hailstorm in Prospect Park ten years ago. The man who promised her a daughter but left only his shoes under the bed.

Mrs. Fontana got up from her kitchen table to check her phone messages. She got eighteen in three hours. One was from her father:

"Honey, I'm worried about you. I think you're spending too much time with Republicans."

Hero Fatigue

Sean Cummins does not want to talk about death anymore. Or tears, or guilt, or hero worship, or the tall tales he thinks people tell about themselves and September 11. He wants to bury it all and move on.

He was sitting in a Manhattan coffee shop on Eighth Avenue drinking tea the other afternoon as the rain fell. For a moment, firefighter Cummins felt serene. "You know, I'm happiest on rainy days," he said, looking into the gray sky. "It goes back to my Irish childhood. The only day on the farm where you could be idle without feeling guilty was on a rainy day."

It has been a year of drought, and on most days he creates household work for himself to keep his mind occupied and the death notices of his friends stuffed away. It seems to work until more corpses are unearthed at Ground Zero or he hears a story told of the days at the Pit that to him seems wildly overblown.

"We're coming on the cold light of dawn," Firefighter Cummins said, unaware that two young women, who had been kissing and holding hands at the next table, had attached themselves to his conversation. "The day they announce the Pit is empty, that the last dust has been swept out, what are we going to be left with? Tears and fifteen thousand body parts, that's what."

Firehouses being what they are, Firefighter Cummins lost some of his best friends on September 11. Dave Fontana was the other half of his firehouse vaudeville act; Lieutenant Eddie D'Atri was in bed when the first plane struck; there was a third man who was working for firefighter Cummins on a replacement shift that morning, a name that he keeps to himself.

Everyone associated with Squad 1 is occupied by unexpected problems. Most of the widows have not gotten the bodies of their husbands back. Another finds herself juggling the responsibilities of being the famous and political widow with the responsibilities of raising a child alone. There is the lone surviving officer straining to keep the old men together while bringing the new ones in. Captains have come and gone. Two men retired. There are strained relationships. Numbness seemed to bloom this spring.

Sean Cummins does not like to speak about what he did at Ground Zero, because when he does, he is invariably tagged a hero— a title, he says, only the dead have earned. "Just wearing a uniform doesn't make you a hero."

His views are representative only of himself, he says. He speaks in generalities and calls no one out by name. Yet when his agony surfaces, it cuts with a strident edge. It is an anger, a confusion from some place that he cannot locate. He keeps silent, mostly, though he has been told silence is bad for his recovery. But when he hears those hero stories, he can't help but make his judgments.

It is a residue that has permeated the department. "They're talking about giving medals to all the firefighters who were down there working after the fact," he said. "Are you kidding me?"

Firefighter Cummins, who transferred out of Squad 1 in February 2002, when he got a position with the prestigious Rescue Company 1 in Manhattan, cannot remember a single hero in all of his days at Ground Zero.

"Someone told me that there was a photograph of me hanging in a gallery," he said. "So my wife and I went to look at it. In the picture,

I'm bloody filthy. That picture is how I choose to remember what I did, rightly or wrongly."

The picture hung on the wall at the Bolivar Arellano Gallery in the East Village. Photograph number 275. He is standing in his denim jacket, stained with soot and blood and dust, staring into his helmet as if something might be augured, as if something might be found in there, a road map, an answer.

The photo might have been taken on day two or day twelve or day twenty-two. Sean Cummins, who has the build of a jockey, is especially trained for tight, enclosed rescues. Like a few dozen others, he was there, hours on end, digging, crawling through burning crevices. On the first day, he and a group of four firefighters found an obese man alive in a smoldering crag.

"That was the only time in my life where I really thought I was going to die," he said. "I was really scared. He was the only guy we found."

At the gallery, there are other photographs of clean people with badges and new gloves and others of unpaid civilians who worked through the nights. The truth of the whole occasion, firefighter Cummins said, is that not every hero wears a badge and not every badge-wearer is a hero.

Speaking intimately with other firefighters across the city, the men in blue now talk about other, not-so-heroic memories of those days on the pile.

In the public mind, anybody who went down there that night or the ensuing days was a hero. The truth is, some of these "heroes" spent hours eating sandwiches and watching television on the third floor of the Marriott Financial Center while others labored below. There was thieving and looting by people on the edges. There was a photographer who hid a body part underneath a traffic cone, ostensibly to photograph it in the golden hour of light.

A fire company was profiled on CBS recently. The film showed the members of that company quartered in their house the entire first evening, apparently under departmental orders. One man went home to bathe with his wife.

Instead of admiration for the work they did, many firefighters wondered if that company had gotten too comfortable on the night of the attack.

These things are buried and lost in the desire to make order of the confusion, to find something good in the bad. But the more time passes, the more Sean Cummins believes how colossal the hero myth has grown.

Beyond those who gave their lives, most rescuers must be placed in the ordinary category. That's where Sean Cummins firmly places himself: ordinary.

Like other department members, he has not gone to psychotherapy, only to one "debriefing" session with a department counselor. He has changed noticeably since September.

Back in late October, he could be found around the edges of the firefighters' wakes, making spooky statements like, "I hope my funeral's on a day like this."

He watched at the taverns as strange young women got on their toes to kiss the men in blue and bought them drinks. The men told big stories. "The truth will come out soon enough," he said then. "Eventually the truth will come out."

Over the past seven months firefighters have been the subjects of television programs. Others have taken free trips, posed for books and so on. Reporters and film crews have overrun the firehouses.

The attention reached its limits long ago. The fire commissioner wants control of the firehouses back, and the news media are no longer allowed into the houses without prior clearance. Many firefighters are taking their vacation days from last year; others are on sick leave. Those left are burning the candle at both ends. They are working overtime instead of spending time with their families. The news media still comes by to bother them.

"I seen guys snapping on stupid things they never would have before," Firefighter Cummins said of the tension and the explosive ventings. "It's not going away."

Sean Cummins is a driven man. He came to the United States in the late eighties. In that time he became a citizen, married, had three children. He has served in the Army and Navy reserves, and is a paratrooper with the Air National Guard. He joined the fire department in 1996, and made Rescue in just six years.

Some of his former housemates grumble that he would not have gotten the appointment had not Rescue 1 also been decimated on September 11.

"Just some hard feelings that don't mean anything, really," he said of the back-chatter. The truth is the transfer was scheduled for September 23, and if the men weren't saying anything about him, then that would be worse than anything they are saying, he figures. "When I walked out the door, I left with a broken heart," he said of his departure from Squad 1. "Life has to move on."

He allowed a reporter to come to his home recently in Rockaway Park, Queens, five blocks from the spot where American Air lines Flight 587 crashed in November, killing 265 people. He was among the first on the scene searching for bodies.

On this day, he was digging a hole in his basement. The kitchen telephone was buried in a linen drawer.

"The reason I let you come over is because I want to take the opportunity to thank those people who came to the firehouse with the food and flags and good thoughts," he said. "The five-year-old who gave a dollar, I'd like to thank him. Understand?"

He silently dug for the next few minutes.

"Okay," he said, looking up from the hole and squinting into the sun. "What do you want to know about the healing?"

A Lonely Son

At first, on September 12, when Aidan Fontana came home from a sleepover, his mother told him that the other firemen were looking for his father, that he was trapped in the rubble and that, with luck, he would be home soon. For weeks he waited for his father to walk through the apartment door. He never did. Eventually, Aidan's mother, Marian, had to tell him, and herself, that Daddy would not be coming home. The boy could not wrap his mind around the idea, alternating between tears and outbursts and silence. He demanded proof.

So a funeral was held on a windy October day. There were bagpipes and fire engines and a coffin, and finally Aidan understood. Until, that is, his father's body was actually found in early December and it had to be explained to the boy that the first funeral wasn't really a funeral.

The boy wanted to know if his father was a skeleton.

Dave Fontana's remains were cremated. His ashes were put in four jars: one for Ireland; one for the beach where he grew up; one for the park where he asked his wife to marry him; one for the cemetery.

At the second funeral, Aidan never looked up from his shoes, shrugged when people touched him. He looked like a little old man in his suit. A hollow, empty little man. He went home to bed sad that night.

With the coming anniversary of the day the world fell down, some in the adult world will try to have September 11, 2002, signify the date on which life moves on. But for the children who, like Aidan, lost a parent, sometimes two parents, or for those who never found the parent's body, some fear that the confusion has left unmedicated sores that will fester. In the long term, child psychologists foresee anxieties, irrational fear of death, aggression, attachment disorders.

In the short term, when the widows from the Squad 1 firehouse talk about their children, they talk about the bad dreams and the empty birthdays, the fights between brothers, the kids having to wear diapers to bed again. There are mass cards mixed in with Pokémon cards, and there are tantrums at school.

Children like Aidan were cheated. His mother can do only so much. She is struggling with her son's grief and her own, as well as representing the families and widows of the fallen firefighters. She doesn't know how to throw a curve ball. She doesn't know paper airplanes or woodcarving.

"He's got his good days and bad days," his mother said as they lay on the couch together watching cartoons.

The only thing that remains of the happy days at the Fontana household is the telephone answering machine message on which Marian speaks and Aidan laughs as his father tickles him.

Aidan had a hard year at school. The kindergarten teacher scolded him because he insisted on playing twin towers with the classroom's wooden blocks. Over and over he built them, and over and over they fell. But Super Aidan always came out untouched, a survivor. Maybe if he had been with his dad that day, he could have saved him, he said. His mother paid a paraprofessional to stay with him through the waning months of the school year.

Aidan is a remarkable boy, said his aunt, Leah Gray. "He's finding ways to work it through," she said. "We were driving in the car once and we were all wearing Squad 1 hats. He would take the hat off his head and say, 'Okay, we have to stop thinking about Daddy.' This would go on for fifteen minutes and then he'd say, 'Okay, put your hats back on. We're going to think about Daddy now.'"

He has a good support network: his mother, his aunt, uncles, grandparents, family friends and some people he may never remember when he grows older. When men come over, the boy instinctively reaches for their hands.

"He's got a lot of good men in his life," said his grandmother Joyce Malerba-Goldstein. "We can be thankful for that."

It seems that the talks with his mother and his therapist are helping him shape the events of the past year into something less than a monster in the closet. When he stood on a surfboard for the first time in December while on vacation in Hawaii, he heard his father clapping from heaven. His father leaves him gifts sometimes, too. Perhaps a little seashell or some sort of sign. A good sunset might remind him of Dad.

Then there was the conversation over a sugar cone at his local ice cream shop recently.

"How are you feeling about your dad and everything?" he was asked.

He thought for a long time and then said: "Well. Ten thousand and ninety-nine firefighters were safe. More than ten thousand. So I feel good and bad. I feel good because my dad will always be with me, and I feel bad that he died and I miss him. And it's very hard to understand. I feel so mad and upset this happened and that's all I know and that's the end."

Ten thousand and ninety-nine. His number was close to the true figure of the uniformed fire department men and women left alive after the awful toll of 343 dead at the World Trade Center (about 11,500). This from a child who can count to ninety.

After his cone, he climbed around the table like a monkey. Some ice cream had dried under his nose. He pointed to the burned-out building next door.

"See that building there?" he said. "It burned the day before the towers fell." It had actually burned months before, but that is how a young mind works, compressing events into Old Testament measurements.

"I know because I saw it. Guys from Ladder One Twenty-two put it out." Dave Fontana was once assigned to Ladder 122.

"I saw it with binoculars. I said, 'Holy smokes! The ice cream store is going to burn down and it's the most famous ice cream store in the whole world.' But the guys from One Twenty-two put it out. They didn't die in that one. They died in the twin towers helping my dad."

Aidan wanted to walk down the street to his school to play on the jungle gym. His classroom window is next to the monkey bars there. He wanted to look inside.

His classroom is at the back of the building, to the left. The halls smelled of disinfectant. Summer school was in session and everything had been rearranged. The summer-school teacher was not his teacher. She was young. He commented on that.

The summer-school teacher asked him if he was a third grader.

"I'm going into first grade," he said.

She was surprised. "You're such a big boy."

"Yeah, like my dad," he answered without pause, without looking at her, as if the existence of his father needed to be explained to strangers.

"I beated my dad in races sometimes. My dad loved basketball, and I beated him a few times. My dad was big."

He poked around the room. Aidan noticed the blocks had been removed. The closets and cubbyholes were empty. He was confused.

"All the stuff's gone," he said. "All my classroom stuff's gone. This was my classroom."

"Well, now we have summer school," the teacher said, unaware that his dad was Lieutenant Dave Fontana. Unaware that a man named Lieutenant Dave Fontana had ever existed.

"Times change," she said.

"Yep," Aidan said, accepting the explanation. "Times change."

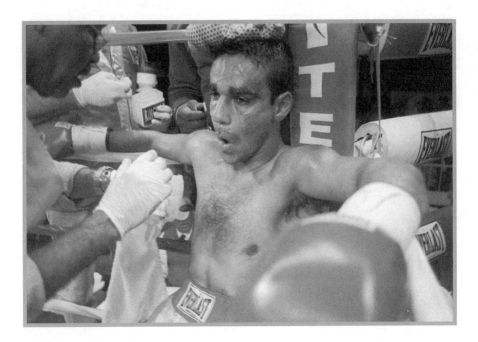

THE
SPORTING LIFE

SHOW me a good loser and I'll show you a loser.

—AN OLD NEW YORK SAYING

The Champ

It would take just one more drink before the place went nuts.

"Gimme a piña colada, Gene," the woman slurred, mostly drunk, her voice box grinding like a cement mixer.

Gene "the Champ" Camp looked stupefied behind his mirrored glasses. He picked up a mug and said, "Howz 'bout a beer?"

The woman belched smoke and the whole bar had a good laugh at that one, seeming to have forgotten that they'd heard it many times before.

These are Gene Camp's people: the stripper, the recovering cokehead, the gambler. He is the closest thing they will know to a star, their Wayne Newton, and he leads this crowd without question. They are regulars and they are middle-aged, at a point "when dreams have become just dreams," like his old friend Francis Deloache says.

But Mr. Camp is different. Mr. Camp has held on to his dreams. And his friends at the Post Time Bar in Elmhurst, Queens, speak with admiration about the lengths he has gone to achieve those dreams.

"He cares about two things," said John St. John, a construction worker with a forearm rippled from repeated use of the hammer and the beer mug. "People and arm wrestling."

Gene Camp is the president, financier, announcer, secretary and stamp licker for the New York Arm Wrestling Association, the sanctioning body for the Golden Arms championship series. Seven arm wrestlers in separate weight classes will be crowned city champion in Manhattan this October.

The association is the biggest arm-wrestling organization in the city because it is the only arm-wrestling organization in the city. The competitors are strictly amateurs and no prize money is awarded. Seven champions from each borough will compete for the city title.

It has been a twenty-year odyssey from barrooms to street fairs, trying to drag a nowhere sport to the pinnacle of Mount Olympus. "It should be part of the Olympics," Mr. Camp said. "I bet Hercules was a hell of an arm wrestler."

Along the way, Mr. Camp, fifty-three, has spent his savings and lost a few women.

The association was formed in the oak-paneled walls of the Post Time in 1977, and Mr. Camp was its first champion. He got the idea for a New York association after watching a televised tournament from a small chicken-ranching town in California.

But the Champ has a dirty little secret: he was never a champ at all, unless you count the shot-put title he won in 1961 at Newtown High School.

"I was real good in the bar, but I never really won nothing professionally," the Champ said. What he did was take a photograph of himself in a muscle shirt and send it out to the local papers declaring himself the Eastern States champion.

"I don't want to be a braggart," he told the *New York Post* in 1977, "but I've never been beaten in my life and I don't intend to be beaten."

None of it was true, of course, but it got his association off the ground. His first tournament was held at the old Sunnyside Gardens Arena in Queens, where Mr. Camp took on all comers and lost to most of them.

"I guess I started believing the hype myself," he said.

Arm wrestling is not the sport of kings. It is a mostly blue-collar activity played in pubs and pool halls around the world. It is a sport for guys who were never good at sports, a second chance to be good at something.

"The athletic field is the only place in life where you cannot lie," Mr. Camp said. "And some guys take that better than others."

In one of New York's most famous arm-wrestling bouts, Mark Gastineau (a defensive lineman for the N.Y. Jets) tore up Studio 54 after he was beaten by a pretty boy who was a hundred pounds lighter. It was a case of a "harmed ego," said the district attorney then prosecuting the case. Mr. Gastineau was later convicted of assault and never answered calls for a rematch. The pretty boy was a champion of Mr. Camp's association.

"If it wasn't for Gene, there wouldn't be arm wrestling in New York," said Jason Vale, one of the top two-hundred-pound arm wrestlers in the country and a protégé of the Champ. "He's like the only game in town."

How long the game will go remains to be seen. The sport had a bubble in popularity ten years ago after the arm wrestling movie *Over the Top*, starring Sylvester Stallone, hit the theaters, but corporate sponsorship has dried up, said H. G. Harmon, president of the United States Arm Wrestling Association, based in Wytheville, Virginia.

"You got a two-part problem with the sponsors," said Mr. Harmon, explaining that his is one of perhaps a dozen arm-wrestling organizations nationwide. "One, some of these guys hold tournaments in sleazy, cheap places and steal the prize money. Two, a lot of these so-called champions refuse to put their titles at stake."

Mr. Camp, on the other hand, has sacrificed everything. He lives in a small apartment in Bayside, Queens, cluttered with papers and arm-wrestling memorabilia, his three-foot shot-put trophy his only company. He has never been married, and several girlfriends have left him because he paid more attention to the sport than to them.

The Champ

Arm wrestling has not made him rich, but that's not the point. He lives for little mentions in newspapers, for the attention in a life where little attention has been paid.

"I'm like a carnival barker," he said. "Give me a mike, I'll get a crowd." Mr. Camp retired after twenty years with the sanitation department and works two bartending jobs to make ends meet. The association loses money. He is looking for a sponsor.

"I gotta make it work," Mr. Camp said, pouring another round. "I'll do anything short of breaking the law to make it work. It gives people a shot to be somebody he never thought he was. Including me."

The last round of drinks does indeed set the barroom off, and a full card of arm-wrestling bouts is quickly arranged. The Champ referees, passes out hot dogs on the house and dances to the Village People.

The ladies love him. Not for his 255-pound frame or his fifty-two-inch chest, prominent under his open-collared shirt. Not for his high-school diploma or his tattered blue Cadillac. Not because he's a winner.

They love him because he brings glamour. The Champ is married to arm wrestling, but it's the ladies high on whiskey who kiss his face.

A Lifetime
of Lifeguarding

The adage that age is a state of mind is a bunch of bunk, said Reggie Jones, who, at the age of seventy-three, may be the oldest lifeguard in the Western Hemisphere. Age, in the opinion of Mr. Jones, is a state of nature.

"You can't beat the Reaper, but you can put him off," he said, and to prove his point, Mr. Jones pulled an old photograph of himself from a chest of drawers inside Lifeguard Shack 5 at Jones Beach State Park on Long Island. It was an old black-and-white of a young Reggie Jones, dated 1944—his first year on the beach—and he looked something like a muscular Sal Mineo. The beach was not named after Mr. Jones, he would like you to know. (It was named after Major Thomas Jones, an eighteenth-century whaler and part-time pirate.) Reggie Jones is, in fact, two years older than the park that Robert Moses built. He is also older than the dark, cake-shaped shack that he works from. The shack has no plumbing or glass windows and houses a half-dozen men like Mr. Jones who have more than thirty-five years on the job.

It is affectionately called Jurassic Park by the other lifeguards at Jones Beach. And these old men with the boyish faces think Ponce de Léon was a fool. Instead of traipsing around the Everglades in search of the fountain of youth, they believe the explorer should have known he was sailing on it.

"You spend a life staring at shells and sand and salt and swells, it does something good to you," said Jay O'Neill, sixty-six, a retired insurance broker who is working his forty-eighth year in the big white chair. "It is the best job I ever had."

It is halfway through the summer season, and on many beaches, lifeguard jobs still go wanting. From Westchester to New York City to the Jersey shore, it seems young people no longer find the clean, glamorous job appealing. Not even for ten dollars an hour. It's gotten so bad that Ocean City, New Jersey, is digging through its personnel files and asking the old-timers to fill the empty observation chairs.

But on the Long Island waters there is a surfeit of young candidates who want to work. The problem here is that the young bulls must wait for the aging pachyderms to ramble off to the tar pits. This season, 120 applicants tried out, eighty qualified and fifty were hired. The job on Long Island is popular.

The reasons are many, the lifeguards say. State parks pay more than others, from eleven dollars an hour for a beginner to twenty dollars for a captain. The state park lifeguards have a union, and they are paid for inclement days. And then there is a certain esprit de corps that comes from working on one of the world's most famous beaches.

"I'd rather watch the tomatoes walk by than watch them grow in the backyard," said Mr. Jones, who has the old habit of pardoning himself before he curses or says something risqué, as he does in a complimentary fashion when beautiful women pass by. "Jeez, I'm a terrible character."

None of the guards can coast on their reputations. Each year, the applicants—new and old—must swim one hundred yards in seventy-five seconds to requalify, and every year Mr. Jones has done it. "I go ocean swimming in the winter," he said. "It's my physical. If I don't drop dead from a heart attack, I'm back for another year."

Henry J. Stern, New York City's parks commissioner, who has had trouble over the last few summers attracting enough qualified people to guard his beaches, was flabbergasted to learn that a man of Mr. Jones's age was still employed as a lifeguard. "How's his vision?" the commissioner asked.

Perfect, he was told.

"Hmmm," said Mr. Stern, who is sixty-five. "I've got to find something to do after I retire."

Of the 240 lifeguards at Jones Beach, one—Mr. Jones—started in the 1940s, nine in the 1950s, thirty-six in the 1960s, fifty-eight in the 1970s, seventy-four in the 1980s and sixty-two in the 1990s. They performed 2,079 rescues at Jones Beach last year, and no one drowned.

"As far as anybody knows, Reggie's the dinosaur of the ocean," said Joe Scalise, the water safety director for the state beaches on Long Island. "He keeps himself in phenomenal shape. He outdoes a lot of the young people."

His skin is clear and cancer free, his mind sharp. He maintains a rigorous training regimen throughout the year that includes running, swimming and weight lifting. With a youthful body, the leathered neck of a turtle, sea-kelp eyebrows, an old hat with a button that reads OLDER THAN DIRT and a grimy seagull feather, Reggie Jones is hard to miss from his perch atop the lifeguard stand. He reckons he has made more than a thousand rescues in his career, including saving a swimmer's toupee and a few sets of dentures.

"The toughest rescue was the fat man who floated out to sea, with me holding on to him," Mr. Jones said. "It was 'forty-seven, in the middle of a fog bank. He had to be three hundred pounds. I got him, though. I never lost anyone."

Mr. Jones met his wife near the Jones Beach concession stands fifty years ago. He is still happily married, still thick-chested, but carries an extra ten pounds and has lost half his hair since then.

Other things have changed in half a century, as well.

Dress, for instance. People used to wear full-body woolens. "Now they were dental floss," Mr. Jones said. "The first bikini walked on the beach around 1952. She nearly caused a riot and the police took her away."

There are minority swimmers at the beach.

The overpasses on the parkways to Jones Beach were deliberately built too low to allow buses to fit under them. "City people got cars now," Mr. Jones observed, which has broadened the beach's accessibility.

Still, the crowds seem to be half the size they once were, he said. "There were no malls then. No air-conditioning. No backyard pools. Everything was closed on Sunday. The beach was the only game in town."

The most egregious change? "The suits got smaller and the people got bigger," he bitterly complained. "America is fat. You should see the stumps they call ankles now. I see women walking around here with enough cellulite hanging off their backsides to deep-fry Pittsburgh."

Landing Jabs to Pay Bills

In the boxing game, the brighter your name the dimmer your entourage.

A Saturday-night bout was being held at the Amazura Ballroom in a dirty corner of Jamaica, Queens, as part of Cedric Kushner's all-Latino show. The Spanish-language television network Telemundo billed the card simply as Boxeo. The arena, normally a disco, was filled with partisans from the Dominican Republic, Puerto Rico and Mexico. The men waved flags of their homeland and the women chewed gum with their mouths unashamedly open. Upstairs in the dressing room, a dozen or so boxers milled around. You could tell the ones with top billing. They had superior bodies and a half-dozen hangers-on from the neighborhood. They had girls in tight skirts rubbing up against them and white men in dark suits telling them how great they were.

On the other side of a cheap curtain, Antonio Oliveros, stripped down to his leopard-skin drawers, lay across a row of rickety cocktail tables. The tables were near the fire exit. It was cold and drafty there, and it smelled like a urinal.

Oliveros was a featherweight listed at the bottom of the card, the first fight of the evening, and he had no entourage to speak of. Just

Marco Antonio Lizarraga, the former Mexican national welterweight champion who was fighting that night under the name Juan Antonio Lopez for six thousand dollars. A masseur who wore a large gold crucifix rubbed camphor into Oliveros's muscles.

The masseur had worn the crucifix tonight, he later confided, in case his man needed a line to the Almighty. This would be Oliveros's second professional fight. He would earn one hundred a round.

One hundred and twenty-two pounds of plodding feet and big punches, Oliveros is but another chapter in New York's rich boxing history. That history is so rich because boxing has always been the sport of the hungry immigrant class, said Hank Kaplan, a boxing historian. Historically, boxing has been considered a way out of the ghetto for blacks and immigrants.

"The poor Irish kids, they were the main group that was heavy into boxing in the early decades of this century, until the other immigrants came," Mr. Kaplan said. "When the Jewish kids came, they took over because they were the new hungry kids, and at the same time the Italians came. The Irish kids got pushed out. That lasted until the end of World War Two. Then came the Puerto Ricans and the blacks. Of course there were always blacks, but they had problems because they were shut out of boxing like they were in all walks of life."

There have been the great Mexican champions, like the bantam Lupe Pintor, the featherweight Salvador Sanchez and the American-bred welterweight Oscar De La Hoya. And for decades, legions of men have crossed the border to serve as human grist for the Friday night "smokers," rough-and-tumble matches in Texas saloons and California nightclubs.

New York had none of them. But if another gauge is needed to measure the increasing Mexican influence in the metropolitan region, consider the names on the fight card Saturday evening: Oliveros, Zubia, Rodriguez.

Outside the ring, Oliveros is a working stiff. He has worked as a picker in the southern fruit orchards, a dishwasher in some highly unrecommended restaurants and now as an itinerant construction worker in the Bronx and in Rockland and Westchester counties.

He dreams of fame and fortune, which he believes he can earn by punishing other men's organs. His first fight ended in a technical draw because of a head butt. At twenty-eight, he is a young fighter, not in age but in experience. This early in his career he cannot afford a blemish on his record. "Losing," he said confidently, "is not an option."

Oliveros is a Mexican without work papers, a man without a bank account and a man with few options. He is tired of the jackhammer, he said, the early mornings spent lifting bricks and spreading cement.

Mr. Lizarraga, who would be fighting as Lopez, sat next to his countryman on a foldout chair dispensing a string of clichés no less true from their overuse.

On individualism: "Go out and fight your fight," he told Oliveros, whose feet were being rubbed.

On duty: "Remember your children."

On strategy: "Be a hunter. Cut the ring in half."

Oliveros had trained at the Omni Health and Fitness Complex in Pelham Manor in Westchester, where aerobics mixes with the serious business of boxing.

Willie Soto, sixty-four, is Oliveros's trainer. He was a professional boxer himself until he was beaten to a pulp one particularly bad evening. His stomach is distended like that of many former athletes disdainful of exercise. But he knows boxing.

"I get a lot of guys coming in here eager to fight, maybe ninety a year," he said. "And they find they don't like getting hit in the face. Maybe one can become a champion. And what does he do? He takes money from the big promoter. He needs money, and I can't pay him. He takes the cake and leaves me. I can't blame him. But I've never made money."

He hopes that Oliveros will be different. If he can do something, Mr. Soto hopes, he won't be left behind.

Oliveros is a little man with a big right hand who came to fighting late. He began in the peach orchards of Georgia five years ago. "I was fighting with the black guys who wanted to take my money," he said. "Sometimes they just wanted the fight."

He walked into Mr. Soto 's gym four years ago and had a decent Golden Gloves amateur career. He has troubles with the fundamentals, though, like the tactic of severing the ring to trap a fleet-footed opponent in the remaining triangle. But what he lacks in skill he makes up in desire.

"I work so much and I can't get a home for my family," he said as he toweled off after a prefight workout. "I'm poor, you know. I need money. Even a hundred a round will help. I'll take that. Rich people don't need to fight."

He lives in the Mexican quarter of New Rochelle, where he shares a two-bedroom apartment with his wife and two children, and another couple and their two children. When he walks in the door, the children climb over him and his wife brings him a soda. The adults discuss finances and day jobs. His wife, Yolanda, sells cosmetics door-to-door. The other man is a landscaper, and his wife is a minimum-wage factory worker.

The Oliveroses earn $2,200 a month and spend about $1,700.

"I'm going to win for my children's education," he said. On the coffee table are a group of second-place trophies from his amateur career.

In the Amazura Ballroom, at 6:51 P.M., the first bout was announced. The boxing inspectors watched as Oliveros had his hands wrapped. A photographer's flash went off.

"Who's this guy?" asked a tobacco-chewing Texan promoter. A reporter answered him.

"He's twenty-eight?" the Texan asked, raising an eyebrow. "He doesn't have a chance. Every guy that steps into the ring thinks he's going to be a champion. But dreams are dreams, and boxing's pretty definitive. Soon as he gets popped in the face, it'll come back to reality."

Oliveros arrived at the apron wearing a poncho that was red, white and green—the colors of the Mexican flag—with his gloves on the shoulders of Mr. Soto.

His opponent was Jhovany Collado, a local product dressed in black with a body carved from granite. It was his professional debut.

Oliveros was raised in Jalisco, Mexico. His favorite boxer is his countryman Julio Cesar Chavez, who fought ninety-one professional bouts before losing. He admires the champ so much that he named his son after him.

Oliveros and Chavez are similar in some ways: They know no direction but forward and have little regard for defense. They are blue-collar fighters, heavy punchers, willful.

The differences are glaring, however. Chavez was known for his left hook, his footwork and his ability to cut the ring in half. Oliveros possesses none of these attributes.

The fight went the distance, and it was a unanimous decision: Collado by three points on every judge's card.

Soto was apoplectic. He kicked the spit bucket over and threatened violence. "The fix was on!" he declared.

Oliveros walked back to the dressing room, his face reddened with welts and scratches. He will not be rich from boxing. He will not be rich from anything, probably.

The doctor checked his eyes with a penlight. He stroked his ribs the way that a horse trader inspects a colt. The doctor nodded his approval, wiped his nose on his coat sleeve and went on to other business.

Oliveros put on his pants and went home to his children, four hundred dollars richer.

Borrowing Mailer's Car, and Other Ring Tales

Jose Torres, author, raconteur and former light heavyweight champion of the world, was telling a story and sipping white wine at the annual Christmas benefit for retired and ruined boxers at Tony Mazzarella's Waterfront Crabhouse in Long Island City.

He was talking about the time, in 1965, when he borrowed Norman Mailer's car. "Well, I ran a red light, you know?" the champ told the table. "And the cop, he wants to see the registration. Well, I don't know where this registration is, see? So they take me downtown.

"Anyway, the sergeant, he calls Mailer's mother and she tells him, 'Norman doesn't loan that car to anyone.' So they arrest me. How do you like that?

"A few months later, Mailer brings his mother to my camp upstate to watch me train for the championship. He tells her to be careful, that I'm a Puerto Rican and liable to become violent. After my workout, his mother and I walk over to the side for a conversation, and I can tell she's very scared, see. I said: 'I respect you for what you did that night with the car, Mrs. Mailer. I hope my own mother would do the same thing.' Well, she was so relieved she gave me a big hug.

"Later in life, when she gave an interview, she called me a no-good bum. How do you like that?"

There were laughs at that story. Eugene the Silent, whose last name is Hairston, heard none of it. He just stared into his plate with his one good eye. The other eyelid had fallen shut years ago. The Silent was oblivious until someone slapped him on the back, too, and he could see they were laughing.

Mr. Hairston, a deaf-mute, was a professional boxer. There were lights in all four corners so he would know when the bell sounded. He had a good career that stretched into the mid-fifties. He drew with Jake LaMotta and won a decision against Kid Gavilan.

Once a year, dozens of old-timers get together for a benefit put on by Ring 8, a fraternal club of pugilists who raise money for canes, dental work and coffins for the old-timers who fought often and never had a pension. Micki Grant and the New Yorkers supplied the swing music. The banquet room was all in tinsel and poinsettias.

I don't regret anything, Mr. Hairston wrote on a notepad with a palsied hand. *And all I really want for Christmas is my two front teeth.* He laughed without sound.

John Britenbruck told a story then. He said he once knocked a man out after having spent an hour in New York Harbor earlier in the afternoon trying to save a drowning boy. This earned him the title of the first guy to take a dive before ever getting into the ring.

"I was fighting one night," Mr. Britenbruck said. "There was a woman in the crowd. She was screaming, 'Kill that bum Britenbruck!'

"After the first round I go back to the corner and ask my trainer, 'Can't you move her back a few rows? I can't hear myself think.'"

"My trainer said, 'John. That's your mother.'"

THE DIAMOND

———— ■ ————

Free Swinger
on the Hudson

NAME: *Derek Bell*

AGE: *31*

COMING FROM: *Houston*

LOOKING FOR: *A championship*

Derek Bell, who is earning $5.2 million as the New York Mets' right fielder in the 2000 season, is taking batting practice a few hours before an evening game with the Atlanta Braves. The crowd has yet to enter Shea Stadium in Flushing. A sweet-faced, corn-fed girl from Somewhere, USA, is standing on the ball field practicing the national anthem over the public address system. She sings earnestly. She sings flat. She is not good. She is resoundingly booed—by the hot dog vendors. "New York's a tough town, yo," says Bell.

He did not plan to come to New York, and New York did not plan to have him. But Derek Bell became Mets property in January as a toss-in, a thirty-one-year-old has-been who batted .236 with twelve home runs and sixty-six rbi last year with the Houston Astros, all career lows. The Mets were forced to take him and his salary as part of the deal that brought the left-handed ace Mike Hampton here. At his news conference in January, D. Bell—as his teammates call

319

him—assured the media that he had a lot left in him. He promised to love New York and promised to make New York love him. He promised to eat in cool restaurants. He promised to find a cool place to live in Manhattan.

New York Lesson number one: "The rent here is really high, yo."

D. Bell likes to live nicely. He has more than a hundred pairs of alligator shoes: black-and-blue wing tips, white-and-coral-and-black wing tips, coral wing tips, black wing tips, white wing tips. He has a six-bedroom house in his hometown, Tampa, five of them filled with orange suits, turquoise suits, green suits and more shoes.

"I got clothes," he explains. "I got to be representing. I don't want to get caught slippin'.'" He has five vehicles—three trucks, a new Mercedes-Benz and a maroon convertible Rolls-Royce. He has a yacht, a speedboat and a fishing boat. He wears a gold-and-diamond baseball pendant, gold-and-diamond studs and a gold-and-diamond watch.

"I mean, I got things, and I needed a place to put them," he states as a matter of fact as he dresses his long, lanky body for the ball game.

So D. Bell went looking for a two-bedroom apartment in January. "I knew New York was expensive, but yo! When I went looking for a two-bedroom, I was thinking somewhere around fourteen or fifteen."

He found a lot of two-bedrooms renting for around fourteen or fifteen a month. The problem was, D. Bell was talking fourteen or fifteen hundred. The real estate agent was talking fourteen or fifteen thousand.

"And then you got to pay the agent a month's commission. I said hell no. I mean, I could afford it, but why should I when I got options?"

The option was keeping most of his stuff in Tampa while bringing his fifty-eight-foot Sea Ray 800 yacht ("How many times I got to say it's not a boat, yo, it's a yacht") to New York. He began living on it in April when the season began. On a couple of occasions, he has sailed it to work at Shea Stadium. It is tied up on the West Side of

Manhattan in a marina close to a popular tourist spot, and he will pay for the slip by doing some publicity for the owner.

"The funny thing is, yo, it's got more room than in the penthouses I was looking at," he says.

Lesson number two: "Never keep the fish."

D. Bell's yacht sits in the Hudson River among the floating bottles and plastic and foam cups. It is leather and smoked glass and has a garage for his Jet Ski, two bedrooms, two full baths, a kitchen and a wall full of electronica. Like many New York apartments, it has only beer in the refrigerator, and the stove has never been used.

On the deck there is a bottle of Hennessy and a leather couch and beyond that is the pier where tourists walk by. A slightly plump white woman sits up there, wearing a skirt, her legs slightly apart.

D. Bell, the fisherman, casts his line: "Hey, pssst. 'Scuse me. You waiting for somebody?"

"Five more minutes," she says. "Five more minutes and I'm getting on your boat."

"You can get on my boat anytime, baby."

She melts into a dopey smile. She keeps tugging down on her top. It's not clear if she knows that this is D. Bell, although his face is unmistakable. The squash-shaped head, the thick goatee, deep lines running across his forehead, the beanpole body. It doesn't matter, because D. Bell knows by now that in New York it's good enough to look as if you're someone worth knowing.

"You need a new friend?" he asks her.

"No telling what I need," she says.

D. Bell spends his time away from the ballpark on his yacht with his head down, a drink in his hands, listening to people whisper, "Is that really him?"

D. Bell is one of the few New York professional athletes to live in Manhattan. He is the only one living on a yacht. He has never really invited the gawking women aboard. It's sort of like catch and release. A tease. He learned that lesson a long time ago. It was April 1994, and D. Bell was playing for the San Diego Padres. He and a team-mate were arrested at East Thirtieth Street and Lexington Avenue for soliciting sex from two undercover policewomen. The players said they were teasing and pleaded not guilty. The charges were dropped six months later for a lack of evidence.

So now D. Bell, who sometimes refers to himself in the third person, rarely goes out. And when he does, he says, "I'm chill." He does not trust the motives of many New York women. He has never been to Central Park, he says. He has never visited a museum. He has never seen a show. His clothes are imported from Cincinnati. "Don't need any of that. Just gimme my hip-hop music and my game and I'm happy."

Lesson number three: "Drive like the cabbies do."

His first month in right field, D. Bell proved to most everybody that he still has something in the tank. He displayed a great glove and a .385 batting average. But it wasn't until May that he got the nerve to drive in the big city. It scared him, he doesn't mind saying. "The way these fools drive, I wasn't sure." But the more he saw of it, the more he liked the challenge.

He brought his truck to New York, and he has the driving figured out.

"There's basically three rules," he says:

1. Whoever has his front end ahead of the other has the right of way.

2. When in doubt use the gas pedal.

3. Never use the brakes.

"Now I drive like a fool anyway possible like the cabbies do. And New Yorkers know you, yo. They know all about ball. I'll be sitting there in traffic and they'll say, like, 'Hey, yo, Derek,' like rootin', you know? It ain't like that in Houston."

In Stadium's Shadow,
Waiting for the Opener

The old man hobbles in on a cane, takes off his coat, shakes off the rain. There is no joy in Yankee Village today. Opening day of the 2000 season has been delayed.

"Why did they call the game off when they didn't call off the war?" Paul Peterson shouts into the empty saloon. "Cold? Now the war was cold, yes, sir." Anticipating bad weather, the New York Yankees announced eighteen hours before Tuesday's home opener that the game would be postponed. With rain and possible snow forecast for Tuesday, the team pushed back the contest against the Texas Rangers for Wednesday.

The proprietors and patrons of the Yankee Tavern, at 161st Street and Gerard Avenue in the shadow of the stadium, had been waiting through the dark, bleak days of winter for Tuesday's gold rush. Especially Paulie Peterson, the seventy-five-year-old crosspatch who lives alone and is delighted when he is able to tell somebody, anybody, to go to hell.

As far back as anyone could remember around here, an opening day had never been called off the day before the game. Not even during the war. Paulie's war.

When they want a game-day report, certain fans do not call the ball club, they call the bar. "No, no, no game today," Joe Bastone, the latest Bastone in a line of Bastones who've owned this place, tells someone on the phone. "It's a stupid thing, I know. But you might as well go to work today. Come tomorrow."

The tavern opened its doors in 1928, five years after the stadium. They served Dutch Schultz beer and bathtub gin during Prohibition. Yankees have always come here to drink. Babe Ruth. Lou Gehrig. Mickey Mantle. Billy Martin. Paulie drank with some of them and today, like many days, he is the first pour at 9:39 A.M. Six minutes do not pass before the rail is stacked with the daily lineup. Paulie on first with his war stories. Eighty-eight-year-old John Roberson on second studying the numbers. Eddie at third reading the box scores. And Lonnie drinking cleanup.

Paulie and John meet here every day. There are no wives anymore, and their apartments can be as lonesome as an empty closet. Companionship is what saloons are for, they say.

They met here more than twenty years ago, in these very chairs. Black man and white man, chattering back and forth like stenotype. They know a lot about each other, but not everything.

"You know, when I came back from the war they let us out in Boston," Paulie says. "Damn Red Sox country. Can you believe that? A Yankee in Red Sox country. I got me a beer and a whiskey and I was glad to get outta there."

"I didn't go to no war," says John, and he shows off the scar that saved him from it. "I'm glad. I didn't want to go." He stayed home and worked the loading docks.

Paulie explodes. "Didn't want to go! Didn't want to go! Damn it, I was glad to go!" He draws sullen and quiet and stares blankly into the mural of Joe DiMaggio.

His eyes begin to cloud. "Dachau," he croaks. "I saw it."

The old man wipes his eyes, tucks a meat sandwich wrapped in foil into his jacket and takes his cane.

There is no joy in the village today as mighty Paulie hobbles away.

A Telescopic Lens
on a Baseball Legend

The baseball career of Sal Yvars is a footnote in the sport's history. Just twelve unremarkable lines in *The Baseball Encyclopedia*.

He played eight years in the major leagues, from '47 to '54, mostly with the New York Giants. He appeared in 210 games and batted .244. He hit ten home runs and amassed forty-two rbi. He made the last out of the 1951 World Series played between his Giants and the Yankees. Yvars (pronounced EE-vars) hit a tailing line drive to right field that was snared by a diving Hank Bauer, ending the game 4 to 3. The Yankees won the Series four games to two.

"I always said, 'Bobby Thomson got us into the World Series, and I got us out,'" Yvars said from his Barcalounger as he replayed the moment on black-and-white videotape. He winced at the catch as if he were being pelted in the face with a handful of sand.

No one ever came calling to inquire about that out or the middling career of a second-string catcher. But the television producers, reporters and book agents began haranguing him last week when *The Wall Street Journal* quoted him and a few of his teammates from the '51 Giants admitting that they had used a telescope and a buzzer system to steal the opposing catcher's signs. The Giants overcame a thirteen-and-a-half-game deficit in ten weeks and won baseball's most memorable pennant race.

The culmination came when Bobby Thomson hit a dramatic one-out, ninth-inning home run off the Brooklyn Dodgers pitcher, Ralph Branca, at the Polo Grounds, catapulting his club to a 5 to 4 victory in the deciding playoff game.

"The shot heard round the world" became the sport's most enduring film clip, with the Giants announcer, Russ Hodges, screaming, "The Giants win the pennant! The Giants win the pennant!" It is still seen on television in the early hours and it is sure to be seen even more with the news story traveling around the world and this year marking the fiftieth anniversary of the event. "I was the guy!" Yvars, seventy-six, stated flatly, his wife, Ann, at his side. "I relayed the signals to the batter. Now, if you're asking me if we could have won the pennant without stealing the signs, I would have to say, 'No way.'"

Yvars explained it this way. A man sat in the center field clubhouse with a telescope nearly five hundred feet away from home plate. When he spied the pitch signal between the catcher's legs, he pressed an electronic buzzer that was wired to the bullpen. The bullpen was in right field and in direct view of the batter. The man on the end of the bullpen bench was Sal Yvars. One buzz meant fastball, two meant off-speed.

"If it was a fastball, I would do nothing, sit still, maybe cross my legs," he said. "If it was off-speed stuff I would toss a ball up and down."

Did Bobby Thomson take your signal on that famous home run?

Yvars is a thoughtful man, a gracious man, a charitable man. He does speaking engagements for retired detectives and insurance salesmen and donates the proceeds to organizations that help children with cancer and spinal cord injuries. He has been telling conventioneers about the stolen signs for the past fifteen years.

He paused for a long moment, thinking how to put it just right.

"I gave him the sign," he said with a smile. "I gave him the sign."

Was it cheating?

Ann, his wife of fifty-three years, stepped in at this point, finishing his thought as spouses do. "Stealing signals with the help of mechanical devices was not outlawed until 1961," she said. "It may have been unscrupulous."

Salvador Yvars was born in Manhattan's Little Italy on February 20, 1924, the son of a Spanish gravedigger and an Italian laundress. They moved to the bottom of the hill in Valhalla, New York, when he was six months old. He grew up poor, like the other Italians in the gulch. There was no bathroom, no shower, and he and his brothers washed in the lake. He and the gulch gang would stare up at the rich folks who lived at the top of the hill, and when they weren't home, the gang would steal their apples and pears.

He starred in football, basketball and baseball at White Plains High School, and Ann D'Aleo must have been the prettiest girl there, Yvars said. He signed with the Giants farm team in 1942 for eighty-five dollars a month but his career was interrupted by the war.

Yvars enlisted in the Air Force, because he wanted to be a fighter pilot. But his eyes watered when they put him in the training centrifuge, and instead, they made him an experimental test dummy. "I could take six and a half Gs without a pressure helmet," he said proudly. "I was built solid."

His first major-league hit came on September 27, 1947. A single to left field off Schoolboy Rowe. He married Ann D'Aleo that same year.

But 1951 was the year. The year he hit .317. The year he went to the World Series. The year he slugged his manager, Leo Durocher, after Durocher's dog urinated on his cleats.

"I never liked him. He abused guys," said Yvars, describing Durocher in a precise locker-room metaphor. "I thought for sure I was gone to the minors. But I guess I was too valuable giving those signs."

He has no regrets, he said, about doing what he did back then. With the pennant money he was able to put a down payment on a house in Valhalla. A house in which he raised four children and still lives. A house at the top of the hill.

Diamonds Aren't Forever

The drizzle fell steadily, the kind of weather that makes an old man ache. The New Jersey air stank of industrial solvents. It was beautiful. It was East Coast baseball.

A group of gray men stood behind the backstop. They were major-league scouts of amateur talent, old-timers who when they meet a young ballplayer have the curious habit of examining his knuckles and inspecting the pads of his fingers. They had come to this industrial patch near the turnpike to see the seventeen-year-old pitcher from St. Peter's Prep, Pete Duda, a right-hander who threw hard and had plenty of room in his chest to grow. Four old men: Eddie Ford; John Hage-mann; Gil Bassetti, who works for the Baltimore Orioles; and a Catholic priest known in New Jersey more for his work behind the plate than in the pulpit. The four began a melancholic discourse about the waning life of a generation of meat-and-potato scouts in the Northeast.

To hear the old-timers, they are an endangered species, for a variety of reasons. Bitterness shapes their theories, but so does cold reality, like the fact that more and more ballplayers are coming from foreign countries.

Some of the scouts think the front offices of major-league baseball teams are now filled with Ivy League bean counters more interested in the bottom line than in the box score. In this age of $250-million con-tracts, the relatively modest money scouts receive—usually about $50,000 a year—still gets plenty of belt-tightening attention.

New York is considered the densest, toughest, most difficult terri-tory in the country to scout for amateur talent. The high school sea-son is short, about six weeks. It is cold and dark and soggy, unlike Florida or California, where kids play year-round on beautifully groomed fields rather than the mud lots and rock piles of the East Coast.

Some big-league stars have come out of the region: John Franco, Manny Ramirez, Jeff Bagwell, Mo Vaughn. But, weighing resources, baseball executives think they are more likely to find the new super-star in the Dominican Republic than in Danbury, Connecticut. So the old Northeastern scouts find themselves expendable or spread increasingly thin.

"Resources are moving south to the Caribbean, Venezuela and now the Pacific Rim," said Al Goldis, assistant to the general manager of the Cincinnati Reds, himself a former scout. He said clubs today tend to go with younger scouts who, armed with computers, can cover more ground. "The New York area has become less important in the scheme of things. The thinking is: Give these young guys a straw hat, a stopwatch and a radar gun and send them on their way."

Mr. Hagemann, sixty-three, spent the last seventeen years comb-ing the backwoods and the blacktop of the region for the Atlanta base-ball club—a Brave in Yankee country. Then, in March, the Atlanta Braves announced the dismissal of ten scouts and minor-league per-sonnel, and Mr. Hagemann, well respected and well paid, was gone.

"I'm a pretty sophisticated man," Mr. Hagemann said. "I know what's happening with corporate America, but I honestly believed baseball was beyond that. I was wrong big-time."

The decision came from New York. The Atlanta Braves became part of the AOL Time Warner conglomerate in January when America Online merged with Time Warner. Since the merger, the company has eliminated nearly twenty-five hundred jobs. One of those on the list of the eliminated was Mr. Hagemann, who was instrumental in the trade for John Smoltz, a skinny nineteen-year-old minor-league pitcher in the Detroit Tigers' farm system. Mr. Smoltz went on to become the National League Cy Young Award winner for the Braves in 1996.

According to Hagemann, he was done in by dot-com guys. Costs did appear to play a role.

"It was a simple monetary decision," said one Braves official who exchanged his frankness for confidentiality. "Sad but true. He cost too much."

"Ah, John, you deserved it," Mr. Ford managed to say through the whole pouch of chewing tobacco wadded in his mouth. "The question is: What took so long to fire you? We've been carrying you for years."

It was a joke, but Mr. Hagemann frowned as though his shoes were pinching his toes. "Yeah," he said. "I went from the penthouse to the outhouse before the first pitch of spring training was thrown."

Mr. Bassetti laughed, sipped his coffee and nodded. The same thing happened to him a few years ago. The Los Angeles Dodgers released him after twenty-five years. "Whole damn game has changed," he said.

Baseball scouts do not make the Hall of Fame. When average fans talk about the greatest of all time, they do not speak the names of Tony Lucadello, who in fifty years of scouting signed fifty big-leaguers to amateur contracts before putting a revolver in his mouth in 1989 on a high school ball field in his hometown, Fostoria, Ohio; Hugh Alexander, known as Uncle Hughie, who had no left hand, couldn't pitch or hit, but knew promise when he saw it; or Ralph DiLullo, who always dreamed of signing a Hall of Famer and once almost did. But the Chicago Cubs were too cheap to sign a kid named Sandy Koufax.

The scout of amateur baseball talent, like John Hagemann, toils away in obscurity, gives his life over to the game. He crosses the country, combs the run-down ball fields, the streets and Little Leagues. He puts a million miles on his car, watches thousands of kids play the game, exists on buckets of fried chicken, sleeps in cheap motels and drinks plenty bad coffee. His wife often eats dinner alone.

Not a single professional game could be played without the amateur scout. He is among the most knowledgeable people about baseball, the one responsible for finding the talent to put on the field.

The first whispers of such talent come from the "bird dogs," the local men, like Mr. Ford, who let the regional scouts know about the talented boys from the neighborhood.

"The modern-day scout, he don't know nothing," said Mr. Ford, who used to scout for the Cubs.

"They don't chew tobacco," he said. "They don't see six or seven games a day. They never played the game, and they couldn't tell a baseball from a watermelon."

For these guys, the days are gone of scouting from behind the tree or the telephone pole or from the playground out in left field. The diamond in the rough, the farm boy or the swamp rat, is rarely found anymore. These days, every scout in the area knows about the big talent. Guys like Manny Ramirez, the Boston Red Sox slugger from Washington Heights, are heavily scouted and are as easy to find as a turkey in a supermarket.

It is the boys out of nowhere, kids like Rich Aurilia, the San Francisco Giants shortstop who leads the National League in hitting and who went to Xaverian High School in Bay Ridge, Brooklyn, who are the true and increasingly rare finds. But who found him? In the scouting world, claims become matters of false credit, lies and pettiness.

"Since a guy gets drafted by a club before he gets signed to a contract, it's hard to know who was the first to spot him," Mr. Hagemann said. "But everybody now wants the credit, because everyone is trying to climb the scouting ladder into the front office. It didn't used to be like that. Guys wanted to be in the field, because they loved the game."

The young guys are little more than data collectors, the old guys say, their objectivity perhaps twisted by recent events. They say the young guys have no feel for the game. The radar gun can tell you the speed of the ball, but it never got a batter out. It doesn't tell you about a kid's aptitude. His head. His body potential. Scouts run in packs now. They share information. It didn't used to be that way, the old guys say.

Mr. Hagemann is unemployed, but still, he can't keep himself from these muddy games. Baseball is what he knows. He was a pitcher for the New York Giants AA fan team in the mid-fifties, just a couple of dozen men away from Leo Durocher's bull pen. The game was there for him when his first wife died of cancer.

"Fifty years of baseball doesn't disappear with a pink slip," he said, his skin still tan from spring training in Florida, an Atlanta Braves World Series ring on his right hand.

"I don't like how they're treating the older guys," Mr. Hagemann said. "The front-office people aren't true baseball men like they were years ago. But the game will do all right. Baseball is bigger than any of us."

Mr. Ford smacked his pal on the back and spit out a puddle of tobacco juice.

THERE GOES
THE NEIGHBORHOOD

WHATEVER else they say about John Gotti, he kept the neighborhood up.

Nickel and Dime
and Quartered to Death

On the gum-stained corner of Thirty-seventh Avenue and Seventy-fourth Street in Jackson Heights is a cheerless little pizza shop. Inside, the temperature reaches 120 degrees and the fluorescent lights are the color of flypaper.

But this does not bother Nino and Nick Lombardo, the two chain-smoking Sicilian-born men who run the store Pizza Boy for their cousin Nick Gambina. "No, no, the work is real nice here, very simpatico," said Nino Lombardo, thirty-eight, who has a Mediterranean accent despite having lived thirty years in the States. "I been doing pizza my whole life. There's just one little problem here. The change. We're being nickel and dime and quartered to death."

On the sidewalk between the front door and the service window are two pay phones, a giant gum-ball machine, a coin-operated kiddie rocket ride and the ubiquitous parking meters. On some slow days, the brothers say, more people might come for change than pizza. It seems like a small matter, Nick Lombardo said, unless you have to deal with it seven days a week, fourteen hours a day. But New York demands that you make a few concessions and a lot of change.

"You know, we believe in the concept that the customer is always right," said Nick, forty-five, who has fifteen years' experience at the shop and offers his burn scars and pizza paunch as a résumé. "But a slice costs $1.45. That's two quarters and a nickel change. We try to give the best for customers, but what are you going to do?"

"Besides, if we mess up, Mama hears about it," Nino said, shoveling two slices with extra cheese into the oven and another cigarette into his mouth.

The shop is celebrating its thirtieth birthday, and business has never been better, the brothers said. Although the neighborhood has changed over the past decade from Irish and Italian to Asian, South Asian and Latino, people are still drawn to the pizza that *The New York Times* once described as "a delicious work of art." Nick was taught to make pizza by his cousin Nick, who brought the recipe from the old world. Cousin Nick learned the "all natural" recipe from his mother, who had it passed down to her from her mother back in Partanna, Sicily.

This is the way things have been at Pizza Boy for thirty years. Copacetic. Nice and regular. Then phones came about four years ago, and that wasn't too bad, Nick said. But then the city extended the parking hours several months ago, Monday through Sunday until ten P.M. Ever since, the brothers said they have had to ration change as if it were their last roll of toilet paper. Their bank charges ten cents for a roll of quarters.

The shop usually goes through four hundred dollars in coins a week, most of it for the meters. And to make matters worse, the traffic police are so vigilant that the middle-aged men have given up their car and have begun delivering pies by pedal.

"I got five hundred dollars in tickets in the last three months. You know how many pies it takes to make up a ticket?" Nick asked. "Fifteen—fifteen pies," he said, exaggerating.

The brothers say they are not complaining. "You can't fight City Hall," Nino said. But as a solution to the problem, the brothers say perhaps meters could operate with a swipe card, like the transit system.

In the meantime, it seems that the brothers will continue to dispense silver by simple criteria. A good-looking woman gets change if she smiles. A man gets change if he is a regular. Children always get four quarters for a dollar for the gum-ball machine. "The gumball machine belongs to me," Nick said.

Elks (Clubs)
Becoming Extinct

There is a building in central Queens that is a temple to the workingman. It is a fading neoclassical castle of brick and plaster. It is five stories high and one floor down, and the American flag that flies above it is the only American flag that can be seen clearly on Queens Boulevard for a mile in either direction.

It is Lodge number 878 of the Benevolent and Protective Order of Elks. To be a member you must be a United States citizen and a man over the age of twenty-one who believes in God. The cornerstone was laid in 1923 and the place was built for $750,000, an astronomical amount at the time. There is a hollow bronze elk on a pedestal in front of the entrance. The place is dying from the inside out.

The interior has those old smells, like those in the public library or the marriage license bureau. There is no sign of life. A ringing telephone goes unanswered. There is a sign near the stairs prohibiting women and non-Elks from climbing farther. On the mezzanine is a sturdy oak door, where an East Indian woman answers the knock. She is a secretary for the New Life Fellowship Church. "God willing, we will own this place soon," she said.

At the end of the week, the Elks Club comes to life. A big screen carries a simulcast from the Belmont Race Track, and a dozen men hang around the first-floor bar waiting for their horses to come in. Most of them are the older crowd: white, retired Teamsters, construction workers and such. They say things like "It's been a while since I been in this jurnt" and "Lemme get a sodie pop" and "Don't be a wise guy, Sammy."

As it is at most men's clubs across the country, the sun is setting on Lodge 878. The building is for sale because the club can't make the $60,000 tax bill. The New Life Fellowship Church, which has been renting the mezzanine for four years, plans to purchase the lodge for around $10 million. One of the sticking points in the deal is that the Elks would like to retain control of the first floor—rent free—for ninety-nine years.

"The whole world's changed," said Patrick Pendergrass, sixty-six, the treasurer of the club and the man who phones the bets to the Off-Track Betting office. "Clubs like this are folding all over the place. It's a piece of America that's dying. We'd like to stay here."

Once, everybody who was somebody and everybody who wanted to be somebody belonged to the club. There were congressmen, district attorneys, local political bosses. The club once had sixty-six hundred members (now there are about six hundred). If you wanted a job in 1960s Queens, you came to the Elks. There was the Elks Bazaar, the borough's social event of the year. There was the raffle of two dozen Cadillacs. There were the eight bowling alleys—with automatic pin setters—in the basement. There were the three bars. There were the drinks and dancing and deals made under the stained-glass skylight. There was the charitable work.

Now there are Fridays and the twenty run-down men who board in the rooms on the top floor. They wear robes and spend the day watching television.

Here's what you're likely to hear at the bar on a Friday afternoon: Maybe things are better for the working man, maybe they're not; it's just that they don't seem better. The wife has to work now, no more coming home for your dinner and then off to the club. The neighbor-hood has changed. The houses are overflowing with third-world immigrants. The club is dying. They say the economy is better. They say the Wall Street money is finally trickling down, that wages are trickling up. But so is inflation. So are taxes.

"It's not my America anymore," said Charlie Novak, fifty-eight, a construction worker and a veteran. "The American kids aren't inter-ested in community anymore. And then again the community is third world."

The statistics agree with Mr. Novak. Fraternal organizations are drying up all around the country. Since the end of the Vietnam War, the Elks' national membership has dropped more than 15 percent, despite opening the club to women five years ago. The Shriners have shrunk from a million members to half a million since 1980. It's a similar story for the Knights of Columbus, the Moose and the Masons.

"Funny thing is," said Mr. Pendergrass, "we keep afloat by cater-ing to the third-world clientele. We do a lot of birthday parties and weddings here."

The older guys who live upstairs wander the halls behind clouds of cigarette smoke, staring blankly, appearing somewhat confused at this new crowd.

"They're from another era," said Eddie DeJesus, Jr., the adminis-trator of the church. "It's odd, isn't it? A church and a fraternal men's organization below. It's so New York. Jesus said love everybody."

Before There Was Dumbo, There Was Pedro's

Pedro Perez has a wife whose name is Carmen and a son whose name is Pedrito (Little Pedro). He keeps them above his restaurant, which is called Pedro's Spanish American Restaurant, in Brooklyn, under the Manhattan Bridge.

Mr. Perez has been in this spot for a long time. Since before the real estate agents called it Dumbo. Way before the refugees from Minneapolis found its bleak shores. Back when the priest got stabbed for his car keys in the lot across the street and cat burglars roamed the rooftops. At sunup, the gas grill is lighted, the beans and rice and coffee are started, merengue slinks from the radio. Carmen Perez works away in the kitchen. It is necessary to put on the fluorescent lights because Pedro's is a cracker box of a restaurant with one solitary window, the top half of which reaches up to Jay Street. The other half is underground.

The lunchtime crowd is mostly Latino workingmen from the garages and the lamp-shade and carpet factories that still pepper the neighborhood. Sometimes the Chinese truck mechanics will come in and complain about the white people who complain about the Chinese mechanics repairing their trucks in the street and making all kinds of racket and filth. It's important to say that the Chinese were here first. That's what the Chinese say.

Mr. Perez got wise and got a liquor license, and now he has an exotic crowd drinking liquor in his restaurant until four in the morning.

"It doesn't matter where they come from," he said of his clientele. "They're honest. Nobody steals anything. It's the only place in the whole neighborhood where you do whatever you please, just like home."

Mr. Perez remodeled a few months ago, but beyond the bar, it's hard to tell where the improvements were made. A damp cold permeates the place, and a fat man could not maneuver his way into the bathroom without becoming jammed in the door frame.

The telephone rings in the bar, but the bartender is told not to answer. Ms. Perez will take it upstairs in the apartment.

At the bar, under the purple light, a customer talks about the old days around the Navy Yard, when guys like Veely and Frankie and Knuckles beat the sailors for kicks and then stole their shoes.

You realize how much of the old neighborhood is still here at Pedro's, mixed in among the Romanians and Panamanians and Frenchmen and Minnesotans, and you listen to the entire world resting on the head of a beer: Milosevic, the rape of Romania, Islamic terrorists, rednecks, Protestants, the symbiosis of the Greeks and Albanians, Afro-Cuban rhythms, smoking causing birth defects, how to save a choking victim. And into the evening.

It seemed easier to beat sailors, a patron says to Mihai Hurezeanu, the barman.

"Yes, those were simpler times," he said.

Bridge of Sighs

During the recent rains, a commuter in Ozone Park got an unsavory surprise while waiting for the number 8 bus beneath the abandoned Long Island Rail Road tracks on 101st Avenue between Ninety-ninth and One Hundredth streets.

She had neglected to look up, where a decade ago nets were strung to keep debris and dust from the crumbling bridge from falling on pedestrians' heads. But the net has never been cleaned, and pigeon droppings have swelled to the size of overstuffed pastry bags. The unsuspecting woman was whitewashed in misery.

"You could tell she wasn't from the area," said Vincent Danise, seventy-one, a knickknack salesman, who saw her from his chair across the street. "Locals wait for the bus in the rain. No one wants to go under there because if that thing breaks, someone is going to be killed by bird crud and rocks, and that would be a terrible way to go."

Local businesspeople and community leaders said they had been lobbying the city not only to change the nets but to tear down the bridge, parts of which turn to dust at the kick of a foot. "It's a danger, a blight and an eyesore," said Betty Mangione, a local merchant. "I've been trying to get action on that thing for twenty years, but no one will listen."

The tracks were built by the LIRR in 1878 as part of the Rockaway Beach line. They have not been used since they were sold to the city in 1953. "The city has given us a lot of excuses," said Community Board 9's district manager, Mary Ann Carey. "Six years ago, they were proposing it as the new express line to Kennedy Airport. Nothing's happened. Not even the net has been changed."

A spokeswoman for the Department of Citywide Administrative Services said that the city would replace the netting by August but that tearing down the bridge was unlikely. "Eventually, we will find a use for it," she said.

The nets were put up in 1988, when Mayor Edward I. Koch came through on a walking tour and was almost struck by falling debris. At the time, John Gotti, the Mafia leader, operated out of the Bergin Hunt and Fish Club, a few blocks from the bridge.

"Whatever else they say about John Gotti, he kept the neighborhood up," said Marion Rescigno, who lives nearby. "He would never have put up with this."

WORDS
TO THE WISE

PEOPLE with too many opinions live alone because opinions are pretty much like onions. They put people off.

When Those
Dancing Days Are Over

She prefers to be called Ellie Babes. She is a former bar-top chorus girl with memories of tangos in Tangiers and merengues in
Madrid, and she is still known in some corners of Brooklyn for her
barroom bop.

"We traveled a lot," she says, flaring her nostrils with pride. "And
when we traveled, we liked to drink." There is, sadly, no we anymore.
Just Ellie Babes and a lifetime of dance tickets floating at the bottom
of a beer glass.

Ellie Pooshejian is sixty-nine. Her dancing days are over and
what's left of the traveling consists of catching two buses from her
apartment in Windsor Terrace to Lundy's clam house in Sheepshead
Bay. Either that or wandering in circles through her neighborhood,
killing the hours in the local taverns. She measures time by the
stroke of the iron bell that tolls from the belfry of the Holy Name
Roman Catholic Church.

"I retired last year and I had to move out of my co-op," she says in
Farrell's, a Windsor Terrace barrelhouse at Prospect Park West and Fifteenth Street. "I felt I had to, because I didn't want to die with property
and leave that pickle for somebody else. I feel like a listing ship."

It is raining and Ellie pokes her head into the bar nervously, like a

hen venturing into a strange barn. Farrell's is a man's domain, a neighborhood living room. Mornings of the first and fifteenth, the oak is
stacked with men staring out the plate glass waiting for the bank across
the street to open so they can cash their Social Security checks.

She is the only woman in the place as the bell peals eight. The
men turn and quickly size her up. She is a brassy little thing, with
a round, sad-eyed Armenian face and a cigarette-scarred voice that
sounds like a board on a sanding belt. She wears leisure slacks and
has beer on her breath.

They make room for her at the rail, and when she captures an ear, she
knows how to hold it. She dispenses ditties the way some scatter seed.

Ellie on politics: "I used to be far left. Now I'm far smarter."

On money: "Hate it. Ruined more people than tuberculosis."

On companionship: "Like bushes without bees. Lonely is worse
than hungry."

On silence: "I heard it once."

On cigarettes: "Forty a day. Pleasure knows no reason."

On work: "I typed a lot of letters for a lot of men."

On religion: "I believe."

This all seems interesting until you notice the men have gone
glaze-eyed. Soon they return to their vulgarities, mutterings and
cursings, their sob stories, tales of woe and done-me-wrongs, stocks
and bonds, beer and basketball. Ellie retires to the corner like so
much furniture.

"I hate being ignored," she says with a hiss. She drains her beer,
snaps her bag shut and heads for the door. A wise guy cites Dylan
Thomas as she passes by:

Do not go gentle into that good night,
Old age should burn and rave at close of day;
Rage, rage against the dying of the light.

"I see you've got an education," she says to him, "but you're not
much on looks."

Latin Lovers
with Free Advice

The only thing you hear about Latin people is that they work like burros, save, save, save and then send the money home," said Cesar Escobar, a well-appointed Peruvian, who was dressed in leather and pointy shoes and held a brandy Alexander in his hand.

"You don't hear about the good times, you know? How we throw our money away for the sweet life and for love? We do it, I tell you. We do it big."

It's the music that makes him do it, Mr. Escobar explained.

It is the devil who resides in the brass horn of the Ralph Irizarry Orchestra, which plays salsa on Wednesday evenings at Willie's Steak House on Westchester Avenue in the Bruckner section of the Bronx.

Everybody goes to Willie's on Wednesdays. The Puerto Ricans, the Dominicans, the Bolivians. It is a regular crowd, both sophisticated and beautiful, that spills out onto the sidewalk. Bankers and artists mix there. The talk is about love, and the patrons at Willie's know how to sweeten the drink of life when it has gone sour.

For instance, Mr. Escobar, forty-seven, a veteran of three wives, had some thoughts on Mayor Giuliani's marital situation, which has become more gruesome and spectacular than a pigeon's drowning in the fountain at Rockefeller Center.

"The mayor, he is Italian," Mr. Escobar said. "This means he is Latin, yes? Now, after twelve years of marriage, a man wants to take another woman. This is natural. You as the man begin to sing one way. She sings another.

"The thing to do here is find a song to sing together. If this is not possible, you go apart and find new songs to sing. I wish I could tell the mayor this, I like him a lot; but he can't see it."

There is another man at Willie's, a Wednesday regular, who sits at the center of the bar and is known as the Godfather. Hedley M. Swaby, seventy-two, is a pristine gentleman who speaks four languages and prefers woolen suits and striped ties.

He is a model for any man in matters of *amor*. When he snaps his fingers, the young women come. His secret?

"Sophistication, flamboyance and an ability to dance," Mr. Swaby said. "Pay attention. A man cannot live without women."

Homeless but Not Helpless
by the Harlem River

Clyde Tensley is not, technically, a homeless man. He lives in a corrugated-steel shack along the Harlem River and has kept the same address for eight years.

"What makes a homeless, homeless?" he asked. "People think homeless equals helpless. But you have helpless people with homes. You got homeless people who are not helpless. Me? I got a home. Home, you see, is in the heart." His domicile lies at the terminus of Marginal Street, a splinter of road beneath the Harlem River Drive. There is a rotting cement factory on Marginal Street, and many people used to live in it. A man named Prince even had electricity. Then a neighbor murdered Prince last summer and everybody moved away. That's the bad part.

The good part includes the big sea turtle who makes her home on the banks of the river, and Mr. Tensley studies her for long periods of time. "It's better to watch the turtle than to watch the TV," he says. Dinner is often caught from the milky green water, and a man could walk around naked if he wanted to.

Lunch at Mr. Tensley's home is served around noon and consists of tall cans of beer and day-old bread. Usually, a friend like Reggie attends.

When he has guests, Mr. Tensley takes out his ironing board and covers it with clean linen. He sets out a candle lamp and teacups and starts a homey little fire in a garbage can.

Raised on the South Carolina coast, Mr. Tensley, forty-eight, is a hospitable man with a slurry manner of speech. He has a wiry build, hands the color of pitch, a flat nose and a bottom plate of ruined teeth framed by a bird-nest beard. He does not accept welfare, and he refuses to sit on street corners with his hand out.

He is a currently a scrap metalist and was previously a pest exterminator, so the abundant river rats don't bother him much. He is, in fact, an authority on their history and habits. "Poetry," he calls it.

Mr. Tensley was married once. It lasted for a year, he says, and in that time she tried to kill him twice. He has no children, no responsibilities beyond himself and has not enjoyed the company of a woman in six years.

"I channel that sexual energy into my philosophy," Mr. Tensley said, draining his can and then snuffing an ember that had settled into his beard. "Life is like trigonometry. You have to have a known point to get to the unknown point."

Reggie said, "I don't know about no trigonometry. But them rats around here crawl up in bed with you like they was some kind of poodle."

A Mentor Shares a Secret
That Really Wasn't

The old English teacher sent an electronic letter recently to his former student, wanting to know why he hadn't returned a composition book assigned to him twenty-nine years ago.

He also wrote to congratulate his student—Ed Keating, the photographer—about a photography prize he had recently won, telling him how he had been admiring his work in the news pages and that he was proud. Warren Allen Smith is remembered as a good teacher from those days at New Canaan High School in Connecticut when youth demanded that you lash out at authority, throw rocks through the downtown bank window and find ways to hurt yourself somehow.

The teacher did not prevent these things entirely, but he did help the young man in small enduring ways. For instance, Mr. Keating does not steal cars anymore.

You don't forget those kinds of teachers: the Mrs. Russos and Mr. Zifkos and Ms. Williamses. And, as Mr. Smith says, those kinds of teachers don't forget you.

A rendezvous was arranged. The men would meet for drinks and supper at Lips, the West Village boudoir that bills itself as the ultimate in drag dining.

Warren Allen Smith, eighty, sat at the corner table looking clean and gray, dressed in dark corduroys, a sweater, an orange oxford shirt, specs, a conservative part in his hair. Above him there were cheap chandeliers, and the place was done up with false flowers and dancing cherubs.

"Nobody wants you when you're old and gray," a drag queen sang.

After cordialities, the old man turned to his former student and asked, "Did you know I was gay?"

"I don't think it was any big secret," his former student said, his eyes large and amused by the question and the atmosphere. No one had tastes and style like Mr. Smith.

"Oh, really?" Mr. Smith seemed disappointed. For thirty-seven years he had lived a dual existence. Most of the year he lived in Connecticut as a closeted man, dedicating himself as the model high school teacher. The rest of the year he spent in New York living his secret life, his captain's paradise, he called it. He even threw burning garbage cans at police cars during the Stonewall riots of 1969. "I thought nobody knew."

They stood at the bar for a cigarette, and Warren Allen Smith, editor of *Who's Who in Hell,* detective of the paranormal, inspector of the male form and beloved educator, attracted the misfits and fatties, and they poured out their hearts and histories to the aged oracle.

Do you know what it's like growing up gay in Long Island? asked one.

Am I too fat to find a man? asked another.

The teacher listened attentively before offering a hopeful quotation from Truman Capote's English teacher: "The football boys might hate you now, but they'll love you later."

The Quantum Leaps of a
Pretty Nice Mind

The Astronomer of Astor Place sat among the punks at the base of the giant steel cube with an expensive bottle of beer between his knees, waving his arms wildly as he lectured on quantum leaps.

"How can electrons disappear in one orbit and show up in another orbit just like that?" he asked. He wanted to accentuate the point by snapping his fingers, but he missed because he was inebriated.

"I'll tell you how!" he told no one in particular. "It's called the time warp. Duh. It's a cup of tea."

The Astronomer is one of those New Yorkers with an obscure, beautiful mind, a person who in his cramped recesses writes music and studies science and reads plays. But once he leaves the orbit of his own private universe, he appears to be nothing more than a grubby miscreant staggering around the Village, shouting into traffic, destined to find his end at the bottom of a pauper's grave.

The universe is a very cold place, with a temperature of negative 454 Fahrenheit, the Astronomer explained. And while most scientists believe that the universe will ultimately expand into a vast void of lifeless cold where not even molecules move, the Astronomer clings to the Nietzschean concept of eternal recurrence, the belief that we will never have to say good-bye, that we will indeed be back.

The optimistic astronomer, between swallows, explained the Big Crunch Theory, where particles having sufficiently slowed down after the Big Bang are attracted back to one another by gravity, which causes them to rush back on each other causing another Big Bang. A cosmic accordion.

"I say the universe will not float away!" the Astronomer insisted. The gutter punks could only snicker.

"Gravity," he said. "I'm talking gravity. Gravity is the tendency of objects wanting to bond. Particles will find each other across the vastness."

"But what causes this attraction?" a solitary observer asked.

"Gravity!" he shouted.

"But what is gravity?" the observer asked. "Your explanation is circular."

"Oh, shut up, stupid! The education I'm giving you is worth twenty thousand dollars. I'm not running a laboratory here."

The frustrating thing about science is that one discovery leads to another question and one never quite fully reaches the Answer. The Astronomer, it seems, deals with these frustrations not only by drinking himself silly by mid-afternoon but by rejecting the newest discoveries.

For instance, the Big Crunch is not held with much regard among astrophysicists, since Einstein's theoretical cosmological constant or "dark energy" was discovered a few years ago by scientists looking out on the end of the universe.

It also appeared that the Astronomer of Astor Place overlooked the very basic Theory of Liquid Attraction.

That is, if one drinks alcoholic liquids from a large glass bottle in a public place, he will invariably attract the police. The Astronomer was issued a summons, the punks scattered and the afternoon lecture was ended.

Acknowledgments

I wish to thank the people whose names and details appear in these pages.

Also:

Frank Parker, Eddie Keating, Alan Feuer, Jesse McKinley and Bob Paris know something about reading and writing.

Dave Smith, Christine Kay, John Landman and Connie Rosenblum are fine editors at *The New York Times*.

Lydia Chavez and Bernard Taper teach young cabinetmakers to build square corners.

Mike Winerip and Earl Wilson are gentlemen.

Michael T. Kaufman is the standard.

Ann Godoff and Sloan Harris: I appreciate your calling.

Evangeline Happy—an elegant woman.

And always, Amy Virginia. The best thing going.

ABOUT THE AUTHOR

CHARLIE LEDUFF became a staff reporter at *The New York Times* in 1999 and has covered everything from New York City bars to the Iraq war. His piece on slaughterhouse workers was part of the *Times* series "How Race Is Lived in America," which won a 2001 Pulitzer Prize. He is now a member of the *Times*'s Los Angeles bureau, and lives with his wife in Hollywood.